Descartes

Also by A. C. Grayling

An Introduction to Philosophical Logic
The Refutation of Scepticism
Berkeley: The Central Arguments
Wittgenstein
China: A Literary Companion
(with Susan Whitfield)
Russell
Moral Values
The Long March to the Fourth of June
(with Xu You Yu as Li Xiao Jun)
The Quarrel of the Age: The Life and Times of William Hazlitt
The Meaning of Things: Applying Philosophy to Life
The Reason of Things: Living with Philosophy
What is Good?: The Search for the Best Way to Live
The Mystery of Things
The Heart of Things: Applying Philosophy to the 21st Century

As Editor

Philosophy: A Guide Through the Subject
Philosophy: Further Through the Subject
Herrick: Lyrics of Love and Desire
The Art of Always Being Right:
Thirty Eight Ways To Win When You Are Defeated

Descartes

*The Life of René Descartes
and Its Place in his Times*

A. C. GRAYLING

First published in Great Britain by The Free Press in 2005
An imprint of Simon & Schuster UK Ltd
A Viacom Company

1 3 5 7 9 10 8 6 4 2

Simon & Schuster UK Ltd
Africa House
64–78 Kingsway
London WC2B 6AH

www.simonsays.co.uk

Simon & Schuster Australia
Sydney

A CIP catalogue record for this book is
available from the British Library.

ISBN 0-7432-3147-3
EAN 9780743231473

Typeset by Rowland Phototypesetting Ltd,
Bury St Edmunds, Suffolk
Printed and bound in Great Britain by
The Bath Press, Bath

For Katie: adeo venusto, ut nil supra

Contents

Acknowledgements		ix
Preface		xiii
	Introduction: Who was Descartes?	1
1	The Awakening	13
2	A Night of Dreams	49
3	The Mystery of the Rosy Cross	81
4	Nine Years of Travel	105
5	Animals on the Moon	141
6	Francine	175
7	The Shape of Snow	183
8	Descartes Contra Voetius	207
9	The Princess of the Passions	227
10	The Queen of Winter	257
	Appendix I: A Note on Descartes' Philosophy	277
	Appendix II: Biographies of Philosophers and Descartes' Biography	295
	Notes	309
	Select Bibliography	335
	Index	341

Acknowledgements

For much appreciated help of various kinds before, during and since the writing of this book, and not necessarily in connection with it, my thanks go to Alex Orenstein, Ken Gemes, John Cottingham, Susan James, Simon Blackburn and John Skorupski. Special thanks go to Naomi Goulder, Andrew Gordon, Edwina Barstow and Catherine Clarke. I am grateful to the staffs of the British Library and the London Library for their help, as always, and to the Dutch friends who pointed out Cartesian scenes among the tulips and canals of Descartes' adopted country.

'I would also have added a word of advice concerning the way to read this book, which is that I would like it first to be read rapidly in its entirety, like a novel, without the reader forcing his attention too much or stopping at the difficulties which he may encounter in it, simply in order to have a broad view of the matters I have treated in it. And after that, if the reader judges that these matters merit examination, and is curious to know their causes, he can read the book a second time, in order to notice the sequence of my reasonings.'

Descartes, 'Letter from the Author',
The Principles of Philosophy

Preface

This book is about the life and times of a genius: René Descartes, a proud, private, sometimes solitary and often prickly man, who had a large impact on the intellectual history of the Western world. Just how large an impact can be gauged from the fact that his writings have been in print for nearly four centuries, and remain to this day on the reading lists of almost every university in the world.

Because Descartes is important for the contribution he made to the development of modern thought, no book about him can fail to say what that contribution is. I do that in the appropriate places here. But my principal aim is to recount what is known of Descartes' life, and to situate his life in its tumultuous times – this latter being something that previous biographies have neglected, with the result that they miss what is possibly a significant aspect of his story. I stress the word 'possibly', for my suggestions amount to no more than a guess. Exploring the guess has made writing about Descartes something of a detective adventure, adding to the illumination and pleasure involved.

As these remarks imply, this is not a specialist tome but a book for the general reader. I stress this for the benefit of my philosophical colleagues. Biographies of philosophers rarely meet with the approval of salaried professionals in the subject. This is because no two academics will always agree on what the right interpretation of *this* or the correct judgement about *that* should be, and when the discussion of someone's thought is summary – even when it is inevitably so as in a general biography – they think the worse of it. Hence the need for this reminder.

But I also remind my colleagues that we professional philosophers have a duty to explain ourselves, our enquiries, and the traditions of thought we spring from and react to; and that one way of doing so is to engage in conversation with non-specialists about our tradition's great figures. Descartes is one of the greatest. To try to make him something more than a name on a book cover, or an item on a reading list, is therefore to try to show that the adventure of thought is a living, important, and consequential thing, and that he and we – and indeed all who read and think, including the readers for whom this book is written – are engaged in that adventure too.

Writing about someone at this distance of time – nearly four centuries – and relying on a highly partial and incomplete record, offers many temptations to speculate. In one respect, as noted, I frankly do this, though with suitable cautions always because, if I am even half right in my guess, I have stumbled upon an intriguing and unappreciated aspect of Descartes' story. It is an aspect that a richer understanding of his time both suggests and, if right, illuminates. For that reason I draw particular attention to Descartes' historical circumstances. In all other respects I adhere closely to the record, profiting from the work done by predecessors in the field, among the latest of them Stephen Gaukroger, Genevieve Rodis-Lewis, and Richard Watson; and of course the excellent scholarly work of John Cottingham, Robert Stoothof and Dugald Murdoch, whose translations and editions of Descartes' work are indispensable. My thanks and admiration go to all these scholars.

One thing all biographers seek is a sense of the person they write about. One listens for a tone of voice, one strives for a sense of the prevailing mindset: the humour or irritation, the warmth or coldness, that reveals something about the individual's inner character. Having lived biographically with Descartes for some years I can say with a degree of assurance that if, by some miracle of time-travel, I were to find myself in the same room with him, I would instantly recognise him. He was secret and proud, had a good opinion of himself – justly so, as his work testifies – and in all but his religious outlook was strongly independent-minded. He lived at his own pace always, which was by no means a hectic one. He might give the impression that he was timid in religious matters and, in particular, afraid of appearing heterodox, whereas in fact it was not timidity but an unswerving faithfulness to his Jesuit-trained Catholic roots. He had a sense of humour, which no truly intelligent mind can lack. When provoked to enmity he was a combative, indeed vituperative, opponent, and was not very good at governing his temper. If his life had not been cut short by illness, he would probably have devoted a proportion of his energies to attaining office and advancement in his social status, having for a long period lived as quiet and retired a life as he could. He was just beginning to get more interested in this surprising direction when he died.

These characteristics make themselves salient in Descartes' doings and his correspondence. Anything more private is hard to glimpse through the thick veils of time, though we see tenderness towards his daughter and, occasionally, to one or other of his friends. These glimpses are attractive and significant. Given the privacy, even secrecy, in which he cloaked himself always, it is certain that the domestic man was considerably less proud and closed, less rebarbative and quarrelsome, than the public man seems.

He was very small in build, perhaps a mere five feet one or two inches in height. He was neither athletic nor graceful and, with his low brow, big nose and long upper lip, none of his various portraits succeed in making him even halfway handsome: but they all picture large, luminous eyes and a steady gaze. Reputation and influence supply all the rest of Descartes' stature in the history of the world: there the lustrous gaze remains, and he stands tall indeed.

Introduction

Who was Descartes?

'The fumes which rise from the bottom of a swamp produce frogs, ants, leeches, and vegetation . . . Cut a groove into a brick, fill it with crushed basil, and put another brick on top to seal the groove. Within a few days the vegetable matter will have turned into scorpions.'[1] So claimed a seventeenth-century savant called Jean–Baptiste Van Helmont. But although Van Helmont lived in the seventeenth century, he belonged far more to its past than its future, for he was one of those whose understanding of the world relied on ideas developed centuries before his own time. The ideas in question belonged to an intellectual tradition that encouraged belief in miracles, spontaneous generation, and phoenixes rising from ashes. In this tradition it was an unquestionable fact that the sun and stars go round a stationary earth, with God's heaven above and hell-fire at the earth's centre. Yet even as Van Helmont premised these notions in his writings, a new world of ideas was coming into existence around him. One of the chief of those bringing about this change was René Descartes.

The world-view containing most of the elements on which

Van Helmont relied, and which Descartes helped to demolish, had taken its start in late antiquity and gathered embellishments as it grew older. Closely associated with the Christian church, it adopted, adapted and assimilated the legacy of classical and, especially, Aristotelian thought, forming itself during the Middle Ages into the elaborate structure of Scholasticism, which was still dominant when the seventeenth century began. So firm was its grip that when the Jesuits formalised their educational policies in their *Ratio Studiorum* of 1586 they could simply state, 'In logic, natural philosophy, ethics and metaphysics, Aristotle's doctrine is to be followed.'

This reflected the instruction issued two decades earlier by Francisco Borgia, head of the Jesuit order, in a memorandum stipulating that '[no one must] defend or teach anything opposed, detracting, or unfavourable to the faith, either in philosophy or theology. Let no one defend anything against the axioms received by the philosophers, such as: there are only four causes, there are only four elements, there are only three principles of natural things, fire is hot and dry, air is humid and hot. Let no one defend such propositions as that natural agents act at a distance without a medium, contrary to the most common opinion of the philosophers and theologians . . . This is not just an admonition, but a teaching that we impose.'[2]

But as Van Helmont and thinkers like him spun their theories from the comfort of their armchairs, reaching deep into Scholasticism's resources for their inspiration and the premises of their reasoning, the revolution in process around them was sweeping those very resources aside, in the same breath therefore challenging the official teaching of the church on matters of faith and philosophy alike. The two key documents of that revolution − documents that shaped Western thought for at least three hundred years afterwards – were the *Discours sur la methode de bien conduire la raison et chercher la verité dans les sciences*, published in 1637, and the *Philosophiae naturalis principia mathematica*, published in 1687. The first was by Descartes, the second by Isaac Newton.

Descartes' *Discourse on Method* – to give this book its standard English title – was an important instrument in providing impulse and direction to the new enquiries, today called the 'natural sciences', by which mankind ultimately gained greater understanding and control of nature. Part of the contribution made by Descartes' *Discourse* was to restore human reason to a status which allowed it to address questions until then regarded by religious orthodoxy as dangerous. In this respect Descartes is to the modern world what Thales, the so-called 'Father of Philosophy', was to the ancient world. The comparison is an illuminating one. Thales asked questions about the nature and origins of the world, and formulated answers that relied solely on reason and observation, making no appeal to supernatural explanations – to gods, legends, myths, or ancient scriptures. He assumed that the world is a place that makes sense, and that the human mind is capable of understanding it. His example unleashed a brilliant epoch of free thought in classical antiquity, which gave birth to the Western tradition.

What Thales achieved for the human mind in ancient times, Descartes contributed to achieving for the human mind at the beginning of the modern age. He is therefore sometimes aptly described as the 'Father of Modern Philosophy' to mark the comparison. He played a key role in helping to rescue enquiry about sublunary things from the stifling and long-frozen grip of religious authority. He did it not by rejecting that authority, for by his own testimony he was a devout

Catholic all his life, but by separating things of heaven from things of earth, so that scientific reason could investigate the latter without anxieties over orthodoxy. This left the things of heaven untouched and unthreatened – so Descartes thought and hoped – by what scientific enquiry discovered.

But it was not only Descartes' ideas about method which had such a seminal impact. His *Discourse* included three essays, one of them about optics, in which the law of refraction was first published (it had been independently discovered by the Dutchman Willibrord Snell fifteen years earlier[3]), another on meteorological phenomena, including the first satisfactory explanation of rainbows, and the third on geometry, in which Descartes presented to the world the foundations of analytic geometry, thereby contributing to the crucial growth of mathematical understanding which, in turn, helped the later progress of the seventeenth-century's scientific revolution.

Thus history remembers René Descartes because he made permanently important contributions both to mathematics and philosophy, thereby counting as one of the major figures in the epoch that gave birth to modern times. He was aware that his achievements in these respects were significant: he had neither reason nor desire to underestimate them. But he also thought of himself as a physicist and a medical scientist, and devoted just as much of his intellectual energy to these spheres of enquiry. One of his abiding hopes was that use of the method of enquiry he had announced in the *Discourse*, and which he believed offered a key to all knowledge, would unlock the secrets of health and long life. Later, in response to the promptings of two royal admirers, he ventured into ethics and moral psychology too. But it is his mathematical and earlier philosophical legacy for which his name now endures, placing him in a pantheon which includes Francis Bacon, Thomas Hobbes, Galileo Galilei, William Harvey, Blaise Pascal, Pierre de Fermat, and other philosophical and scientific luminaries of the first half of the seventeenth century.

Descartes was born in Touraine, France in 1596, and after living most of his adult life in the United Provinces of the free Netherlands, died in Stockholm, Sweden in 1650. His life therefore falls, chronologically and geographically, within the scope of that vast and momentous complex of events which the history books inadequately call 'the Counter-Reformation' and the 'Thirty Years War'. In these events he was, in ways to be discussed, not just a spectator but a participant. The legacy of these events still blights the world, in more and less indirect ways; but Descartes' intellectual work transcended them.

Given that Descartes' fame is so richly merited, it is odd now to think that it suffered a temporary eclipse among some of the *philosophes* of his own country in the eighteenth century, when Voltaire and others regarded him as outmoded by Newton and Locke. Philosophical fame, it is true to say, is to some extent the function of fashion, as exemplified by the fact that Descartes' two greatest philosophical contemporaries, Bacon and Hobbes, have retained less than their due in the university curricula which are chiefly responsible for sustaining philosophical reputations. When I was an undergraduate, courses in the history of modern philosophy were typically labelled 'From Bacon and Descartes to Kant'; now Bacon has gone from the syllabus, to become undeservedly a footnote in the history and the philosophy of science. Likewise, Hobbes appears to retain interest only for political theorists, whereas his views in metaphysics and epistemology are effectively the inspiration for Locke's philosophy, to such an extent that the latter was even charged with plagiarism[4]. Descartes, by contrast, stands so firmly in the curriculum that he is often the first philosopher studied in detail by undergraduates, and his celebrated *Meditations on First Philosophy* is a classic both as an introductory text and as a focus of scholarly discussion.

The fate of Descartes' major philosophical contemporaries reflects another curious fact about posthumous reputations. Although genuine merit often survives the neglect and calumny of its own time, contemporary renown is equally as often taken by posterity to be a reason to praise also, while contemporary attacks on a reputation can unjustly block the applause posterity ought to give. This latter is also part of what happened to Bacon and Hobbes, the first because of a bribery scandal late in his life, the second because he was an atheist, and atheism was once regarded with flesh-crawling horror: for what depths of depravity, what murders and dalliances with evil, could an atheist not stoop to? Descartes' high standing with many of his contemporaries, by contrast, continued unabated with his successors, ensuring (despite Voltaire) a continuous reputation ever since.

Although Descartes has been lucky with the judgement of time, he has had mixed fortunes as regards his biographers. The work on which all subsequent biography has principally depended is the too-often unreliable but suggestive early account by Adrien Baillet, *La Vie de Monsieur Descartes*, published in two volumes in 1691. It makes use of much lost material, which we know Baillet does not always accurately employ or even quote, because we have occasional independent checks and can see that he trimmed and shaped his sources to give a slant – frequently a too-positive one – of his own. But it is the fullest of the early sources, and is indispensable.

Baillet's account, however, was not the earliest. Just three years after Descartes' death Daniel Lipstorp, a German savant, gave a brief biographical sketch in his *Specimina*, using extremely valuable first-hand material collected from among Descartes' Dutch acquaintances. The other contemporary biographer was Pierre Borel, who in his *Vitae Renati Cartesii summi philosophi Compendium* (the first edition of 1653 is lost; we have the second edition, published in 1656) gives a certain amount of information – perhaps more than is accurate – about Descartes' military career. Since much of Borel's information came from Descartes' friend Etienne de Villebressieu, scientist and engineer to the King of France, it is nonetheless a useful source.

In 1910 Charles Adam, one of the editors of Descartes' collected works, published his *Descartes: sa vie, son oeuvre*. He improved upon Baillet and the other early sources because of his intimate knowledge of Descartes' writings, especially the letters, and he had of course the advantage of longer hindsight, and of the nuggets of information embedded in several intervening centuries of gossip and legend.

Since Adam's book there have appeared a few minor biographies, mainly French and almost all tendentious,[5] but there has only been one really significant one: Stephen Gaukroger's comprehensive and scholarly account, *Descartes: An Intellectual Biography* (1995). Gaukroger devotes more space to surveys and assessments of Descartes' work – all of it: including a great deal of uncompromising mathematics – than to purely biographical matters, about which he is commendably circumspect given the uneven reliability of the sources. Consequently, his book is a biography for specialists, and he would himself, I am sure, agree that it makes heavily technical demands on its readers. To date there has not been a satisfactory non-specialist biography devoted to the general reader: a gap that the following pages, with due modesty, aspire to fill.

I have learned and profited from almost all the forerunners in the field, and came especially to appreciate the work of Adams and Gaukroger, together with an achievement worth repeating the praises of: the edition of Descartes' works translated into English and edited by John Cottingham, Robert Stoothof and Dugald Murdoch. My debts in the history of science and the general history of the first half of the seventeenth century are paid in the bibliography, but I should mention here an old classic which was thrilling and illuminating to re-read, and which gave me many clues to follow in pursuing an hypothesis about Descartes' early career. This is C. V. Wedgwood's *The Thirty Years War*, first published in 1938 as the clouds regathered over the legacy of that earlier epic struggle.

In light of the animadversions cast above (and in the endnotes) upon some of Descartes' less disciplined biographers, I feel a certain hesitancy in turning now to advance an hypothesis I formulated while researching Descartes' life. It is necessary to mention it here, right at the outset, because it applies to much that is puzzling and hidden in the first half of Descartes' adult life, approximately the dozen or so years between the completion of his formal education and the early part of his sojourn in the United Provinces (the free part of the

Netherlands). As the sequel will report, at the outset of this period Descartes joined the armies first of Prince William of Nassau and then Duke Maximilian of Bavaria, taking part in some capacity in the opening events of the Thirty Years War and, while doing so and afterwards, travelling very widely in central, eastern and southern Europe. The details of Descartes' military service and travels are extremely scanty; he himself did not speak or write about them, except in the vaguest and most passing terms. In this, together with the manner of life he subsequently chose, lie the seeds of a mystery.

The year 1628 was pregnant with significance for politics and war in Europe. In that year Descartes, after a private audience with the notorious Cardinal Berulle – then one of the leading figures in French politics – decided to go into permanent, and apparently self-imposed, exile in the United Provinces, moving frequently from one address to another and for a long time keeping his whereabouts secret. The standard explanation of this is that he desired privacy and seclusion for his philosophical work, and chose the United Provinces because he found the climate, both meteorological and social, congenial for it. Some add or substitute the idea that he wished to keep hidden from his family, which disapproved of his choice of career.

My suggestion is rather different. It is that Descartes was a spy. More circumstantially put, my suggestion is that he was in some way engaged in intelligence activities or secret work during the period of his military service and travels. It was because of this, I further suggest, that Cardinal Berulle warned him that he was no longer welcome in France. The thought is by no means far-fetched and, if correct, goes a long way to explain some of the many curiosities and inexplicabilities of Descartes' life and doings.

The case for this tentative hypothesis rests on evidence that emerges as the story unfolds. But a background point to it is as follows: many intellectuals and clerics at this period engaged in intelligence activity because they were well fitted for the task by their command of languages, especially of the universal language Latin, and the fact that they corresponded widely and travelled more than any other class apart from aristocrats and merchants (but these latter did not have nearly as good access to political circles as scholars and clerics did). Some well-known examples support the thesis. Christopher Marlowe was stabbed to death in Deptford in 1593 because, it is thought on good grounds, he was engaged in espionage of some kind. The celebrated Huygens family engaged in intelligence for the British and the House of Orange throughout the seventeenth century. Peter Paul Rubens was an agent for the Habsburg interest in the Spanish Netherlands. Other examples could be cited, but the point is sufficiently made by these.

If Descartes was an agent of some kind, he was by far most probably so in the Jesuit interest. The Jesuits were on the side – more: were instigators and coadjutors – of the effort by the Habsburg rulers of the Holy Roman Empire (the misnamed and complex empire of mainly German states) to reclaim for Roman Catholicism those parts of Europe lost to Protestantism as a result of the Reformation in the preceding century. That, in large part, was what the bloody and terrible Thirty Years War (1618–48) was about, and its chief prosecutor, Emperor Ferdinand II, had a Jesuit confessor and advisor, Wilhelm Lamormaini, who was the conduit between the throne and the Jesuit Order.

For various reasons of their own, both France (chiefly because of its hostility to Habsburg Spain, and anxieties about the European balance of power) and intermittantly the Papacy were opposed to the Holy Roman Emperor's endeavours, and indeed the former opposed them with arms; which means that if Descartes were an agent in the Jesuit–Habsburg interest, he could not have been comfortable with the policy adopted by his own country. As an unwavering and orthodox Catholic, educated by the Jesuits and always anxious for their approval and protection, and yet living as an independent layman, Descartes was a natural candidate for employment by them. Moreover, even though Descartes came into a share of his mother's estate in early adulthood, his income from it cannot have matched the level at which he lived: which makes one wonder where the extra money came from.

Now, I do not know whether Descartes was indeed a spy or agent, and I would not bet my house on the notion. So I am neither asserting nor claiming that it is so; I am merely mooting the possibility, in the chapters to follow pointing out how this hypothesis helps to explain gaps and puzzles in Descartes' story. At least it is a plausible hypothesis, and merits its place in his tale.

Descartes was once actually accused by some of his enemies in the United Provinces of being a spy. But although this might be taken as evidence of a contemporary suspicion that strengthens the case, I suspect that, in that instance, mere malice was the motive (see the account of Descartes' quarrel with one Gisbert Voetius in Chapter 8 below). Still: smoke requires fire, and it happens that I came across these allegations only after beginning to wonder about the full meaning of Descartes' chosen motto, 'The hidden life is best.'

1

The Awakening

The world René Descartes entered on 31 March 1596 was not a peaceful one. Europe was convulsed by religious conflicts, yet at the very same time mankind's greatest and most powerful achievement – science – was in the process of being born. Whereas the religious conflicts represented the death throes of one epoch in history, the scientific revolution marked the birth of another – the period we call modern times. It was because the Reformation and Counter-Reformation were tearing holes in the certainties of religious belief that the scientific revolution could begin, by allowing the light of secular reason to shine through the gashes; and once people started to see by that light it became inextinguishable. Despite the terrors of intolerance, persecution, and recurrent bitter war, the turn of the seventeenth century was therefore a time rich in promise. Descartes entered it just at the right moment, because his interests and gifts tallied exactly with what was required for the longer-term intellectual revolution then beginning to happen.

Descartes did not write an autobiography, but in his seminal *Discourse on Method* he reminisced about his education, which, when he looked back on it, seemed to him not as good as it might have been. He thought this despite having been a pupil at the best and most famous school of the day, the Jesuit college of La Flèche in France's Anjou province, now part of the Pays de la Loire. In the *Discourse* Descartes described his education in equivocal terms to provide a foil for his own mature views about how enquiry should be conducted in mathematics, science and philosophy. He believed that he had discovered a powerful method for finding the truth about everything, and his *Discourse* was written both to describe and to demonstrate that method. The question of method was an important one in his day; most thinkers, including Francis Bacon in England and the Rosicrucians scattered about Europe, were eager to find an easy, direct and infallible way of discovering the truth about things, some of them because they wished to help the advancement of learning, others because they wished to turn common metals into gold or to find the secret of longevity; and most of them because they desired a combination of both – Descartes among them.

The autobiographical details in the *Discourse* (and occasionally in Descartes' letters) are very sketchy, but they are of course useful for subsequent biographers, and highly characteristic of Descartes' way of doing things, for he always believed that if his readers could see things through his eyes, thus retracing the path he had taken to his insights, they could not possibly disagree with him. In Descartes' other famous work, the *Meditations on First Philosophy* – the book on which almost all students of philosophy in the Western world still cut their teeth – the argument is set out from the point of view of an 'I', ostensibly Descartes himself, reporting his doubts, reasons and conclusions; but in fact this is a device in which each reader is himself or herself the 'I' of the adventure, seeing things from a vantage point inside Descartes' mind, and thus from the outset sharing his perspective.

Although what Descartes says about his early intellectual development is fascinating, it has to be treated with the usual amount of caution required by all autobiography. Auto-biographies are frequently unreliable documents, a fact that biographers enjoy because they like discovering independent information which shows that autobiographers have been sculpting their lives into shapes either more agreeable than the truth, or perhaps closer to what they felt was (so to speak) the real reality, which only they could see because only they had lived it. Then again, autobiographies are generally written by people who have reason to believe that the story of their lives will interest others, and such people – most of them achievers, succeeders, discoverers or creators – have personalities to match; which is another reason (to paraphrase Bing Crosby's famous 'Mister In-Between') why they might 'accentuate the positive and eliminate the negative' too far.

Descartes does a certain amount of accentuating and elimin-ating in his various autobiographical remarks, for example stating that his mother died a few hours after his birth, whereas in fact she died fourteen months later. But what he says in the *Discourse* about his education and mental development is almost certainly accurate, though sketchy; and it is the basis of most of what we most solidly know about his early life.

But of course that life began before Descartes went to La Flèche, and it is pertinent briefly to note something of his origins.

★   ★   ★

In the year Descartes was born Shakespeare's *Richard II* and
A Midsummer Night's Dream were first performed, El Greco's
famously bleak and stormy *View of Toledo* was painted, and
three other births took place of people whose lives were to
have an impact, directly and otherwise, on Descartes' own:
Frederick V, Elector of the Rhine Palatinate and briefly King
of Bohemia (the 'Winter King' of 1618–19); Frederick's wife
Elizabeth Stuart of Scotland (Frederick was born on 16 August
1596 and Elizabeth on 19 August); and the poet and scholar
Constantijn Huygens, who thirty years later became Descartes'
friend and protector in the free Dutch lands of the United
Provinces, today called the Netherlands or Holland.

If the language of the English class system were used to
describe Descartes' family background, he would be said to
come from well-off upper-middle-class stock comprised mainly
of doctors and lawyers, a number of them holding senior
official positions in the regional civil service of the royal
government. One of Descartes' recent forebears had been
mayor of Tours, another had been treasurer of that city's cath-
edral. A third (on Descartes' mother's side) had even for a time
been physician to Queen Eleanor, wife of King Francois I of
France. And a fourth, still more grandly yet, had been physician
to Catherine de Medici, mother of all the last three Valois
kings of France. This medical ancestor later became physician
to the duc de Montpensier, and dedicated a little book about
fevers to him; so there was authorship and science as well as
law and medicine in the family genes.

The Descartes family and their relations were thus well
established and flourishing, with money, position and property
in those beautiful stretches of France known as Touraine and
Poitou. It was here that Descartes was born and raised – born in

Touraine at La Haye (now, in the interests of the tourist indus-
try, renamed Descartes), and brought up across the provincial
border in Poitou at his great-uncle's house in Chatellerault.
In France at that time people of Descartes' class were regarded
as minor nobility, and if they owned property they could
give themselves a title – which Descartes himself for a time did,
calling himself 'sieur du Perron' because he inherited from his
mother a small farm at Perron. Like the equivalent expression
'lord of the manor', which in English usage is a description
rather than a title of nobility, such appellations could be bought
and sold along with the corresponding property. When he
entered his inheritance Descartes exchanged both his parcel of
land and its associated title for cash to meet his needs.

As this suggests, Descartes did not share the dynastic interests
of his father Joachim or his older brother Pierre. Joachim was
a distinguished lawyer whose own father had been a successful
doctor well known in provincial circles, and at the time of
Descartes' birth he held an official position in the high court for
Brittany at Rennes. (Such courts had multiple functions; as well
as being courts in the usual sense, they oversaw administration
of the law for their region and heard petitions to the crown.
They were called 'Parlements', misleadingly for English speak-
ers.) Joachim expected his sons Pierre and René to follow him
in the family tradition, adopting respectable professions, marrying well, and by both means adding to the family's portfolio of
dignities and properties. René, the younger son, disappointed
him; Pierre obliged handsomely by becoming a replica of his
father. There were other children too, only one of whom – a
daughter called Jeanne – survived infancy.

It was in his grandmother's house on the banks of the River
Creuse in La Haye that René Descartes first saw light, and it

was in the town's Catholic church of Saint-Georges that he was baptised three days later, on 3 April 1596. A significant footnote to these innocuous facts is that Saint-Georges was his grandmother's parish church only because a closer church, Notre Dame, had been granted to the town's Protestants seven years before. So Descartes' first public act, that of being baptised, took place in a manner determined by the great religious divisions of the time.

Another footnote concerns a legend – the evidence suggests that it was invented long after the philosopher became famous – to the effect that Descartes was born in a country ditch halfway between La Haye and Chatellerault. The story has it that his mother was en route from Chatellerault to her mother's house in La Haye, a distance of eighteen miles, and was overtaken by her labour pangs at the exact halfway point, outside a farm called La Sybilliere (providing a suitably prophetic association for the birth of a great thinker). This 'halfway point' detail has the tinge of fiction to it, as does the additional detail that Descartes' mother was so weakened by giving birth that she had to rest at La Sybilliere for two nights, thus explaining why three whole days elapsed before Descartes was baptised. The most probable reason for the 'delay', of course, is that Descartes' various godparents had to be informed, and then had to travel to La Haye. The eighteen miles separating Chatellerault and La Haye was a day's journey; so a messenger sent, and his return journey with the prospective godparents, would itself take two days.

Fourteen months after Descartes' birth his mother was again at his grandmother's house in La Haye for a lying-in. This time the outcome was fatal. Descartes' mother died on 13 May 1597, six days after giving birth to a baby boy, who followed her into the grave a mere three days later. At the time of this tragedy Descartes' father Joachim was at his duties in the Parlement at Rennes, and young Descartes himself was most probably still with his wet-nurse. What happened after this direful event is a blank in the record, though it is probable that all three of the children, Pierre, Jeanne and René, went to live with their grandmother at La Haye for a time, and that the boys then moved to Chatellerault to be raised by their great-uncle Michel Ferrand (who was also René's godfather). Joachim remarried three years after being widowed, moved to Rennes to be close to his duties, and raised a new family of children, leaving his first family behind with their mother's relatives.

This was not a bad arrangement. Descartes' great-uncle-cum-godfather Michel Ferrand was a substantial citizen. During the negotiations preceding the epochal Edict of Nantes in 1598 (the Edict giving protection to France's Protestants), Ferrand was lieutenant-general of Chatellerault – an office corresponding to that of mayor, though much grander-sounding – and it was in his town that the Protestants of all France met to discuss the provisions of the Edict before it was enacted. He was still lieutenant-general in 1605 when another national meeting of Protestants took place there to protest against Catholic violations of the Edict. The man in charge of the 1598 Edict negotiations was the King's first minister, Maximilien de Béthune, duc de Sully. It is not very likely that Ferrand was involved in any direct capacity with the discussions themselves, but he was probably Sully's host, and certainly would have been responsible for the local organisation of the event.

One historian of Poitou, Alfred Barbier, claimed in an 1897 study that Michel Ferrand was a staunch Catholic who opposed concessions to the Huguenots.[1] This seems improbable. Poitou had the largest Huguenot population of any French province (nearly a million by the mid-seventeenth century), and relations between Poitevin Catholics and Huguenots had been consistently good right from the beginning of the Reformation. As a leading public figure in a town with a large and influential Huguenot population, Ferrand was unlikely to have been anything but tolerant, if only because he could not afford to be otherwise. And if so, his was a good house to be brought up in.

It was not only the example of tolerance that made Ferrand's house a good one to be raised in, it was the physical environment of La Haye and Chatellerault too. The beauty of that region of France, and its warm summers, was one of the last things Descartes spoke about when he was dying, showing that the impression it left on him was a deep one. Farms and gardens, and the ubiquitous hedges after which the village of his birth was named, stood between half-timbered houses, those still remaining tile-roofed now but probably thatched then. Rodis-Lewis perceptively notes that the swiftly turbulent river Creuse that runs through La Haye must have given Descartes his first ideas about the motion of matter, while the everyday occurrences and avocations of rural life provided him with similes he later used in constructing his scientific theories. He had seen bundles of damp hay steaming from the spontaneous heat generated within them, and new wine boiling when left to ferment on pomace (the pulp left after pressing). He had seen how wind, blowing through a hedge, carries off leaves and straw caught in the branches, and how dust is raised by the feet of passers-by. And he had watched milk being churned until it separates into cream and butter, and grains being sieved. Each of these mundane examples appear in his scientific writings as illustrations of such phenomena as 'cardiac heat' (Descartes says that it is no more mystifying than the spontaneous heat in hay and fermenting wine); the way 'subtle matter' passes through interstices in coarser matter (the wind through the hedges); and how the 'humours' of the body work like sieves separating oats from rye.[2]

These indirect glimpses of the world of Descartes' childhood so perceptively garnered by Rodis-Lewis are, with a very few others, the only ones that relate specifically to his early experience. Descartes otherwise says little about his childhood. He refers to it no more than a half-dozen times, and, except for the autobiographical snippets in the *Discourse*, always in passing merely. He tells us that because he was born in the 'gardens of Touraine' he preferred a mild climate. In a letter, he says that his health was poor as a child because he had inherited a dry cough from his mother and was always pale, prompting his doctors into pessimism about his chances of surviving into adulthood. But he adds that by the time he reached his twenties he had grown ruddy and robust, and for the most part enjoyed good health thereafter. In another letter he recalls having a tenderness for a girl with a mild affliction, which had a permanent effect on him: 'When I was a child,' he wrote, 'I was in love with a girl of my own age who was slightly cross-eyed; consequently whenever I looked at her unfocused eyes the impression of that vision of her on my brain was so linked to what aroused the passion of love that, for long afterwards, whenever I saw cross-eyed people I felt more inclined to love them than others.'[3]

But though the references are fleeting they are suggestive. Take for example Descartes' comment about inheriting poor health from his mother. The letter in which this occurs speaks also of his mother's death, misdating it to shortly after his birth. Written in the early summer of 1645 to Princess Elizabeth of Bohemia, with whom he had been having an absorbing correspondence and indeed friendship since 1642, it offers advice on the Princess's health – she had been suffering from a cough and a fever – and says, 'The most common cause of a slow fever is sadness . . . My mother died a few days after my birth from a disease of the lungs caused by distress. From her I inherited a dry cough and a pale complexion, which remained with me until I was over twenty, so that all the doctors who saw me until that time condemned me to a youthful death. But I have always been inclined to look at things from the most favourable angle and to make my chief happiness depend upon me alone; and I think this inclination gradually overcame the weakness which was effectively part of my constitution.'[4] This passage suggests that as a boy and youth Descartes was, though his health was delicate, fortunate enough to have a naturally positive, independent and reflective outlook. All three traits served him well for the next chapter in his story, which was his going as a boarder to the newly-founded and immensely prestigious Jesuit college of La Flèche in Anjou, not far from his home in Chatellerault.

Despite the critical remarks Descartes made in the *Discourse on Method* about his education at La Flèche, he himself recognised it as the outstanding school of his day. Twenty-two years after leaving it, and a year after the *Discourse* was published, he replied to a request for advice on where the best schooling was to be found by singing the praises of La Flèche. The school attracted 'so many young people from all parts of France,'

Descartes wrote, 'and they form such a varied mixture, that by conversing with them one learns almost as much as if one travelled far.' He praised also the 'equality maintained by the Jesuits among themselves, treating almost in the same fashion the highest born and the lowliest.' And the clincher for him was that 'there is no place on earth where philosophy is better taught than at La Flèche.' And this mattered because although not everything taught in philosophy 'is as true as the gospels, nevertheless, because philosophy is the key to the other sciences, it is extremely useful to have studied the whole philosophy curriculum in the manner it is taught in Jesuit institutions, before undertaking to raise one's mind above pedantry in order to make oneself wise in the right way.'[5]

The founding of La Flèche in 1604, when Descartes was eight years old, is in itself a notable event, given the religious and political complexities of the day. Its story is inseparable from that of its royal founder, Henri IV, and inseparable too from Descartes' story, in many different ways additional to the obvious one of his being educated there.

Henri IV was one of France's most remarkable kings. Born in the Protestant faith in 1553 to Antoine de Bourbon, he was regarded by the Huguenots as the nominal head of their cause. In August 1570 the Huguenots and the Valois king of France, Charles IX, reached an agreement aimed at ending eight years of intermittently violent hostility between the country's Catholics and Protestants. They signed a treaty subsequently known as the Peace of Saint-Germain. To mark the occasion Charles IX betrothed his sister Margaret of Valois to Henri de Bourbon, a gesture intended not merely to symbolise but to cement the rapprochement between the two sides of the religious divide – or so it seemed.

The marriage between Henri and Margaret took place two years later, on 18 August 1572. Six days after the wedding celebrations, on the night of the feast of St Bartholomew, an appalling episode in France's history occurred: a massacre of Huguenots. It had long been meditated by Charles IX's advisors and especially his mother, the chilling and dangerous Catherine de Medici. The massacre started when the Huguenots' effective leader, the Admiral de Coligny, was murdered outside his house in Paris by royal troops, and with him a number of Huguenot nobles. Then the killing spread to Huguenot households elsewhere in Paris. Front doors were smashed down, whole families within murdered, their houses looted. A spate of royal orders to provincial cities encouraged officials to subject local Huguenots to the same treatment. Lyons, Toulouse, Bordeaux, and Rouen saw frightful slaughters; the river Rhone carried so many corpses from Lyons down to Arles that the Arlesians could not drink the water for three months afterwards. Instructions from Paris reached local officials in such a sporadic way that the massacres in Toulouse and Bordeaux took place respectively a month and two months after the initial events in Paris.

Henri reacted by hastily converting to Catholicism. Nevertheless his father-in-law, the king, or more accurately the king's mother, Catherine de Medici, did not trust him, and kept him under house-arrest at court. In 1576 Henri escaped, reverted to Protestantism, and took arms against the Catholic monarchy as again one of the leaders of the Huguenot cause. Repeated outbreaks of fighting over the next several years at last prompted Spain to send troops to aid the French Catholic side; but by the time they did so Charles IX had died, his brother Henri III had succeeded him, and Henri de Bourbon had become heir to the throne because of the death of Henri III's immediate heir presumptive, Francois duc d'Alençon. Henri III, last of the Valois kings, was assassinated in 1589, and Henri de Bourbon succeeded him. But in order to assert his rights as Henri IV, he had to fight France's Catholics yet again. He defeated them and then besieged Paris, but could not take the city until, in 1593, he converted to Catholicism a second time, saying (so legend famously has it), 'Paris is worth a Mass.' The city therefore opened its gates to him, and his victory was complete.

More importantly, though, Henri IV won the peace that eventually followed. By means of the Edict of Nantes, which granted a large measure of religious freedom to Huguenots – a freedom they enjoyed for nearly a century afterwards – and successful economic policies, Henri IV restored France to order and prosperity in an astonishingly short time.

And then, in 1603, Henri invited the Jesuits to return to France. He had banished them eight years earlier because one of their number had attempted to assassinate him. Now he not only welcomed them back but patronised them handsomely. He took a confessor from among them, and gave them the palace of La Flèche – his birthplace – so that they could open a school in it. He was deeply attached to La Flèche, leaving instructions in his will that both his and his wife's hearts were to be buried in its chapel. But his interest in the idea of founding a Jesuit college was not merely sentimental. He paid for the necessary renovations and alterations to the palace, and interested himself in the rules and curriculum for the pupils. He had always been keen to improve education, before-hand appointing regents for various colleges and providing salaries for teachers. Now he went further, entrusting an elite institution wholly to the Jesuits, whose idea of 'total education' impressed him – a conception of education as a moulding of the whole intellect and personality by what might now be called 'immersion' techniques (the pupils did not spend much time holidaying at home with their families in the course of a year), and by encouragement and reward rather than the more traditional method of the birch.

Such was the institution Descartes entered in the spring of 1606, aged ten. His older brother Pierre was at La Flèche too. The two boys were known to the college's first rector, Père Chastellier, a native of Poitou, and to its second rector, Père Etienne Charlet, who was a relation of Descartes' mother. The Descartes boys were not, therefore, going into the keeping of strangers. Evidence that the Jesuit fathers were kind at least to Descartes himself is attested by the fact that when, nearly four decades later, he wrote to Père Charlet, he did so in warmly affectionate terms, calling him 'my second father'.[6]

Kindness has its appropriate limits, however. Descartes' earlier biographers repeated a story alleging that because of his delicate constitution he was allowed to stay in bed until noon each day, a habit that remained with him throughout life. It is true that as an adult Descartes spent his mornings thinking and writing in bed, but the idea of a ten-year-old at boarding school staying in bed until lunchtime seems improbable not only for the early seventeenth century, but even with a 'second father' as the college's rector. Descartes was not the son of a grand nobleman (such – and there were quite a few at La Flèche – were housed in the main college buildings with their servants), and he therefore lived with the majority of the 1,200 pupils in one or other of the ordinary boarding houses scattered

round the village in the neighbourhood of the college. The
legend of school mornings abed is doubtless a result of Chinese
whispers: Descartes must have told someone that his preference
for mornings in bed was acquired at an early age, and this was
transmuted into a legend about an improbable indulgence at
school.

Still, the irrepressible Baillet offers us reason to believe that
Descartes stood out among his school-fellows. When Henri IV
was assassinated on 14 May 1610, his heart was brought to La
Flèche according to his stated wish, and Baillet tells us that
Descartes was one of twenty-four boys chosen to take part in
the final ceremony of interment, after the heart in its urn had
been carried in procession through the black-draped college
buildings, accompanied by members of the royal family,
nobility, priests, and a guard-of-honour of archers, all clad in
profound mourning. A great arch was erected for the cortège to
pass through, and the central court of the college was decorated
with Henri IV's royal insignia and depictions of his soul being
wafted to heaven by angels.

Did Descartes help to carry the urn containing Henri's heart?
His intellectual gifts might well have singled him out among his
schoolfellows, and a mark of that distinction might equally well
have resulted in his being chosen as one of two dozen acolytes
to attend the murdered king's heart as it went to the chapel.
But Baillet himself gives us cause for doubting the veracity of
the story when he says that the twenty-four youths in question
were 'gentlemen' students. Descartes, like the majority of his
fellow students, indeed came from the gentry; but among this
number were some five hundred sons of dukes, marquises,
counts and other noblemen, and distinctions of rank were
taken seriously. Since nothing else is reported of Descartes

being singled out for special attention at the school, a grain of salt is obviously needed here. The porters of the urn containing Henri's heart were without doubt sons of ranking noblemen, and Baillet's claim that Descartes was among them has to be treated as legend-making.

The interment of Henri's heart at La Flèche was nevertheless significant for Descartes. Henri IV had been murdered by a Jesuit called Ravillac, so there is black irony in the fact that, by his own wish, the king was buried by Jesuits among the Jesuits, whom he had patronised and supported with such generosity. The staff of La Flèche assiduously honoured Henri's memory with festivities and competitions on the anniversary of his murder for as long as the college thereafter lasted; but nothing could expunge the fact that the many assassination attempts made on Henri IV were motivated, as the final successful one was, by suspicion of him as a once-Protestant who, in pursuit of his policy of containing the Habsburg power in its Spanish and German empires, sided with Protestant interests everywhere in Europe. The Jesuits, as already noted, were the advisors and encouragers of the Habsburgs who, like their Jesuit mentors, saw themselves as the champions of the Catholic church, and who were soon to plunge Europe into three decades of hideous war in an effort – ultimately un-successful – to reclaim for Catholicism all territories lost to Protestantism.

In short, Henri IV had nourished a viper in his bosom by sponsoring the Jesuits, and had been killed by its bite at last. Descartes, Jesuit-educated and for years afterwards a loyal adherent of the Jesuit interest, might (as suggested in the Introduction) have served the Jesuit-Habsburg interest against his own country. Given the historical circumstances and the great issue of the day, there were probably many unfaithful hearts in the courts of La Flèche on the day that the dead king's own heart arrived there for burial.

One of the principal ways that the Jesuit movement sought to defend, fortify and potentiate the Catholic cause was by educating boys in such a manner as to make them secure in the faith forever. They saw themselves as soldiers in the van of the Counter-Reformation and, accordingly, one of their prime goals was to barricade young minds against heresy. By means of fine discipline, a military-style structure, and high standards, the Society had forged itself into a formidable instrument since its inception in the mid-sixteenth century. From its seminaries, including the prestigious Collegio Romano, it sent out an army of scholars and teachers to champion the faith. Given Descartes' lifelong adherence to the Catholic faith and to the Jesuit interest, he counts as a signal example of the success of their methods.

If the Society was in the front line for the Catholic cause, its teachers were crucial front-line troops for the Society itself, and it mattered greatly that they should succeed in the vital task allotted to them. They therefore thought carefully about education, and the methods they adopted now seem impressively modern. In the schools run by their rivals, the Benedictines, boys were kept at their books for long exhausting hours and drilled incessantly. The Jesuits' teaching manual, the *Ratio studiorum*, took from Quintilian the comparison of a boy's mind with a narrow-necked bottle: try to pour in too much too fast and little will get into the body of the bottle, but pour slowly and carefully, and the bottle will be filled. The Jesuits took the simile to heart. Using prizes and badges to mark achievement, allowing the boys to enjoy games, dancing and theatrical activities, giving each of them personal attention, promoting discussion, allowing the boys to govern themselves to some extent through a prefectorial system – by such means they won their pupils' confidence and therefore taught them well.

The main forms of instruction were the study of texts, daily review of lessons, weekly debates and discussions, and monthly formal debates in which the participants were given marks for their performance. Everything happened in Latin; use of French was forbidden on pain of punishment. Apart from the fact that Latin was the *lingua franca* of all educated people, it was especially associated with the Roman Catholic church, in whose view the body of the faithful were one people under their earthly monarch, the Pope, sharing one language and one culture. Interestingly, some Catholic thinkers went so far as to suggest that use of vernaculars constituted a sin because it subverted the integrity of Christendom. Later, Descartes chose to publish in the vernacular, which in the light of these delicate questions counts as a significant gesture.

A pupil's first five years at La Flèche were dedicated to the classical tongues and their literature, beginning with 'grammar' and ending with 'rhetoric'. In the sixth, seventh and eighth years, if they stayed that long, boys studied philosophy, mathematics and science. In the first five years the main focus was the style of the classical authors rather than the content of their writings. In Descartes' day, as throughout the Renaissance, the most admired Latin writer was Cicero, whose texts were widely used as models of excellence for style and rhetorical structure.

Most boys spent only five years at La Flèche, because what they acquired in that time was enough for university entrance. But some universities were hostile to the Jesuits and refused to admit their pupils, so the Jesuits made sure that the upper years of some of their colleges could more than adequately take the place of a university education. Descartes benefited from this arrangement. In 1611, when his five years of studying 'letters' was over, he took the advanced curriculum, studying Aristotle's logic in the first year, science and mathematics in the second, and metaphysics and ethics in the third.

This was the education Descartes described twenty years later in his *Discourse on Method*. 'From my childhood I have been nourished on letters,' he wrote, meaning the classical languages and their literatures, 'and because I was persuaded that by their means one could acquire a clear and certain knowledge of all that is useful in life, I was extremely eager to learn them. But as soon as I had completed the course of study at the end of which one is normally admitted to the ranks of the learned, I completely changed my opinion. For I found that I had gained nothing from my attempts to become educated, except for an increasing recognition of my ignorance. And yet I was at one of the most famous schools in Europe, where I thought there must be learned men if any existed on earth.'[7]

This looks like a damning indictment of La Flèche, and on the face of it Descartes might be taken to mean that he had wasted his eight years there. But that is not what he meant. In the same passage he says he had made good use of the college library, reading beyond the curriculum; that he had not been accounted slow-witted by his teachers and peers; and that on leaving La Flèche he found the world to be as well equipped with intelligent people as at any time in history – and yet still it was clear that 'there was no knowledge in the world such as I had previously been led to hope for.' So it was not the particular fault of La Flèche that his expectations were disappointed. It was the general fact that letters, and what passed in his day for philosophy and science, were either limited in value (this, he meant, was especially true of letters) or stood on shaky ground (this, he meant, was especially true of philosophy and science). He appreciated all these subjects as far as they went; he enjoyed stories and poetry, fables and oratory; and above all he loved mathematics. 'I delighted in mathematics because of the certainty and self-evidence of its reasonings. But I did not yet notice its real use; and since I thought it was of service only in the mechanical arts, I was surprised that nothing more exalted had been built upon such firm and solid foundations.'[8]

It was for this reason, he said, that he decided to abandon the study of letters, and to avoid metaphysics because it had been cultivated for centuries by the best minds and yet was still embroiled in disputes and doubts. Nor did he think he could venture into the sciences, which stood on the shaky foundations of metaphysics. And there was no question of involvement with what he called 'the false sciences' of alchemy, magic and astrology, of which he was frankly contemptuous. So, he wrote, 'as soon as I was old enough to emerge from the control of my teachers, I entirely abandoned the study of letters. Resolving to seek no knowledge other than that which could be found in myself or else in the great book of the world, I spent the rest of my youth travelling, visiting courts and armies, mixing with people of diverse temperaments and ranks, gathering various experiences, testing myself in the situations which fortune offered me, and at all times reflecting on whatever came my way so as to derive some profit from it.' The reason he gave for this empirical and pragmatic decision is as pertinent now as then: 'For it seemed to me that much more truth could be found in the reasonings which a man makes concerning matters that concern him than in those which some scholar makes in his study about speculative matters. For the consequences of the former will soon punish the man if he judges wrongly, whereas the latter have no practical consequences and no importance for the scholar except that perhaps the further they are from common sense the more pride will he take in them, since he will have had to use much more skill and ingenuity in trying to render them plausible.'

Despite what these autobiographical remarks suggest, Descartes did not go travelling immediately after La Flèche. He left the college in the summer of 1614, aged eighteen, and his next documented appearance occurs in November 1616, when he graduated from the University of Poitiers with a degree in civil and canon law. All his biographers assume that he spent just one year at Poitiers, and therefore cite Baillet's claim that the missing year or even fourteen months between Descartes' quitting La Flèche and beginning his studies at Poitiers was spent in Paris; but not in the way of youth, with its predictable and even required sowing of oats, but in retreat at Saint-Germain-en-Lay, then a small village on the city's outskirts. Some speculate that Descartes was busy suffering a nervous breakdown, as David Hume and many other brilliant people have done when young – such a thing being almost a rite of passage for the creative intellect. But there is no evidence to support the idea, although it has a romantic attraction, and nothing in Descartes' later writings on the emotions suggests otherwise – these writings being where he would allude to his own example of emotional turmoil if he had suffered any, given his fondness for the autobiographical technique when explaining his views.

It is of course possible that Descartes had a breakdown, or even an illness of some kind, but it is somewhat more possible that he was indeed sowing some oats in the capital city, perhaps acquiring the taste for gambling later imputed to him; and yet more possible still that a degree in canon and civil law took more than just one year of study, and that the whole of the 'missing' year was spent over laborious texts in Poitiers. This latter, I suggest, was exactly the case. The source of Baillet's characteristically embroidered and inflated story about a 'year' in retreat on the outskirts of Paris might have been that Descartes, for some reason, spent part of the summer at Saint-Germain-en-Lay immediately after leaving La Flèche and before going up at Poitiers University in the autumn of 1614. Baillet, in retrospective obeisance to Descartes' genius, would see a sequestration at Saint-Germain as full of significance for the burgeoning young mind, far more interesting than swotting up *jus scriptum* and *jus publicum, jus commune et speciale* and *jus universale et particulare* at Poitiers. There can be no prizes for guessing what Descartes thought about all this *jus*, given his later strictures on the contrast between useful and useless knowledge; but at this juncture he had not quite ruled out pursuing a legal career at some future point and thus following in the well-heeled footsteps of his father and brother. Eight years later, in 1625, he wrote to his father asking whether he might apply for the post of lieutenant-general of Chatellerault (the job once held by his great-uncle Michel Ferrand) which required a legal background.[9] But he had little intention of doing so immediately, nor of seeking a position in the Parlement. One good reason was the minimum age requirement for entrance to a Parlement, even though, as his brother Pierre had done, he might have entered the profession in some other capacity first to gain experience.

If Descartes did indeed spend time at Saint-Germain-en-Lay, perhaps in those summer holidays between school and university as just suggested, an interesting connection between its sole tourist attraction and his later theories offers itself. Saint-Germain was the home of a royal pleasure garden designed by the Francini brothers, whose speciality was fountains – but not just of splashing water, for their expertise ran to hydraulic statues that moved, played music, danced, and even (reputedly) spoke. The garden was a labyrinth of grottos and mysterious passages containing water-powered organs, mechanical birds, and the moving speaking statues: a garden of wonders, and perhaps also of alarms, if Descartes indeed wandered neurasthenically there.[10] More interestingly, though, the garden suggests part of the inspiration for some of Descartes' later theories about animals as soulless automata, biological machines without consciousness, who experience neither sensations nor emotions, though appearing to; mere robots barking and mewing, eating and running, as if blindly powered by Francini pumps, and no more conscious than they.

After graduating from Poitiers in November 1616 Descartes next appears in the guise of a young godparent, signing the baptismal register in both October and November of 1617 at the church in Sucé. This small town stood near the property that his increasingly well-off father had bought some years before: the estate of Chavagne-en-Sucé, a commodious chateau set in fertile farmland among wooded hills. This suggests that Descartes spent the year after graduating from Poitiers at his father's house, perhaps assisting with the farm or his father's legal business, or reading, or all three, while considering what to do next. He might also have entered into an informal apprenticeship with a local doctor, out of curiosity; he later reported that he had studied some medicine as well as law when young. Of course, he could have attended medical and anatomical lectures at Poitiers, though formally registered as a law student. If so, a two-year stay at the university becomes more probable still, unless Descartes was given (like Baillet) to inflationary reminiscences, turning attendance at a few lectures into a study of medicine. That is unlikely.

In any event, the answer to Descartes' question about what he should do next was soon found. He decided to join an army. Note the wording: not 'the' army, but 'an' army. There were plenty to choose from. The one he chose belonged to Maurice of Nassau, Prince of Orange, arguably the greatest general of the day. (He thought so himself; he generously acknowledged that the famous Ambrogio Spinola, a Genoese who commanded the King of Spain's armies, was *second* best in the world.)

To enlist in Maurice's army Descartes travelled to Breda, just over the border from the Spanish Netherlands in the United Provinces of the free Netherlands. He arrived there in the summer of 1618, intending to cut something of a dash it seems, because he styled himself 'sieur du Perron' after the small property his mother had left to him and which had now come into his possession.[11]

His choice of Breda is partly explained by the fact that it was the base of a de facto military school, where military engineering and other technical skills of the art of war were taught.[12] Descartes' facility with mathematics evidently inclined him to the idea of learning how to build such defences as bastions, ravelins, hornworks, and the like, and to construct siege camps, make temporary bridges and pontoons, calculate artillery ranges, dig mines (for placing explosives under city walls), and more.

It was a fateful decision, for in the town of Breda one day Descartes met a man who was to give his life its first nudge in the direction of its later great achievements – not the definitive nudge, for it still took some years for Descartes to settle to the vocation of philosophy, but the first major push. It was an accidental meeting too, and an improbable one, given that the Jesuit-educated Catholic Frenchman Descartes was there in Protestant Dutch Breda, standing in front of a poster pasted to a wall in a street, when the man in question happened to be passing by but stopped to look at the poster also. The man Descartes thus encountered was Isaac Beeckman.

An account of the significant friendship between Descartes and Beeckman must, however, wait, because it is first necessary to speculate a little about any other reasons – that is, beyond a suddenly-acquired desire to be a military engineer, and in a Protestant army – that the Jesuit-educated Catholic Frenchman Descartes (or for that matter, any Jesuit-educated Catholic) might have for enlisting in the forces of a Protestant prince whose country was coming to the end of a short armed truce with its bitterest enemy, the Jesuit-supported Catholic

Habsburg power of Spain. A glimpse into the absorbing history of the circumstances helps to point the question: the reader must now entertain a couple of pages of history to set the scene for some of the mystery in Descartes' life.

Descartes had deliberately stepped into a situation by then over seventy years in the making. In January 1579 the seven Protestant northern provinces of the Netherlands, which was then in its entirety under Spanish dominion, made a declaration of mutual support, thereby forming themselves into the 'Union of Utrecht'. This was a response to a similar declaration jointly made by the Netherlands' Catholic southern provinces, which wished to affirm their allegiance to the Spanish crown and the Catholic faith and which had therefore formed themselves into the 'Union of Arras'. The seven dissenting Protestant provinces in the Union of Utrecht were Holland, Zeeland, Utrecht, Gelderland, Overijssel, Friesland and Groningen (without its city).

The semi-formal nature of this pair of unions was ominous for the future of Spanish hegemony in the region. Within just two years the members of the Union of Utrecht had declared themselves independent of the Spanish crown by the Oath of Abjuration (1581), and a protracted war began. The longer term outcome of that war (and a fact of great significance to Descartes personally, as later events proved) was that the United Provinces – as the Dutch republic of the northern provinces became known – managed to secure their independence from Spain. The United Provinces flourished mightily in the late sixteenth and seventeenth centuries, becoming immensely rich as a result of their overseas trade and empire, with a superlative domestic cultural tradition in consequence. This was the great age of Dutch painting; the country's relative liberty of thought and life encouraged thinkers, scientists and writers to settle there, and political exiles with them. It was, literally as well as figuratively, the Dutch Golden Age.

By contrast, most of the part of the Netherlands that remained under Catholic Spanish control eventually became Belgium.

Phillip II of Spain tried hard to reconquer the United Provinces, but Spain was already a moribund force, though dying slowly, and eventually Phillip II realised that the task was beyond him. By the time he had reached this decision in the late 1590s the United Provinces had built formidable defences along the line of the Maas and Waal rivers, and had developed a flourishing and growing trade with the Mediterranean lands, Spanish America, and Indonesia. In the hope at least of limiting the United Provinces' progress, Phillip II turned the Spanish Netherlands into a semi-autonomous state under his daughter Isabella and her husband (and cousin) Archduke Albert of Austria, who had already been in post as governor-general at Brussels for several years. The husband and wife team became known as 'the Archdukes', and although effectively under the control of the Spanish crown, they little by little increased their margin of competence, though never seeking to make the Spanish Netherlands wholly independent.

It was the Archdukes who hired Spinola to lead their army – a bold choice, because Spinola was a banker from Genoa and had never had military experience; people joked that he was a general before he was a soldier, and this was perfectly true. But he turned out to be a general of genius, and gave the United Provinces a few grey hairs before, in 1609, helping the Archdukes to arrange a twelve-year truce with them, which effectively recognised the United Provinces' independence.

This move infuriated Phillip II's successor as King of Spain, Phillip III, who hated the idea of peace with the rebel Dutch Calvinists. But Phillip III was in no position to insist: Spain was bankrupt and unable to raise further loans, and moreover was on the brink of war with Venice: a most uncomfortable combination. After some enforced reflection, Phillip III was made to see that a dozen years of peace in the Netherlands might help to rebuild Spanish finances; the Dutch (so the Archdukes and Spinola told him soothingly) could be reconquered thereafter.

When Descartes arrived in Breda, therefore, in the summer of 1618, the United Provinces had been at peace with its Catholic neighbour for nine years, and no military adventures were immediately in prospect. But the United Provinces was in an interesting state politically. Maurice of Nassau had just succeeded to the Princedom of Orange in that year, having previously been Count Maurice of Nassau. He was captain-general of the federal army and Stadhouder of five of the seven free provinces (his cousin William-Louis was Stadhouder of the other two). Already some transprovincial institutions had grown up: the mint, the council of state for military affairs, the admiralty, and an audit board. But each of the seven provinces had its own independent assembly, each of which in turn sent delegates to the federal assembly, called the States-General. This was a small body, consisting usually of less than a dozen members. All its decisions had to be referred back to the provincial assemblies for ratification – a time-consuming and frequently divisive business, not least because the provincial assemblies themselves had to consult the magistrates of their larger towns and the nobility in their rural areas before reaching any decisions.

This might have been a recipe for more paralysis and divisiveness if it were not that the richest province, Holland, in virtue of providing two-thirds of the United Provinces' tax revenue, usually had its way in most decisions, even major ones opposed by some of the other provinces. That in fact was what happened when the truce with the Archdukes was pending in 1609: some provinces, their hard-line Calvinist clergy to the fore, were as opposed to peace as Spain's Phillip III himself, and for mirror-image reasons. Also the United Provinces had enjoyed the expertise and canniness for some years of the States-General's leading permanent official, Johan van Oldenbarnevelt, who with the aid of a trusty standing committee arranged the agenda for meetings, before which he negotiated, cajoled, persuaded and twisted arms, and during which he took the chair – thus observing (or trying to) Sun Tzu's advice only to go into battle when the victory has already been won.

Still, among so much fissiparating potential there was sure to be something really dangerous to the internal peace and unity of the Provinces, and – inevitably, one must suppose – religion provided it. In 1605 two theologians at the University of Leiden fell out over the question of predestination. One, a strict and zealous Calvinist called Francis Gomarus, held that each individual is saved or damned from the beginning of time. Jacob Arminius, a liberal Reformed theologian, held that human beings have free will. Professors and students took sides; so eventually did the cloth workers of Leiden; and neither academics nor clothworkers were above throwing stones and breaking heads in defence of their preferred view. As civil unrest welled up, Oldenbarnevelt grew concerned; he called together a meeting of leading clergy to discuss a revision of the Reformed Church's Catechism and Confession of Faith, in order to settle matters. The clergymen angrily refused to consider changing the Confession, which to them was sacrosanct, and they told Oldenbarnevelt that the civil authorities must not dare to interfere with matters of doctrine.

All this happened during the first decade of the seventeenth century, at the end of which Arminius died. But his followers were determined to continue the fight. They presented a 'Remonstrance' to the assembly of the leading province, Holland, calling for a revision of the Confession of Faith, and demanding that church and state matters be kept completely separate. The Gomarists hit back with a 'Counter-Remonstrance', which included a demand that all Arminians should be discharged from their teaching and preaching posts. The Arminians asked Oldenbarnevelt for his help; the great jurist Hugo Grotius, then chief magistrate of Rotterdam, attacked the Gomarists for threatening the safety of the state, the church's unity, and worst of all the principal of freedom of conscience.

What made matters worse from the Gomarist point of view was that Roman Catholics, or at any rate most of them, were also believers in free will. In the pro-Gomarist section of the public mind this put Arminians into the same unspeakably vile category as Catholics. As a result Arminian ministers and their churches were attacked by mobs. Riots and disorder increased, and began to spread to other matters besides, as when in 1616 Delft saw several days of rioting over corn taxes, during which barricades were erected in the streets and the houses of the rich were stoned.

Maurice of Nassau began to tell his friends that the dispute over predestination would only be settled by civil war. He and Oldenbarnevelt disagreed about how matters should be handled. Indeed, they quarrelled; and the quarrel brought into the open the real difference between them. Oldenbarnevelt was an Arminian, Maurice a Gomarist; and he now publicly took the Gomarists' side. As a result their cause began to get the upper hand. In towns with an Arminian preacher large crowds marched out to places where they could hear a Gomarist minister instead. Harassment of Arminians increased, and Maurice instructed his troops to do nothing to protect them.

As matters grew worse Oldenbarnevelt decided that he had to act in the interests of public order. He persuaded the assembly of Holland to authorise each town in the province to raise *waardgelders*, in effect police or militia companies, if the local authorities thought they were necessary. The *waardgelders* were to swear loyalty to the town. Unfortunately, the same proclamation stated that soldiers in the federal army who were paid by Holland had a primary loyalty to Holland rather than to the whole United Provinces. This provision incensed Maurice; he saw it as a personal affront, and a direct challenge to his power. Under his direction, the States-General voted by five provinces to two to disband the *waardgelder* companies and he immediately put the order into effect, going with a large force to Utrecht and disarming its *waardgelders*, and then purging the city of Arminians and installing Gomarists in their place. That happened in July 1618; in August the towns of Holland submitted to Maurice, who repeated what he had done at Utrecht, at the same time placing Oldenbarnevelt and Hugo Grotius under arrest.

These events were happening just as the young Descartes arrived in the United Provinces in the summer of 1618. Given that the whole of Europe had been watching agog as the quarrel between Arminians and Gomarists heated to boiling point, there is no way that Descartes could have been unaware of the tense situation prevailing there. Nor could he have been unaware that an important crisis in the affair was impending. Nowhere else in Europe were such matters at that moment so delicately poised, or so important to the fate of Reformation and Counter-Reformation alike. Still, it might have been pure coincidence that Descartes chose that very moment to go there – rather than, say, being sent there for a purpose.

What Prince Maurice did next effectively settled the future of the Dutch republic in both its religious and political character, and influenced the course of European history. He convened a great assembly of Calvinist divines, with representatives from Germany, Switzerland and England joining their Dutch counterparts in a general synod at Dort (otherwise known as Dordrecht). After debates lasting six months, the synod condemned Arminians as heretics and as 'disturbers of the peace' both in church and state. Instantly, about two hundred Dutch Arminian ministers were dismissed from their posts, nearly half of whom went into exile. Maurice also sacked Oldenbarnevelt's followers in official posts in all the provinces, replacing them with new and inexperienced personnel, by this means drawing more power into his own hands. Grotius was sentenced to life imprisonment (he escaped two years later), and Oldenbarnevelt was condemned to death. He went the very next day, 13 May 1619, to the scaffold, carrying himself with great dignity. He was seventy-two years of age.

These events were watched with thrilled interest all over Europe, which by and large accepted Maurice's representation of the affair as an attempt by Oldenbarnevelt and his Arminian supporters to seize power. It had indeed been a power struggle, for Maurice himself was intent on strengthening his grip on the United Provinces and had ambitions to be named King. Oldenbarnevelt stood in the way of that hope – although as matters proved, so did the republican instincts of the Dutch in general. Still, Dutch painters depicted the surrender of the *waardgelders* as military victories for Maurice. Within months the English playwrights John Fletcher and Philip Massinger had brought their 'Sir John Van Olden Barnevelt' to the stage in London. Merchants there and elsewhere in Europe – and in certain of the other Dutch provinces too – were delighted that the old statesman had gone, because his canny policies had advantaged the merchants of Holland at their expense. And Calvinists everywhere believed that their view of Christianity had a great new champion in Maurice and that they were therefore poised to prevail.

But with the experienced Oldenbarnevelt gone, and the less canny Maurice supreme in the United Provinces, this rejoicing was not merely premature but misplaced. What it really meant was that Spain, and by extension the Habsburg cause, had been given a marvellous chance to wrest back the initiative in international affairs. And just at that moment in 1618–19 events elsewhere in Europe were building towards an explosion of the volatile elements brewed by religious differences.

So why was it that Descartes chose to go to the United Provinces in the summer of 1618, in the middle of the great upsets taking place there, as a volunteer in the army of the United Provinces, stationed in one of that army's main training depots? On the face of it there are good innocuous answers. One is that he wished to benefit from a solid grounding in the science of military engineering, in an army which was regarded as one of the most modern and effective of the day as a result of

Maurice's innovations. Another is that he went to join one of the two French regiments in Maurice's army, led respectively by Baron de Courtmour and Gaspard de Chastillon. The regimental lists have long been lost, so there is no independent confirmation of this; and neither Descartes nor any of his early biographers said which regiment, if any, he joined in Breda.

It might of course be another coincidence that Descartes left Maurice's army, and the United Provinces, two weeks after Oldenbarnevelt's execution in May 1619. The fact that he was in the country during the Synod of Dort, and quitted it when matters were definitively over is, however, suggestive. According to my tentative surmise about his employment as an intelligence agent, the possibility is this: he could have been sent as a pair of eyes and ears to observe how matters stood in the Breda garrison of Maurice's army while the Arminian difficulties were going on. He would certainly not have been alone in doing such work in the United Provinces; there were doubtless scores of Jesuit or Habsburg (or both; and certainly Spanish or Spanish Netherlandish) eyes all over the country, and the possibility that Descartes was one of them cannot be completely fanciful.

In any event, when Descartes left the Netherlands it was to join another army intent on another, and by then pressing, task of hostilities. This second army was a Catholic one, led by Duke Maximilian of Bavaria on behalf of the Holy Roman Emperor, and Descartes enlisted just as it was en route for Bohemia to avenge the 'Defenestration of Prague'. This was the incident which, with Duke Maximilian's victory at the Battle of the White Mountain outside Prague, precipitated the Thirty Years War. And once again it was not as someone in a combatant role such as pikeman, halbadier or cavalryman that Descartes went with Duke Maximilian's troops to that epochal battle, but in some never-specified non-combatant capacity: engineer perhaps – or perhaps still, as a spy.

Before decamping to the Czech lands with Descartes in Maximilian's army, however, the main event in Descartes' intellectual life during his stay in Breda must be returned to, this being the chance meeting, already mentioned, with Isaac Beeckman. Because of the significance of this encounter for Descartes' later career, all biographers rightly dwell on it.

While walking through Breda on 10 November 1618 (the date is significant as we shall see), Descartes came across a publicly-displayed poster describing a mathematical problem and challenging readers to find its solution. Descartes' mathematical facility at school, and his reviving interest in the subject because of the mathematics in his military engineering studies, prompted him to stop and read the poster. As he tried to make out what the problem was (it was written in Flemish), a stranger stopped to read it too. Descartes asked him whether he could translate the Flemish into Latin. The stranger indeed could; and he and Descartes got talking.

The man was Beeckman, who recorded the event in his diary for 11 November. A 'Frenchman from Poitou' had tried a bit of mathematical sophistry on him, Beeckman wrote; but as they found that they had many like-minded interests, and were 'the only people in Breda who could speak Latin', they took an instant liking to each other.[13] During the remaining six months of Descartes' stay their friendship grew intense. To it is owed the later direction of Descartes' intellectual career, and the basis of his fame.

2

A Night of Dreams

Isaac Beeckman was seven years older than Descartes. He was a qualified physician who had left medicine for teaching, and who later (from 1627) became the rector of the Latin School at Dordrecht, which under his leadership developed into the most prestigious school in the Netherlands. He was also a mathematician and scientist of considerable parts. In cosmology he was a Copernican, and in physics a 'corpuscularian' – that is, an atomist in the seventeenth-century sense, as opposed to the classical sense of Democritus and Leucippus.[1] Corpuscularianism and atomism share the premise that matter ultimately consists of tiny particles (atomism held that these particles cannot themselves be broken down into tinier particles; they are the bottom rung of reality), and that therefore all macroscopic phenomena are to be understood by reference to their microscopic parts and structure. This theory formed the basis of Beeckman's thinking. His studies in dynamics early led him – independently of Galileo – to understand the principle of inertia, and to see that bodies fall with identical velocities in a vacuum. He agreed with Harvey on the circulation of the blood, and in 1626 he stated the relation between volume and pressure in a given quantity of air, and correlatively understood that water rises in a pump because of air pressure rather than nature's supposed 'abhorrence of a vacuum', which was the standard alternative explanation. As this shows, he was perceptive and knowledgeable, and his scientific insights were underpinned by mathematics.

Happily for Descartes and for history, this intelligent and accomplished man happened to be in Breda in November 1618. He was there visiting a relative and investigating a matrimonial prospect (in his diary he reports in rather business-like terms that he was there to 'assist Uncle Peter, and for courtship as well'). In the same diary pages, Beeckman explains the instant mutual attraction that sprang up between the young Frenchman and himself on the tenth day of that month: it was because they found that they shared a 'physico-mathematical' approach to scientific questions. '[Descartes] says he has never met anyone other than me who pursues enquiry in the way I do, combining Physics and Mathematics in an exact way; and for my part, I have never spoken with anyone other than him who does the same,' he wrote.[2] The result was a warmly affectionate friendship and a close intellectual co-operation.

Beeckman was far ahead of Descartes in scientific knowledge at the time they met, but he did not have the same high level of facility in mathematics. This made them a good match; for as Beeckman educated Descartes in science by setting him problems in acoustics, mechanics and hydrostatics, he in turn profited from the younger man's mathematical skills. Beeckman's interests were practical ones, centred chiefly in mechanics, and because his fundamental assumption was that macroscopic phenomena are produced by the motions and interactions of corpuscles (considered as agglomerations of atoms), he needed the mathematical input that would make that model more exact in its various applications. This Descartes provided, for several different topics suggested by Beeckman. One topic was harmonics, and Descartes' work here resulted in a little treatise called the *Compendium Musicae,* giving an arithmetical account of the nature of consonance. It started from enquiries Beeckman had earlier made into harmonics and a theory of sound. Descartes' dedication to Beeckman in this treatise reveals just how much he was the latter's pupil at this stage: 'I release the offspring of my mind to the bears, to go to you as a souvenir of our intimacy and as the surest affirmation of my affection for you, on condition that you keep it eternally hidden in the drawers of your desk so it will not affront men's judgement. They would not avert their eyes from its imperfections, as I am sure you will do.'

The second topic was the mathematical description of falling bodies. Here Descartes did not fully understand what Beeckman intended, and his proffered solutions were incorrect. Beeckman put them right, and Descartes doubtlessly learned from the episode.

The third and most notable topic was hydrostatics (the foundations of fluid dynamics), which Beeckman presented again in problem form, this time in a set of four. And this time Descartes' response contained something significant. In looking for solutions to Beeckman's problems he germinated seeds of ideas and techniques which, much later, flowered into some of his most significant work.[3] One commentator wrote that in this early endeavour 'certain concepts and modes of argument appear . . . which [came to] constitute the essence of Cartesian micro-mechanism in optics, cosmology,

51

physiology, and natural philosophy generally, after being refined over the next fifteen years through practice, criticism, and deliberate metaphysical reconstruction.'[4]

The hydrostatics case is the best example of how the friends collaborated, and how therefore Beeckman helped shape Descartes' thought. When Beeckman set Descartes problems he also suggested the rough outline of solutions, which Descartes then proceeded to formulate in detail. The actual person-to-person contact between the two men was restricted to just the first two months (more accurately, six weeks) of their friendship, for Beeckman had to leave Breda at the end of December 1618. Thereafter, the two corresponded. Five of Descartes' letters to Beeckman written during the first half of 1619 are extant. They also testify to the mutual warmth between them. 'I shall honour you as the inspiration of my studies and their first author,' Descartes told Beeckman in a letter of 23 April 1619. 'You are indeed the one who has shaken me out of my nonchalance and made me remember what I had learned and almost forgotten. When my mind strayed far from serious concerns, it was you who guided it back down the right path. If, therefore, by accident I propose something which is not contemptible, you have every right to claim it for yourself. For my part I shall not forget to send it to you, not only so you can profit from it, but that so you can correct it.'

In one of the first letters Descartes sent Beeckman, written on 24 January of that year, he wrote, 'Love me, and be assured that I would forget the Muses before I forgot you, because they unite me to you by a bond of eternal affection.' And as the hydrostatics solutions show, the closeness of the friendship was not only important for stimulating Descartes' intellectual development, but for the direction it took. Beeckman gave Descartes' mind its first impulse towards the arena in which it made its best contributions, even if it was not until a decade later that Descartes settled systematically to the task of working out and writing down his ideas. Descartes was the smitten pupil in this relationship, a fact that is relevant to what happened ten years later – a deeply unpleasant falling-out between them which did Descartes himself little credit.

Despite its passionate beginnings, however, the friendship moderated to normal temperature almost as rapidly as it had begun, for in the summer of 1619 Descartes left Breda to embark on a curiously circuitous journey to join the army of Maximilian of Bavaria. The occupations and adventures of this journey might have caused him to write less to Beeckman, but they did not dim his now rewakened interest in science and mathematics. He continued to think hard about the latter especially, and to experiment with the compass (a simple two-pronged version of this instrument is familiar to all schoolroom geometers) which mathematicians of the time employed to carry out arithmetical and geometrical calculations. Galileo had published a pamphlet in 1606 to show how compasses can be used to do some of the things that electronic calculators now do (work out interest, extract square roots, and so on). With great ingenuity Descartes saw how different kinds of compasses can be used to deal with a variety of mathematical problems, and – even more significantly – he explained the underlying principles in algebraic terms. (The mathematically-minded will be interested to know that in a letter to Beeckman Descartes described a compass for trisecting angles, and other compasses for finding conic and cylindrical sections, and most importantly a version of the ancient 'mesolabe' compass of Eratosthenes

which he used for finding solutions to cubic equations.[5])
Despite what the technical commentators on Descartes' work
describe as his frequent carelessness, his ingenuity is unquestionable, as is the significance of some of his innovations:
for this early work showed that he was on the brink of realising
that apparently quite diverse kinds of mathematical problems
can be handled by reducing them to a form where their
solution is attainable by simpler techniques.

What Descartes was doing in the summer and autumn of 1619
is sketched prospectively in a letter to Beeckman, written at
the end of March that year, describing his travel plans. He
was going, he said, to join Duke Maximilian's army in
Bohemia, but the uncertain state of affairs in Germany meant
that he would have to take a very circuitous route, sailing from
Amsterdam through the Baltic Sea to Danzig, and going overland thence through Poland to Hungary and Austria, and so
on to Bohemia – a long way round the circumference of a
large circle. A glance at a contemporary map shows that he thus
avoided Protestant German states and kept to Catholic territory
– and in the later stages exclusively Habsburg Catholic territory
– for all the overland part of the journey. How far south
he intended to penetrate into Hungary and Austria, or how
far south he actually went, is open to question; perhaps, if the
hypothesis that he was an intelligence agent is correct, he had
business in Vienna – delivering or collecting documents, or
meeting someone. Under this supposition his journey makes
sense: he would have been well placed by it to make direct
contact with Jesuit minders close to the Habsburg court, either
to deliver papers or a verbal report, or to receive instructions or

collect papers for delivery elsewhere. He may even have had something to do en route through Poland.

One suggestive fact is that Descartes was present in Frankfurt on 9 September 1619 to witness the coronation of the new Holy Roman Emperor, Ferdinand II. Why was he there? He neither held office in any government or embassy, nor was he a member of a company of soldiers or cavalrymen detailed to participate in the ceremonies. Was he one of the idle spectators? Possibly; but if so he made a mighty journey to be one, and nowhere in his writings or in early accounts of his life is there a record of sufficient enthusiasm for Ferdinand II to make it credible that he was some kind of Imperial fan. The most likely explanation is that he was present at the coronation on business, as a non-clerical participant midway between high official and lowly soldier. What capacity could that have been?

The place and the event – Frankfurt, and the coronation – were full of meaning because, until a few years earlier, Prague had been the centre of Habsburg power, having been chosen as imperial capital by the eccentric Rudolf II, patron of Archimboldo (Rudolf II had died five years before, in 1612). It was now the seat of a challenger to Ferdinand II's authority as Emperor, and rival to his claim to be King of Bohemia also. This rebel, as Ferdinand II saw him, was Frederick, the Elector Palatine, husband of Elizabeth, daughter of the English and Scottish King James I and VI. The Bohemians had declared Frederick their king and protector, and Ferdinand II naturally took exception. But Ferdinand also had larger fish to fry, and saw the Bohemian difficulty as an excellent opportunity to inaugurate his more ambitious project: to reclaim for Catholicism the lands lost to Protestantism.

The situation into which Descartes thus ventured, travelling right into its very heart, was extraordinarily fraught. Europe trembled on the edge of a precipice, the abyss being religious conflict prosecuted by force of arms – and when it tumbled over the result was thirty years of terrible war in which the bloodshed, rapine, waste and misery were unprecedented in European history, and which ended by laying the foundations for later wars and atrocities from whose consequences, four and a half centuries later, it still suffers.

This war lasted almost all the rest of Descartes' life. His silence about it in his later writings and letters is deafening: the silence perhaps of someone who had seen enough of it and knew too much about it. Given that Descartes was somehow involved in the early years of the war, that it was a reason why he later chose to live in self-imposed exile in the United Provinces, and that it is the not-so-distant backdrop to all his endeavours and achievements, its beginnings merit – indeed demand – description: and so I undertake a detour here to give one.

The long roots of the war lay of course in the Reformation and Counter-Reformation themselves, but the proximate causes can be traced to an incident that took place in 1606 (the year that Descartes first went to La Flèche) in the small city of Donauworth on the Rhine. The city's Catholic minority organised a religious procession aimed at defying the Lutheran-dominated city council, which had forbidden public manifestations of their faith. The inevitable result was a riot. The then Holy Roman Emperor, Rudolf II, took the opportunity to reclaim Donauworth for Catholicism by revoking the city's privileges, expelling most Lutherans from the council and appointing a Catholic majority in their place. He thus directly breached the terms of the Peace of Augsburg of 1555, which had established the principle *cuius regio eius religio*, 'the religion of the ruler is the religion of the subjects'. The principle merely formalised what had been the de facto situation in Germany before 1555, but its official recognition brought an uneasy peace after years of war – and in addition, though incidentally, gave both Catholic and Protestant princes a strengthened hand against whoever happened to be holding the imperial office.

Rudolf II also decided to remove Donauworth from the 'Swabian circle' – a 'circle' being an administrative district of the Empire, of which there were ten in all – into the 'Bavarian circle'. The director of the Swabian circle was a Lutheran; the director of the Bavarian circle was none other than the formidable Duke Maximilian, Descartes' commander and one of the Counter-Reformation's most zealous champions.

Rudolf's extremely provocative measures angered the Empire's Lutheran and Calvinist princes. Despite their internal differences of opinion over doctrine and other matters, they therefore decided to form a self-protective league, the 'Evangelical Union'. It was formally declared in 1608, with Frederick IV the Elector Palatine as its leader. He was, on the face of things, a natural choice for this role; he was a Calvinist eager to resist Catholic encroachments, and he was an important prince because he held electoral office (there were seven electors who, putatively, chose a new emperor when the previous one died, although the Habsburg's hold on the office was so complete that the title never left the family). But his son Frederick V was a bad choice to succeed him, because he was timid and not especially bright, and therefore relied heavily on the advice of others, especially his chief counsellor, Christian of Anhalt. Had Christian himself been more astute, the younger Frederick's reliance on him would have been no bad thing. But for all his charm and great – too great – self-confidence, Christian of Anhalt was not equal to the dangers of the time, which he exacerbated by his ambition. Either the Elector of Brandenburg or the Elector of Saxony would have been better leaders for the Evangelical Union; but they were both Lutherans who disliked Calvinists as much as they disliked Catholics – this was especially true of Elector John George of Saxony – and some historians argue that neither of these Electors anyway thought the situation was as grave as Frederick V and other Protestant rulers made out.

Another intriguing detail from the point of view of Descartes' later involvement in these affairs is that Henri IV of France had promised in 1608 to act as the Evangelical Union's patron – not out of religious motives (he was then in his second and final phase as a Catholic) but in order to preserve the balance of power against the Habsburgs. This placed Descartes' home country against the power supported by the Jesuits. But religious affiliation was then the determining factor in loyalties; to think in terms of national loyalties would be an anachronism, even if something different – ethnic and linguistic affiliations – often counted for something. Descartes, accordingly, might more naturally have sided with the Jesuit view of the Catholic cause than with the political interests of France.

In response to the formation of the Protestant princes' Evangelical Union, the Catholic princes formed their own league whose leader, naturally enough, was Descartes' commander, Duke Maximilian. The Catholic League was officially sponsored by Rudolf II's cousin, Philip III of Spain. Rudolf II, despite his actions in Donauworth, had to appear to be largely neutral towards both the Catholic and the Protestant interests in the Empire, in an effort not to polarise matters too far, which is one reason why he left the role of sponsor to his Habsburg cousin. But in any case, by this time, because Rudolf's eccentricity and lack of grip had gone too far, his brother Matthias was effectively serving as Emperor, though with not noticeably greater skill.

But polarisation was the inevitable result of the formation of two leagues so opposed in temperament, outlook and belief. When the Duke of Julich and Cleves died, the two leagues quarrelled not so much over which prince should inherit the territory as which religion should inherit it. The deceased duke had been Catholic, but his nearest heirs by blood were both Lutherans – Philip Ludwig of Neuberg, and the Elector of Brandenburg. To add to the problems, the duchy of Julich and Cleves sat astride the tenuous land link between the Spanish Habsburg possessions of Milan and Brussels (the 'Spanish Road' through the heart of Europe, supplying the Spanish Netherlands with goods and troops). The Catholics were therefore very anxious not to lose it to a Protestant prince.

In this bristling situation the Evangelical Union looked to France's Henri IV, the Catholic League looked to Spain's Philip III, and war loomed. But then Henri IV was conveniently assassinated, his heart going to Descartes' school, La Flèche, for burial. His widow Marie de Medici became regent (Louis XIII being too young to reign) and immediately effected a rapprochement with Spain, at a stroke removing the Evangelical Union's main support. In those circumstances the Union saw little future in standing up to the Catholic League. But almost immediately another twist occurred: Philip Ludwig of Neuberg, taking a leaf out of the freshly murdered Henri IV's book, decided to convert to Catholicism and to offer to marry Duke Maximilian's daughter. The way was thus paved for a compromise: the duchy was partitioned by the terms of the Treaty of Xanten in 1614, Philip Ludwig receiving Julich for his son, and Cleves going to the Elector of Brandenburg.

This vertiginous series of events did not however remove the threat of war, it merely delayed it. All that was required for a great conflict to occur was a trigger. It came just four years later, when Descartes was in Breda and the intelligence agents of Christian of Anhalt reported their belief that the Empire would collapse when Rudolf II's successor, Matthias, died. Christian's agents thought this because the divisions created by the ineptitude and eccentricity of Rudolf II had not been managed, and certainly not overcome, by anything Matthias succeeded in doing during his short reign since 1612. The Empire's sprawling possessions ranged not only over the German electorates and duchies but also Austria, Carinthia, Carniola, the Tyrol, Styria, Bohemia and Hungary – an inchoate jigsaw of languages, ethnicities and faiths. Much of Hungary was in Ottoman hands, and the rest was an almost wholly independent fiefdom under its Magyar nobility. Bohemia presented the most complex problem of all: with its dependent provinces of Moravia, Lusatia and Silesia it had four different capital cities and therefore four different parliaments (called Diets). The population of Bohemia and its provinces was predominantly Slav and Protestant, though with a mixture of both Protestant and Catholic Germans, and its monarchy was elective. This last factor was a particular irritant to the Habsburgs because they had to pay scrupulous attention to local traditions in order to keep the Bohemian crown in Habsburg hands.

★   ★   ★

When Descartes undertook his circuitous journey from Breda
to Frankfurt in 1619, it was through some of these unsettled
fragments of the Habsburg's eastern holdings, Silesia and the
Austrian-dependent provinces among them.

None of the Holy Roman emperors in the decades before
1618 had succeeded in establishing unified control over the
whole of their heterogeneous and fractious empire, nor even
genuine authority in any of the self-governing parts. Sometimes they opted for repression, as Rudolf II had done in
Donauworth, and sometimes they opted for concession, as
when Rudolf gave a Letter of Majesty to the Bohemian Diets
reinforcing their independence. Both repression and concession weakened the Empire further. So when Emperor
Matthias died, Christian of Anhalt – chancellor, remember, to
Elector Frederick V of the Palatinate – thought the hour had
come to take advantage. It was a mistake; he had not reckoned
with the man chosen by Matthias as his successor: Ferdinand of
Styria, the new Emperor Ferdinand II, whose coronation
Descartes attended in Frankfurt in September 1619.

Descartes' journey to Bohemia was a direct result of a
determination this new emperor had formed, long before
his coronation, to deal with the situation in Prague. His pre-
decessor Matthias had angered the Bohemians by appointing
Catholics to leading posts on the Council of Regents there. The
new regents' first act was to require that all Bohemian religious
bodies should revert to the terms of their original foundation,
thus at a stroke returning all Protestant churches to Catholic
control, complete with their endowments and other property.
The Bohemian Protestants immediately rebelled. On 22 May
1618 they marched on Prague Castle, took the two leading
members of the Council of Regents, by name Martinitz and

Slavata, and threw them out of a window. This was the famous 'Defenestration of Prague'. The two regents fell twenty feet into a pile of rubbish, so the only injury they sustained was to their dignity. (Catholics put it about that they had been caught and gently lowered by angels.)

The damage to Bohemia was far greater than that to its erstwhile regents. By manhandling the Emperor's representatives the Bohemians had impugned his authority. They realised that there was no going back, so they went forward. They set up a board of thirty deputies to administer the kingdom, called on the dependent provinces to join them in a new confederation, and raised an army. They issued a demand to the Emperor that the provinces should henceforth be autonomous and that all offices should go to Protestants. These were not terms a Habsburg emperor was likely to accept.

Matthias died in March 1619, and the process of Ferdinand's official election began. He had the three archbishop-electors in his pocket, and he had his own vote as supposed King of Bohemia. If the Protestant electors of Saxony, Brandenburg and the Palatinate had supported an alternative candidate, the Thirty Years War just might have been averted. But there was no obvious alternative to Ferdinand, and the three Protestant electors – one Calvinist, two Lutheran – were, as usual, at odds with one another. It was an expression of their impotence and disunity that they all eventually sided with tradition and voted for Ferdinand.

While this was going on, however, the Bohemian Estates were considering what to do with the throne vacated by Matthias's death and destined, if precedent were followed, for Ferdinand II. In the new circumstances created by the Defenestration they were intent on taking an independent path and voting themselves a Protestant king. They chose Frederick of the Palatinate. Thus, as one among very many consequences, was Descartes' destination after Breda determined. As with the coronation of Ferdinand and the Synod of Dort, the Bohemian crisis was the tense focus of all Europe's attention; and in all these cases Descartes was involved, on the margins, in some unnoticed capacity – but *there*.

Deliberating whether to accept the offer of the Bohemian crown, Frederick sought the advice of his father-in-law, James I and VI of England and Scotland, he sought the advice of his fellow-members of the Evangelical Union, and he consulted his own council. They all strongly advised him not to do it. In the face of such overwhelming discouragement a wiser man would have done the opposite of what Frederick chose to do. But there were two people who had a much nearer way to his heart: Elizabeth Stuart, his wife, and his chancellor Christian of Anhalt. Playing on his sincere Protestantism and, as we shall see, relying on the prophecies and promises offered by the study of arcana in which Christian and Frederick both indulged, they encouraged him to accept. 'It is a divine calling I must not disobey,' he grandly announced.

The revolt of Bohemia was accordingly complete; and the trigger for the Thirty Years War had been pulled. Ferdinand II regarded Frederick V's position and possessions as forfeit by the treason of his acceptance. He promised the Upper Palatinate and its associated Electoral office to Maximilian of Bavaria. He promised the Lower Palatinate (lying west of the Rhine, conveniently for the 'Spanish road') to Spain. He offered Lusatia to its neighbouring prince, Elector John George of Saxony. In this way several armies – of Spain, of Maximilian, and of Saxony – became available to him. Descartes enrolled in the second of these, thereby taking (figurative) arms in Emperor Ferdinand II's cause.

As these armies massed, Frederick V arrived in Prague with his German Calvinist entourage, to whom the Bohemian Lutherans immediately took a dislike. Sweden, Venice, Denmark and the United Provinces of the Netherlands had all recognised Frederick's accession to the throne of Bohemia as a way of thumbing a nose at Ferdinand II, but they had no intention of sending troops to help him. His father-in-law James of England and Scotland abandoned him. So Frederick's natural timidity and hesitancy, his Calvinism, his German followers, and his lack of international support, quickly combined to show the Bohemians that they had grievously erred in choosing him.

Frederick is known as 'the Winter King' because he enjoyed his new dominions for a very brief time, from the winter of 1619 to the autumn of 1620. This latter date is when the short campaign to overwhelm Frederick began. His Palatinate possessions fell without a struggle to the plundering armies of Spain and Maximilian. John George of Saxony helped himself painlessly to Lusatia. And on 8 November 1620, in a single easy morning on the White Mountain outside Prague, Maximilian's army of 20,000 men under their canny commander Count Tilly – Descartes somewhere among them – overcame the 15,000 soldiers of Christian of Anhalt. The two ignominious hours of Christian's defeat represented the last vestige of Palatinate-Bohemian resistance. Frederick fled into exile, and a savage repression of the Bohemian Protestants followed, together with a complete subjection of Bohemia and Moravia to the Imperial crown.

Descartes was at the Battle of the White Mountain, according to Baillet, in some non-combatant capacity – Baillet says he was there as an 'observer'.[6] How long he remained during the persecution of Protestants is hard to say. Many Bohemian leaders were executed, and Protestant clergy were outlawed and their chapels destroyed. The Jesuits flooded in, taking control of schools and universities. The whole country was returned to Catholicism at the edge of the sword. Baillet says that after the Battle of the White Mountain Descartes was with the Imperial troops commanded by the comte du Bucquoy when they captured and destroyed the town of Hradisch in Moravia; and likewise with other towns on Bucquoy's punitive progress. There was nothing pretty about these events: rape and massacre were commonplaces of them, as a strategy of terror and subjugation. Nothing in Descartes' writings recalls any of it; which of course tells us neither that he saw any of it, nor that he did not see any of it.

These events looked very much like a triumph for Ferdinand II and the Catholic cause, and must have seemed so to Descartes at the time. But in truth it was the beginning of the opposite. France could not stand by while Habsburg strength waxed, and in the far north of Europe the burgeoning and ambitious power of Sweden was growing uneasy at the danger to its Protestant co-religionists – and at the same time saw opportunity in this danger: opportunity to extend its own empire. Ferdinand II had in effect stirred the hornets against himself by these victories; so instead of reasserting Catholic dominion of Europe, he had set in train the events that would, over the next three decades, eventually and permanently lose it.

★   ★   ★

While these excitements were brewing in military and political affairs, others no less momentous were happening inside Descartes' head. There is no incongruity here, between the endeavours of armies and the collapse of nations on the one hand, and on the other hand the growing seeds of ideas in a philosopher's mind; for these latter not only have as much power as the former to change history, but – in sober truth – usually much more power. Which has had the greater effect on the world: the new Europe of 'nation states' forged by the Thirty Years War that began at the Battle of the White Mountain, or the scientific revolution – a revolution Descartes played a significant part in – which occurred even as that war raged? Of course, the two things cannot be separated, just as Descartes' story cannot be told without reference to both.

In line with this necessary dualism of outer and inner history, therefore, it is time to return from the origins of the Thirty Years War to the mental development of René Descartes.

Almost exactly a calendar year before 'assisting' (as the French expression would have it) at the Battle of the White Mountain, Descartes had what he later described as an intellectual epiphany, a vision of a scientific and philosophical method which, he thought, would unlock all knowledge. According to Baillet this event took place on 10 November 1619, and it consisted of a day of meditation in a stove-heated room, followed by a night of extraordinary dreams which so impressed Descartes that he wrote them down in a notebook which he subsequently carried wherever he went.

The meditations of that luminous day began, Descartes himself tells us, with the reflection that the best works are those devised and carried out by a single individual, rather than those put together from the endeavours of many. Evidently Descartes had in mind something akin to the point of describing a camel as a committee-designed horse. The same, he thought, must be true of the sciences; knowledge 'made up and put together piece by piece from the opinions of many different people never comes as close to truth as the simple reasoning that a man of good sense naturally applies to whatever he encounters'. To free our minds from the influence of our appetites and what others told us as we were growing up, therefore, we must make a clean sweep of our existing notions and begin to build again from the foundations.[7]

These thoughts mark a significant moment in the history of thought. They encapsulate a realisation that methods of enquiry need to be placed on a scientific basis. Like Francis Bacon in England some years before him, but with large differences in emphasis, Descartes was in this way recognising that to sort the sheep from the goats among methods of enquiry – that is, to ensure that each in the pairings of chemistry and alchemy, astronomy and astrology, medicine and magic, are kept apart by right methods of enquiry – some work needed to be done to identify what those methods are. In his classic *Meditations on First Philosophy* written twenty-two years later, Descartes described the task in these terms: 'Some years ago I was struck by the large number of falsehoods that I had accepted as true in my childhood, and by the highly doubtful nature of the whole edifice that I had subsequently based upon them. I realised that it was necessary, once in the course of my life, to demolish everything completely and start again right from the foundations if I wanted to establish anything at all in the sciences that was stable and likely to last.'[8] In the *Discourse*, written five years before the *Meditations*, he alludes to this realisation, but instead of proceeding to undertake the difficult foundational task it describes – a task left to the *Meditations* itself – he lists a set of rules to live by while he carries that task out.

As noted, Baillet dated the day of insights and subsequent night of dreams to 10 November 1619. In his notebooks exactly a year and a day later, effectively the anniversary of this momentous date, Descartes wrote in the margin next to his record of the dreams: '11 November 1620. I began to understand the foundation of the wonderful discovery.' The dates are intriguing. If the momentous day was indeed 10 November 1619 then Descartes was recalling it just three days after the Battle of the White Mountain, presumably still in the vicinity of Prague and, if so, then in the midst of the tumult and confusion of the city's fall and the victorious army's seizure of control over it.

Baillet and most subsequent biographers locate the momentous day and night of 10 November 1619 as occurring at Ulm, a town in the state of Neuberg on the road between Frankfurt and Vienna. Descartes himself tells us in his *Discourse,* written seventeen years later, that he was travelling from the Emperor's coronation in Frankfurt to rejoin (note 'rejoin') the army in Bohemia when he was detained in quarters by 'the onset of winter'. The winter of 1619 must have been an early one indeed, for Ferdinand II was crowned on 9 September. Descartes' own words are: 'At that time I was in Germany, where I had been called by the wars that are not yet ended there. While I was returning to the army from the coronation of the Emperor, the onset of winter detained me in quarters where, finding no conversation to divert me and fortunately having no cares or passions to trouble me, I stayed shut up alone in a stove-heated room, where I was completely free to converse with myself about my own thoughts.'[9]

It is intriguing to look at the famous series of dreams Descartes had on the night following this day of insights. Our knowledge of them is derived from an early notebook, now lost but known to Baillet and the philosopher Leibniz, which contained passages of fascinating autobiographical reminiscence which has not only mesmerised subsequent biographers, but even provided material for psychoanalytic speculation.[10] Fragments of the notebook survive because Leibniz transcribed several passages from it, impressed and perhaps amused by their content: for the series of dreams seemed so deeply portentous to Descartes that he wrote them down very carefully, and analysed them for their meaning.

There were three dreams, or – more accurately – two dreams with a peculiar intervening event which no-one has previously explained but which can now be understood, thanks to the advance of medical understanding in neurology. All day Descartes had been in a state of high enthusiasm – so he tells us in the notebook entry, somewhat different from the meditative version given in the *Discourse* – thinking about method as the key to all knowledge, and believing that deep truths about it were within his grasp. As his notebook tells us and as his peculiar 'second dream' confirms, he went to bed in an exhausted, excited and feverish state, and soon after falling asleep had the first dream.[11]

In it Descartes 'felt his imagination struck by the representation of some phantoms, which frightened him so much that, thinking that he was walking in the streets, he had to lean to his left in order to reach his destination, because he felt a great weakness in his right side and could not hold himself upright. He tried to straighten himself, feeling ashamed to walk in this fashion, but he was hit by turbulent blasts as if of a whirlwind, which spun him round three or four times on his left foot. Even this was not what alarmed him; the difficulty he had in struggling along made him feel that he was going to fall at every step. Noticing a school open along his route he went in, seeking refuge and a remedy for his problem. He tried to reach the school chapel, where his first thought was to pray. But realising that he had passed an acquaintance without greeting him, he sought to retrace his steps to pay his respects, but was violently repulsed by the wind blowing into the chapel. At the same time he saw another person in the school courtyard, who addressed him by name and politely told him that if he wished to find Monsieur N he had something to give him. Descartes took it that the thing in question was a melon from a foreign country. What was more surprising was that the people clustering around that person in order to talk with him were straight and steady on their feet, although he himself was still bent over and unsteady on the same ground. Having almost knocked him over a number of times, the wind had greatly lessened.'

Then, Baillet tells us, Descartes woke and found that he had a real pain in his side, which made him think that the dream had been caused by an evil spirit sent to seduce him. He turned over immediately onto his right side – having slept and dreamed while lying on his left – and asked God to protect him from any evil effects of the dream, and to preserve him from the miseries he might suffer in punishment for his sins, which he acknowledged were great enough – though he had lived a life largely blameless in the eyes of men – to merit thunderbolts from heaven falling on his head.

After nearly two hours of meditation on the vicissitudes of

this life, Baillet continues, Descartes fell asleep again, only to have an instant new 'dream' which woke him with a fright. 'He thought he heard a sudden, loud noise, which he took for thunder. Terrified, he immediately woke. Upon opening his eyes he noticed sparks of fire scattered about the room. He had experienced this phenomenon many times before, and it did not seem strange to him that when he woke in the night his eyes sparkled enough for him to see objects close to him.' After a little while his fears faded away, and he fell back into sleep, only to dream again – a peaceful dream this time, with nothing fearful in it.

In this third dream Descartes found a book on his table, without knowing who had put it there. He opened it, and found that it was a dictionary, which pleased him greatly, as promising to be very useful. At the same moment he noticed another new book, again without knowing where it had come from. It turned out to be a collection of poems by different authors, called *Corpus Poetarum*. Curious to read some of it, Descartes opened it and chanced upon the line, *quod vitae sectabor iter?* 'What way in life shall I follow?'

Just then he noticed a stranger, who gave him a piece of poetry which began with the words 'Yes and No', recommending it as an excellent poem. Descartes said that he recognised the line as coming from one of the *Idylls* of Ausonius, and that it was included in the large poetry anthology lying on the table. To show the poem to the stranger he began leafing through the anthology, boasting that he knew its order and arrangement perfectly. While he searched for the poem the stranger asked where he had acquired the anthology. Descartes replied that he did not know, but that just a short time before he had been leafing through another book which had since disappeared, and there too he neither knew who had brought it or taken it away. He was still searching for Ausonius's 'Yes and No' when he saw the first book – the dictionary – reappear at the other end of the table; but he noticed that this time it was not as complete as when he had looked at it earlier.

At last he found Ausonius's poems in the anthology, but 'Yes and No' was not among them. Never mind, Descartes told the stranger, I know a better poem by Ausonius, beginning 'What way shall I follow in life?' The stranger begged to see it, so Descartes set about searching the pages again. As he did so he came across several portraits engraved in copperplate, which made him remark that the book was very handsome; but before he could find the poem both book and stranger suddenly disappeared.

This third dream did not waken Descartes, Baillet reports, but even as he slept he wondered whether it was a dream or a vision, and he began to interpret it. 'He judged that the dictionary could only mean all the sciences gathered together and that the anthology of poets entitled the *Corpus Poetarum* represented, in a more particular and distinct way, the union of Philosophy and Wisdom.'

And then, on waking at last, Descartes proceeded to interpret his dreams fully. The poetry anthology he understood to represent Revelation and Enthusiasm, 'for the favours of which he did not despair,' says Baillet. By 'Yes and No' he understood Truth and Falsehood in human enquiry and science. 'Seeing that the interpretation of these things accorded so well with his inclinations,' Baillet continues, 'he was so bold as to believe that the Spirit of Truth had wished, by means of this dream, to open to him the treasures of all the sciences.' (The 'Spirit of Truth' is presumably God.)

And then Baillet hints that Descartes took the dreams to be prophetic, for he adds: 'It remained only to explain the little copperplate portraits he had seen in the second book. He looked for no further explanation of them following the visit, later that same day, of an Italian painter.' This suggestion – that Descartes believed that the future could be foretold – is an intriguing one, because although Descartes was devout enough in his ostensible commitment to Catholic Christianity (he was faultless in avowed orthopraxy – that is, orthodox behaviour and observance – and gave no reasons for anyone to think differently about his orthodoxy), belief in prognostication sits ill with the otherwise robust rationality of his scientific outlook. Perhaps, though, the early date of the notebook from which Baillet extracted this account is sufficient explanation.

One final point about the dreams is that the second of them, the bang that woke Descartes and the sparks that floated in the darkness about him when he opened his eyes, have by turns puzzled and excited commentators. Neurology now recognises a harmless event which it labels (obviously feeling no need for a Latinic formulation) 'exploding head syndrome'. As this frank appellation suggests, it involves a subject 'hearing' a loud noise like an explosion or a pistol-shot inside his head soon after falling asleep, an event which naturally wakens him. No pathology precedes, or harmful sequelae attend, such events, which seem to occur mainly when the subject of them is tired or stressed. They are some sort of neurological discharge, similar in cause perhaps to what produces the sense of tripping just as one falls asleep. In the margins of sleep a variety of curious subjective neurological phenomena occur, and it is easy enough to see how they might be interpreted as significant events, until one learns how common they are and how little they mean.[12]

No-one who has ever written about Descartes doubts that these dreams occurred, and in the way that he describes them. But an intriguing, and indeed puzzling, fact is that Descartes' dreams closely resemble two accounts of dreams published not long before Descartes had his own dreams. Because the earlier accounts are connected to a crucial matter – the Rosicrucian furore of the years just before and after 1620 – I leave discussion of them to the next chapter, where the extraordinary case of Rosicrucianism and its relation to Descartes is considered. But the fact that accounts of dreams very like Descartes' own were published not long before he had them, has to prompt questions. Was it coincidence that Descartes dreamed as he did? Were his dreams prompted by those he had read about? Or were the 'dreams' fictions, adapted from the published accounts to provide Descartes with a way of saying something that could not be said *en clair*?

Descartes described the insights of the day preceding the dreams collectively as a 'wonderful discovery', and they prompted him to try to write a treatise, perhaps a very early version of his *Rules for the Direction of the Mind*. But he abandoned the attempt after a couple of months.

The emphasis Descartes himself placed on his discovery and dreams at the time they occurred is probably best understood as an expression of enthusiasm by a gifted young man with grand hopes, whose ambition was at that point greater in form than content, as all early ambition by nature is. Even so, it offers an interesting picture of the confident and independent-minded twenty-three-year-old military engineer and possible Jesuit agent, day-dreaming about being a great scientific discoverer, conceiving the beginnings of ideas and methods that would make them come true, and starting upon his first efforts to work them out and write them down.

Such sentiments are familiar enough among the ambitious, but an example drawn from another philosophical biography might illuminate them further. In the early twentieth century, when manned flight was just beginning, the physicist Ludwig Boltzmann said that the new science of aeronautics required 'heroes and geniuses' for its advancement – heroes to risk their necks in the flimsy new flying machines, geniuses to understand the principles of aerodynamics that sometimes kept them aloft. Inspired by this vision, the young Ludwig Wittgenstein conceived a passionate desire to be an aeronaut in order thereby to be a hero-genius. It is easy to imagine any ambitious individual enjoying similar sentiments appropriate to his or her time – and especially in the dawn of the scientific revolution. The youthful Descartes felt something like this. His night of dreams was evidently so significant a moment for his aspirations that, as already mentioned, he kept his record of them with him for the rest of his life. As events proved, they were not idle aspirations; under the impetus of the interest generated by Beeckman, he was conscious of his powers and their possibilities. Although it took time for the latter to be realised fully, his day of discoveries and night of dreams evidently left him confident that their realisation would surely come.

Above all, the day in the stove-heated room confirmed for Descartes the answer to Ausonius's question, 'What way in life shall I follow?' In the *Discourse* he writes, still as if referring to the deliberations of that significant day, '[I reviewed] the various occupations which men have in this life, in order to choose the best. Without wishing to say anything about the occupations of others,[13] I thought I could do no better than to continue with the very one I was engaged in, and devote my whole life to cultivating my reason and advancing as far as I could in the knowledge of the truth, following the method I had prescribed for myself. Since beginning to use this method I have felt such extreme contentment that I do not think one could enjoy any sweeter or purer one in this life.'[14] It is striking that in a letter written just a few months before his death, he repeated his commitment to this aspiration.[15]

The notes Descartes made in the aftermath of the day of insights and night of dreams show that the aspiration was fully formed even by then. And indeed they give evidence of a re-markable consistency in his outlook and ambitions. He begins them by saying, 'the fear of God is the beginning of wisdom.' This marks his commitment, to which he unwaveringly clung, never to stray from at least the appearance of orthodoxy. He then says that he is going to advance upon the world's stage 'masked', as actors do in order to conceal their flushed faces. He says that when he was young he was inspired by others' discoveries to wonder whether he could make discoveries on his own account, without the aid of books. And then he says that in answering this with an emphatic 'Yes', he saw how it could be done by means of fixed methodological rules. Science, he wrote, is like a woman: she is respected if she remains modestly by her husband's side, but vilified if she gives herself promiscuously to everyone. The sciences are masked; when their masks are removed they will be seen in all their beauty. Whoever sees how the sciences are connected will find it as easy to grasp them all as it is easy to remember the sequence of numbers.[16]

In writing of his discoveries in the stove-heated room,

Descartes touched only briefly on the all-important question of method, but described the four general principles he vowed to observe in all his studies: 'First, never to accept anything as true unless I had evident knowledge of its truth: that is, carefully to avoid precipitate conclusions and preconceptions, and to include nothing more in my judgements than what presented itself to my mind so clearly and so distinctly that I had no occasion to doubt it.' Secondly, 'to divide each of the difficulties I examined into as many parts as possible and as may be required in order to resolve them better.' Thirdly, 'to direct my thoughts in an orderly manner, by beginning with the simplest and most easily known objects in order to ascend little by little, step by step, to knowledge of the most complex.' Fourth and lastly, 'throughout to make enumerations so complete, and reviews so comprehensive, that I could be sure of leaving nothing out.'[17] Despite their generality, the rules are good ones. Descartes valued them; he claimed that his advances in geometry and algebra resulted from his strict observance of them.[18]

Useful too are the rules-of-thumb Descartes sketched for himself as guides for living while he was undertaking his researches – also devised, so he says in the *Discourse*, while meditating in his stove-heated room. Apart from their intrinsic merits they have biographical interest too. Genevieve Rodis-Lewis reports that not long before her own account of Descartes was written, she learned that a collector in Neuburg had found a copy of a book famous, or rather notorious, in its time, Pierre Charron's *Traite de la sagesse*, which apparently had been given to Descartes as a gift in 1619.[19] The copy found by the Neuberg collector is inscribed 'to the most learned, dear friend and little brother, René Descartes'. It is signed 'Father Jean B. Molitor SJ', and it is dated 'end of year 1619'. Competent judges say they do not think the inscription is a forgery. Assuming it to be genuine, the inscription locates Descartes near Ulm at the close of that year, and more interestingly still places in his hands a book that anticipates some of his later ideas.

Pierre Charron was a theologian and philosopher who used scepticism about the possibility of science and human knowledge to privilege faith in their place, thus promoting strict adherence to Catholicism. He was a celebrated preacher, and from 1594 served as chaplain to Henri IV's wife Margaret. He was a close friend of Montaigne, another employer of scepticism as a weapon of enquiry. He died in 1603, and his *Traité* was put on the Index of Prohibited Books by the Church in 1606. But it was still in circulation when Descartes was given a copy, though the fact that the person who gave it to him was a Jesuit raises an eyebrow: why would a Jesuit priest give a young protégé a book proscribed by the Church?

Charron began from the claim 'I do not know', premising a form of ignorance and doubt that is, he wrote, 'more learned and certain, more noble and generous, than all the knowledge and certainty' of would-be savants and scientists, for it opens the path to true knowledge by faith, in that it leaves one's mind clear for God to 'engrave the truth upon it.'[20] If Descartes read this it must have given him a large hint for later constructing his own answer to the question, 'What can be known with certainty?', for he does so by doubting everything that admits of the least possible doubt, in order to see what such doubting will leave behind – for any residue would by definition be indubitable, which is to say: certain. This is exactly the strategy he carries out most fully in his *Meditations on First Philosophy*.

In addition to demonstrating a method of seeking truth from sceptical beginnings, Charron offered guidance on the great question of how best to live. His advice was 'to follow and observe the laws, customs and ceremonies of the country in which one finds oneself.'[21] This is echoed in Descartes' own first principle. 'I formed for myself a provisional moral code consisting of just three or four maxims, which I should like to tell you about. The first was to obey the laws and customs of my country, holding constantly to the religion in which by God's grace I had been instructed from my childhood, and governing myself in all other matters according to the most moderate and least extreme opinions.'[22] This last thought is a version of Charron's injunction 'never to act against God or Nature' in following the customs of a given country.

Charron also enjoined submitting judgement and faith to the tutelage of reason, and employing an 'internal reserve' in carrying out obligations. Descartes' other maxims differ in content but not in spirit from these. They are: to be firm in following a chosen course of action, 'to master myself rather than fortune' (a principle of Stoic ethics, of which Descartes later showed himself a votary), and – as noted earlier – to 'cultivate my reason, and to advance as far as I could in the knowledge of the truth'.

Descartes, in short, followed Charron's lead both in devising a personal code of ethics and in employing the methodology of scepticism as a starting-point for enquiry. The parallels offer an intriguing glimpse into the formation of his thought. That is a significant enough gain in its own right. But the circumstances also provide another glimpse into his life, showing him in Ulm in the winter of 1619, on intimate terms with the Jesuit community, called a 'little brother' by one of them, and again admired, as Beeckman had admired him, for his powers of intellect.

But if one asks: why was Descartes in Ulm at that time, making such leisurely efforts to 'rejoin' the army of Duke Maximilian? What was he doing with the Jesuits there, those busy commandos fighting for the cause of Catholicism and the Habsburgs? One possibility is that Descartes' interests, and perhaps even duties as an agent of pro-Habsburg Jesuit endeavours, had something to do with a movement associated with Frederick of the Palatinate: the mysterious and more than half-legendary 'Brotherhood of the Rosy Cross'.

3

The Mystery of the Rosy Cross

Forming a picture of Descartes' doings in the significant period between the time he left Breda in the spring of 1619 and his presence in Prague at the end of 1620 requires considering a subject that, until now, biographers and commentators have mentioned only in passing. It concerns the matter of the Rosicrucian furore of the years between 1612 and 1623, and it has particular relevance to the hypothesis that Descartes might have been a servant of the Jesuit interest in the unsettled circumstances of the age.

Thoughts about Rosicrucianism would have no relevance to Descartes were it not for two striking facts: that he himself implies an interest in it, and that many of the people he dealt with then and later, including some of his closest friends, were likewise interested. It would be too much to call any of them, or indeed anyone, 'Rosicrucians', because there seems never to have existed an organised or formal Rosicrucian movement as such. Rather, many people were stimulated by Rosicrucian ideas, and many among these felt sympathy with its tenets and goals. It is only in this courtesy sense that a 'loose and self-selecting fraternity' existed, though for convenience those who expressed sympathy for or solidarity with Rosicrucian ideals might as well be called Rosicrucians.

Once the picture we try to draw of Descartes' life at this period is allowed to include Rosicrucianism, it becomes complex in an intriguing way. This is because Rosicrucianism, and other movements associated variously with Protestantism, esoteric knowledge, the occult, alchemy and magic, were enthusiastically supported by Frederick, Elector Palatine, and suffered a devastating blow with his defeat at the White Mountain in 1620. Thereafter the Catholic church, with Jesuits leading the way, was indefatigable in demonising Rosicrucianism and anything to do with magic, Hermeticism, the Cabala, and the occult in general, fomenting unease about alleged nefarious activities involving some or all these things in the early 1620s to such an extent that, after the great 1623 panic over Rosicrucianism in France, these 'movements' (insofar as there were any such in the first place, to survive in any form), and especially Rosicrucianism, vanished underground.

Moreover, one of the leading hammers of Rosicrucianism was Marin Mersenne, the man who made Descartes famous by publicising his genius, and who remained not only his friend but in effect his secretary, keeping him in touch with the whole scientific and philosophical world from the late 1620s onwards. So vehement was Mersenne's assault on Rosicrucianism that his very public battle with Robert Fludd kept the entire intellectual world of Europe agog for years.

The questions that crowd round in light of these considerations are: what was Descartes' involvement with Rosicrucianism? Was he perhaps briefly tempted by it in 1618–19, but then rejected it? This might be a plausible scenario given that although he could have been initially curious about what it promised – a key to the secrets of Nature – he was later the principal architect of a style of thought that opposed and (largely) defeated everything represented by interest in Freemasonry, the Cabala, Hermeticism, and other styles of pseudoscience like them.

Or was Descartes' interest in Rosicrucianism professional, in the sense that he was investigating it and its votaries as an agent (if so, doubtless just one of many) of the Jesuit interest? Was he, this is to ask, spying on the Rosicrucians he met? For as we shall shortly see, the documents which set the Rosicrucian furore going were not only Protestant in orientation, but expressly anti-Jesuit, and indeed offered themselves as manifestos for a brotherhood that would constitute an alternative to the Jesuit movement.

To shed some light on these questions, and to see if what they suggest about Descartes might be merely fanciful, two things are necessary: a sketch of the Rosicrucian story, and a consideration of the nature and extent of Descartes' place in it – at this juncture focusing mainly but not exclusively on the year and a half between the early summer of 1619 when he left Breda, and November 1620 when he 'observed' the defeat of Frederick V (and with him Rosicrucian hopes) at the Battle of the White Mountain.

The proximate source of the Rosicrucian excitements of the decade or so after 1612 is the publication of three books, the *Fama Fraternitatis* published in 1614 but known in manuscript for some years beforehand, the *Confessio Fraternitatis* published in 1615, and *The Chemical Wedding of Christian Rosencreutz* published in 1616 – all years when Descartes was a senior pupil at La Flèche, or studying law at the university in Poitiers. But as Frances Yates shows in her study of the Rosicrucian story, the ideas and aims of the Rosicrucian manifestos had long roots back into the Renaissance, almost all of them passing in one way or another through the intellectual cincture of a very remarkable man, the English polymath Dr John Dee.[1]

In the later Renaissance a heady mixture of notions, beliefs and practices from cabalistic, occult, astrological, alchemical, hermetic and magical sources had thrived, promising aficionados gains of almost Faust-like proportions in knowledge of the mysteries of nature and Heaven, if only they could find the Method, the secret, the code or technique for unlocking the gates of wisdom. Because this ebullition of ideas was exceedingly non-orthodox in religious terms, it was strongly opposed by the Catholic church, whose storm troops, the Jesuits, took the lead in combating it. When the intoxicating pot-pourri of 'magia, cabala, alchymia' reached a head in the Rosicrucian documents on either side of 1615, a definitive clash with the forces of orthodoxy was inevitable. It came; and within a decade Rosicrucianism had been so discredited and demonised that, insofar as it survived at all as an idea among an informal coincidence of people inspired by its ideals, it went underground and turned into a rumour, a memory, and a legend.

But Rosicrucianism never fully died away, at least in the attenuated sense of a belief in secret pathways to knowledge. When Isaac Newton, decades later, devoted more time trying to fathom what he believed must be the numerological code of the Bible than he spent on physics, he was following close to well-trodden footprints. In the eighteenth century and subsequent interest in arcana and the occult, and with the proliferation of Freemasonry, supposed Rosicrucian themes revived.

The *Fama Fraternitatis* and *Confessio Fraternitatis* are invitations to join an allegedly newly revived Fraternity or Order founded by 'Brother Christian Rosencreutz', who (so these books claimed) had travelled in the East and brought back from it all manner of arcane wisdom. The *Fama* and *Confessio* were anonymous tracts, but *The Chemical Wedding of Christian Rosencreutz* has been securely attributed to a gifted Lutheran pastor from Wurttemberg called Johan Valentin Andreae, the author of a number of other works, including plays and an autobiography.

Andreae's home state of Wurttemberg was ruled by an Anglophile duke, Frederick I, who had been awarded the Order of the Garter by Elizabeth I, and who was intensely interested in alchemy and the occult.[2] After Elizabeth's death James I and VI continued her pro-German Protestant policy, which was aimed, as was that of Henri IV of France, at countering Habsburg power. Wurttemberg neighboured the Palatinate, whose Elector, as the previous chapter shows, married James's daughter Elizabeth in 1613. The marriage took place with enormous pomp and fanfare, occasioning plays, pamphlets and songs. When Elector Frederick took his bride home to the Palatinate a company of English actors and musicians went with them, performing at the celebrations arranged for the journey and the homecoming at Heidelberg. The significance of the family alliance between James and Frederick – the latter being head, remember, of the Protestant Union – was obvious to all Europe; though in fact it turned out to mean nothing, for James abandoned Frederick when the latter needed help following his ill-starred acceptance of the Bohemian crown.

Elector Frederick's chancellor, Christian of Anhalt, was also an enthusiast for occult, Paracelsist and alchemical studies. He was a patron of a master in these arts, Oswald Crollius – who was Christian's physician, and had dedicated a book to him – and friend to another, Peter Wok of Rosenberg.[3] Because of his position in the Palatinate court, Christian was able to encourage a climate of thought friendly to these interests, thereby propagating further the influence of John Dee who, with Edward Kelley, had visited the German states in the 1580s. Dee lived for a time in Bohemia under the patronage of the eccentric Emperor Rudolph II, and then visited the Palatinate and other German states during his return journey to England in 1589. As advisor to (and spy for) Elizabeth I, and author of widely celebrated and admired works, Dee's journey through the German states caused a sensation, with savants and aristocrats alike flocking to meet him. Most of the cabalistic, hermetic, alchemical and mystical works published in subsequent decades bore the mark of his influence, especially of his *Monas Hieroglyphica* which sets out his eclectic mystical brand of alchemy and philosophy.

Two Dee-inspired works which, in their turn, influenced the Rosicrucian documents were Henricus Khunrath's *Amphitheatre of Eternal Wisdom*, and Simon Studion's strange vatic work entitled *Naometria,* published in 1604. This latter bore the symbol of a rose with a cross at its centre, which some enquirers see as prefiguring the Rosicrucian documents of a decade later. Studion's *Naometria* predicted that 1620 was to be an apocalyptic year in which the Antichrists of Pope and Mahomet would finally be defeated – a prophecy that doubtless had its part to play in encouraging Christian of Anhalt to lead Elector Frederick into his fateful errors.

Khunrath's *Amphitheatre* was published in 1609, and Dee's influence on it is palpable. In turn, its own influence on the Rosicrucian documents is direct. 'In Khunrath's work we meet with the characteristic phraseology of the manifestos,' writes Yates, 'the everlasting emphasis on macrocosm and microcosm, the stress on Magia, Cabala, and Alchymia as in some way combining to form a religious philosophy which promises a new dawn for mankind.'[4]

When the *Confessio* appeared in 1615 it was accompanied by a pamphlet entitled 'A Brief Consideration of More Secret Philosophy', intended as an explication of some of the *Confessio*'s themes. It is drawn almost entirely from Dee's *Monas Hieroglyphica*, which it frequently quotes at great length. Andreae's *Chemical Wedding* has, both on its title-page and in the text itself, Dee's then instantly recognisable 'Monas' symbol. So, as all these indications imply, the thread linking Dee, his influence in the German Protestant states, and the documents of the Rosy Cross, is a tight one; and Bohemia and the Palatinate is where enquiry into mystical routes to knowledge connect with politics, religious controversy, and international relations. In Yates's words, '[The] Rosicrucian publications belong to the movements around the Elector Palatine, the movements building him up towards the Bohemian adventure. The chief stirring spirit behind these movements was Christian of Anhalt, whose connections in Bohemia belonged right in the circles where the Dee influence would have been known and fostered.'[5]

The long title of the *Fama Fraternitatis* reads: 'Universal and General Reformation of the whole wide world; together with the *Fama Fraternitatis* of the Laudable Fraternity of the Rosy Cross, written to all the Learned and Rulers of Europe; also a short reply sent by Herr Haselmayer, for which he was seized by the Jesuits and put in irons on a galley. Now put forth and communicated to all true hearts.' It begins with a heady declaration that 'in these latter days' a great promise was being fulfilled: the revelation of the secrets of nature. We may, says the *Fama*, 'boast of the happy time, wherein there is discovered unto us the half part of the world, which was heretofore unknown and hidden, but [God] hath also made manifest unto us many wonderful and never heretofore seen works and creatures of Nature, and moreover hath raised men, imbued with great wisdom, who might partly renew and reduce all arts (in this our age spotted and imperfect) to perfection; so that man might finally understand his own nobleness and worth, and why he is called Microcosmus, and how far his knowledge extendeth into Nature.'[6]

In telling the story of Brother Rosencreutz's journey to the East gathering knowledge, the *Fama* stresses that the East's epistemological superiority results from the fact that its wise men communicate with one another and share their findings, whereas although there are many 'magicians, Cabalists, physicians and philosophers' in Germany, they do not collaborate, thus inhibiting the growth of knowledge.

Rosencreutz's journey is dated by the *Fama* to the fifteenth century. On his return to Europe his teachings were laughed at, so he started a secret society to preserve and propagate what he had learned. This select group of Illuminati devoted themselves to healing the sick for free, and to study. For a time the vault where Brother Rosencreutz was buried was kept secret; its recent discovery, with all the treasures and secret books it contains, heralds the moment for Europe to awake and enjoy a 'general reformation'. The vault, says the *Fama*, was reopened in 1604.

The *Fama* and the *Confessio* generated immense excitement and controversy throughout Europe. They were variously quoted, defended, attacked, believed in, and rejected as spurious; but widely read, whether by friend or foe. Significantly, the foes included those who were alert to the dangerous implications of the *Fama*'s talk of imminent 'alterations' to the Holy Roman Empire, which (it said) the brotherhood of the Rosy Cross would help to bring about 'with secret aid'. It was widely understood that references to such changes alluded to the Elector Frederick as head of the Protestant Union; references to the 'Lion' – Frederick's emblem – as the agent of that prospective change made the allusion explicit. When Frederick was defeated at the Battle of the White Mountain any number of bitter attacks on him and Christian of Anhalt followed, together with caricatures, cartoons and lampoons explicitly mocking their association with Rosicrucianism. [7]

But although the Rosicrucian idea had many enemies, among them serious scholars like Andreas Libavius and formidable critics like the pseudonymous 'Menapius' and 'Irenaeus Agnostus', it also had a wildly enthusiastic would-be following, and scores of publications appeared in the wake of the *Fama* and *Confessio* by people hoping to be noticed by the secret brethren and therefore invited to join them. There were even straightforward appeals from people anxious to learn more and to be admitted to the Rosicrucian secrets. There were also many publications by people who seemed to be Rosicrucians themselves, or at least to know a lot about their ideas – for example Theophilus Schweighardt, 'Joseph Stellatus' (a pseudonym), 'Julianus de Campis' (another pseudonym), and others. One apparent Illuminatus singled out by Yates as having a profound insider's grasp of Rosicrucian ideas is 'Florentinus de Valentia' who, in a studied reply to an anti-Rosicrucian publication by 'Menapius', showed excellent knowledge of architecture, music, navigation, geometry, fine arts, mathematics and astronomy. In describing the sciences as being in need of reformation – and in the process displaying the influence of Francis Bacon (apparent in other Rosicrucian documents too) – 'Florentinus' says that astronomy is very imperfect, astrology uncertain, physics lacks experimental support, and ethics needs re-examination.[8]

These comments by 'Florentinus' are astute, and remind one that for all the admixture of Cabala and Hermeticism and the like there was a deeply serious streak in Rosicrucian thinking. Nor was it impious, by standards other than those applied by orthodox Christians of all denominations. 'Florentinus' insists – and appears sincere, even earnest, in doing so – that the Rosicrucian aim is to understand nature as 'God's book', containing everything man needs in order to recover knowledge lost because of the Fall. (The idea of studying nature as reading God's book was iterated a century later by George Berkeley.[9])

Indeed, two positives are obvious to anyone now looking at the spate of Rosicrucian literature with an unprejudiced eye. One was the encouragement it gave to scientific enquiry into nature. The other was its rejection of Aristotelian physics and metaphysics. Both of these features were anathema to the Roman Catholic church, which feared the new sciences and fiercely defended Aristotelian thought. The intimate connection between Catholic orthodoxy and Imperial power meant that critics were quick to condemn Rosicrucian ideas as subversive, and they meant subversive equally of the religious and temporal orders.

The maelstrom of literature for and against Rosicrucianism abruptly ceased in 1620, for the reasons amply given by Yates in her study: namely, the connection of Rosicrucian hopes with Palatinate ambitions and their failure at the Battle of the White Mountain. In 1621 there appeared a pamphlet entitled 'A Warning Against the Rosicrucian Vermin'. Its message was not, in the light of the previous years' controversies, new; but it was an especially significant document for another reason: its place of publication. The 'Warning' was published at Heidelberg, the erstwhile capital of Frederick, Elector Palatine, but a city now firmly under occupation by the Habsburg armies. In the same year appeared a work called *Palma Triumphalis,* a paean to the miracles of the Catholic church, published in the major Jesuit centre of Ingoldstadt and dedicated to the Emperor Ferdinand II. Among other things, the *Palma* attacks the Rosicrucians, ridiculing their pretension to 'restore all sciences, transmute metals, and prolong human life'.[10]

After the Battle of the White Mountain the political hopes associated with Rosicrucianism were dead, but apart from its invisible lingering down the centuries to follow, the 'movement' had one major final spasm in it. In 1623 posters suddenly appeared in Paris announcing that the Brothers of the Rose Cross were in town, 'making a visible and invisible stay . . . We show and teach without books or marks how to speak all languages of the countries where we wish to be, and to draw men from error and death.' The result was panic, together with a 'hurricane of rumour' as Gabriel Naude phrased it in his 'Instruction to France about the truth of the Rose Cross

Brothers', published as a response to the excitements of 1623 in that same year. Reaction to the supposed presence of Rosicrucians in France involved attempts to demonise them thoroughly; they were said to have abjured Christianity and the Church, and to prostrate themselves before Satan, who appeared to them in splendour.

Naude's attack on Rosicrucianism is interesting because it is moderate and well-informed. He placed it firmly in the Hermetic tradition of the Renaissance, and described it as promising the imminence of an age of discoveries involving a great 'instauration' or renewal of knowledge. Use of the term 'instauration' reflects acquaintance with Francis Bacon's works, two of the most important of which had only recently been published.[11] Naude's intention was of course to oppose Rosicrucianism; after recounting what it stands for he remarks, 'Behold, gentlemen, the huntress Diana whom Actaeon presents to you naked.' In this myth the goddess Diana, supremely chaste and loth to be seen naked by a male, whether god or man, was bathing when the unfortunate hunter Actaeon stumbled upon her. To punish him Diana turned him into a stag and set his own hounds to tear him to pieces. The meaning of the reference is thus plain: Rosicrucians are false savants pretending to reveal the truth. Naude ends by agreeing with the Jesuit condemnation of the Rosicrucians, and applauding Libavius for having conclusively refuted them.

The chief hammer of Rosicrucianism, and indeed of all the tendencies of thought like it or linked with it, such as Hermeticism, Cabala, magic, alchemy, and the like, was – as already noted – Marin Mersenne. His part in the controversy is described below. Mersenne's emphatic opposition to Rosicrucianism is an important matter because of his association with Descartes, whose intriguingly ambiguous association with the 'movement' must now be explored.

We left Descartes at Ulm in the tense summer of 1620 while everything here under discussion – Frederick and Bohemia, the Rosicrucian furore – was coming to a head. According to Baillet, who is almost but not, as we shall see, quite our only guide in these matters, Descartes heard about the Brotherhood of the Rosy Cross during the winter of 1619–20, shortly after his day of inspiration and night of dreams. (The notion that he heard of the Rosicrucians only then is completely implausible: they had been a major topic of general conversation since his schooldays.) Accordingly, says Baillet, he decided to try to find them, because they offered a new wisdom and true science, which is exactly what he himself was after. So he went to Germany in search of them, settling at Ulm for the summer. There he met one Johann Faulhaber, author of a work called *Mysterium Mathematicum sive Cabalistica et Philosophica Inventio*, dedicated to the Brothers of the Rosy Cross and published at Ulm in 1615. (Baillet fails to see, or to mention, that this might have been one main reason why Descartes chose to visit Ulm specifically. The other reason was that in June 1620 negotiations between the Protestant and Catholic leagues were taking place there, and the city was full of diplomats and spies.) Then Baillet reports that Descartes went to Bohemia with Duke Maximilian's army, 'observed' the fateful Battle of the White Mountain, accompanied the army on its work of suppression in Moravia and Hungary (which included – a fact significant enough to repeat – being present at the capture and destruction of Hradisch in Moravia, effected by the Imperial

army under the savage comte du Bucquoy), and then afterwards set off on two years of travels through various parts of
central Europe, northern Germany, and the Catholic Netherlands. What he was doing during these travels, who he was
visiting, and why, Baillet leaves wholly unexplained.

All we next know is that Descartes visited his family home
in Poitou two years later, in 1622, to deal with some family
business – among other things, to sell the small farm at Perron
inherited from his mother – and that another year later, again
his intervening whereabouts unknown, he appeared in Paris –
just as the Rosicrucian scare of 1623 was breaking out there.
The innocence of Baillet's account, masterly or otherwise, is
worth quoting. When Descartes arrived in Paris, Baillet tells us:

> ... the affairs of the luckless Count Palatine, who had
> been elected King of Bohemia ... and the transfer of the
> Electorate from Count Palatine to the Duke of Bavaria,
> which had been made at Ratisbon on the previous 15th
> of February [1623], were obsessing public discussion.[12]
> Descartes could tell his friends a great deal about these
> matters, but in return they told him news of something that
> was giving them much anxiety, for all that it seemed in-
> credible. It was that for several days there had been talk all
> round Paris about the Brothers of the Rose Cross, and it was
> beginning to be said that he [Descartes] was one of their
> number. Descartes was surprised at this news because such a
> thing was not conformable with his character, nor with his
> inclination to think of the Rosicrucians as impostors and
> dreamers. In Paris people called them the Invisibles ... six of
> them had come to Paris and lodged at the Marais, but they
> could not communicate with people, or be communicated

94

with, except by joining thought to will in a way un-detectable by the senses.

The accident of their arrival in Paris at the same time as Descartes could have had an unfortunate effect on his reputation if he had kept himself closeted or lived solitarily, as he was wont to do on his travels. But he refuted those who wished to calumniate him through this conjunction of events, by making himself visible to everyone, and particularly to his friends, who needed no other argument to convince them that he was not one of the Rosicrucians or Invisibles. He used the same argument about invisibility to explain why he had been unable to find any of them in Germany.[13]

Baillet then adds that Descartes' visibility and untroubled dismissal of allegations that he was a Rosicrucian 'served to calm the agitation of his friend Father Mersenne,' who had been especially upset by the rumour because, unlike those who thought the Rosicrucians a mere myth, he was convinced of their reality and the danger they posed, having read 'what several Germans, and Robert Fludd, the Englishman, had written in their favour'.[14]

Well: it might indeed have been pure coincidence that the Rosicrucian scare in Paris erupted just as news of the fate of Frederick of the Palatinate was being discussed; and it might also have been pure coincidence that Descartes arrived in Paris at the same time as the Rosicrucian scare began, after some years of travelling around Europe looking for Rosicrucians; and yet more of a coincidence that his name was associated with Rosicrucianism. But a good deal of additional, though circumstantial, evidence strengthens the thought that he was not so uninvolved as he was keen to make his Paris friends think. That evidence suggests either that he was – as hypothesised – an agent, most probably for the Jesuits, investigating or keeping an eye on actual or alleged Rosicrucians, or that he was indeed one of them (or for a time wished to be). That additional evidence is as follows.

First there is the testimony of Descartes' notebook, the *Olympica,* known to Baillet and Leibniz but since lost, in which his portentous dreams of 10 November 1619 were recorded. The vicissitudes of the text of that notebook are extraordinary; the original was lost after Leibniz's use of it, then Leibniz's transcriptions of parts of it were lost after a French scholar of the nineteenth century had published an edition of them. What we now have is a version prepared by Adam in the early twentieth century. Assuming therefore that we have reliable versions of the following passages, they cannot but intrigue, so enigmatic and suggestive are they:

Polybius Cosmopolitanus's *Thesaurus Mathematicus* teaches the true ways of resolving all difficulties of this science and demonstrates that the human mind can go no further in this respect. This calls forth hesitation and rejects the recklessness of those who promise to perform miracles in all sciences. It also supports the agonising work of many who (F. Rosi Cruc), entangled night and day in some Gordian knots of that discipline, exhaust their minds in vain. This work is offered again to the savants of all the world, and especially to the most celebrated F. R. C. in G [Fraternity of the Rosi-Crucians in Germany].

Now the sciences have been masked; they would appear in all their beauty, if their masks were to be removed. For to anyone who sees clearly the chains linking the sciences, it will seem no more difficult to keep them in mind than to remember the series of numbers.[15]

These passages appear to tell us that Descartes planned to write a book to be called *Thesaurus Mathematicus* under the pseudonym 'Polybius Cosmopolitanus', and to dedicate it to the Fraternity of the Rosy Cross. That 'Polybius' is a pseudonym Descartes actually used is made plausible by the fact that Johann Faulhaber describes the clever young French mathematician who visited him in the summer of 1620 as using that name.

Moreover, the dreams reported in Descartes' celebrated notebook have remarkable parallels with a Rosicrucian work published in 1619, the *Raptus Philosophicus* by Rudophilus Staurophorus, in which a young man ponders which way to go at a crossroads, meets a woman who informs him that she is Nature and shows him a book containing all knowledge, but whose contents have yet to be methodically arranged.[16] Gaukroger carefully observes that there is no certainty that Descartes read Staurophorus, and points out that the conceit their accounts share was commonplace – a parting of the ways in the quest for knowledge, a person (usually a woman) who personifies or points the way to wisdom – commonplace enough for it to be possible that they both made independent use of it.

But if it was not Staurophorus' *Raptus* which provided a model for Descartes' dreams or 'dreams', it could well have been Andreae's *Chemical Wedding* itself, in which Rosencreutz hears a trumpet blast (Descartes' 'bang') that announces the angel of truth; his way is made difficult by a powerful opposing wind, but he gains access to a castle where he finds acquaintances and a giant globe in which the stars are visible even by daylight. Moreover he finds an incomplete encyclopaedia, and someone asks him, 'Where are you going?' The parallels with Descartes' dreams are striking.

If neither source inspired Descartes' dreams, the similarities constitute a very remarkable coincidence. To it must be added the fact that Descartes knew a surprising number of people who were Rosicrucians, or who were sympathetic to their ideals. One such was Jacob Wassenar, a Rosicrucian he was friendly with in the United Provinces later. In 1624 a treatise called *Historich Verhal* by one Nicolaes Wassenar actually named Descartes as a Rosicrucian. Nicolaes Wassenar is thought to be Jacob Wassenar's father. Another later friend with Rosicrucian associations was Cornelius van Hooghelande, a physician with an interest in alchemy. Descartes was closely associated with van Hooghelande throughout his years in the United Provinces. Both van Hooghelande and his father were frank about their sympathies for Rosicrucianism. When Descartes went to Sweden in 1649 he left his private papers with van Hooghelande for safekeeping.

Moreover, Descartes corresponded with the Englishman John Pell, who with Samuel Hartlib and Theodore Haak was one of the 'Invisible College' that eventually became the Royal Society in London. Later Freemasons claimed that the Royal Society was a Masonic lodge in all but name, and point out that Rosicrucianism and Freemasonry were at that time intimately connected. Theodore Haak, moreover, was born in the Palatinate, where members of his family had been counsellors to the Elector. His family left the Palatinate after the Bohemian disaster at the White Mountain. He was educated at Oxford and Cambridge, and later became a naturalised Englishman. He undertook translation work and even spying for the government in London, and when Frederick's son was restored to the throne of the Palatinate in 1648 he was asked to be the new Elector's secretary, but refused. His continental connections – among other things he helped Protestant clergy expelled from Bohemia and the Palatinate – were paralleled by those of Hartlib who, apart from his scientific interests, was also celebrated for the welcome and help he gave exiles from the continent. Educated itinerants and exiles, displaced by the Thirty Years War, were one source of the rich fabric of exchanges of ideas (and intelligence) current in Europe during the first half of the seventeenth century.

These Rosicrucian connections with Descartes have prompted some, from the fanciful Daniel Huet writing in the 1690s to the sober Adam writing in the early twentieth century, and on to the usually sceptical Watson in the late twentieth century, to conclude that Descartes was himself a Rosicrucian. Huet reminds one how easily fanciful theories arise: he claims that Descartes did not die in 1650, but let it be thought that he had done so, that he thereupon arranged a fake funeral, and went to live in secret in the far north of Sweden in order to pursue the Rosicrucian study of occult sciences. Huet, and those who follow him in this fantasy, cite letters purportedly written by Descartes to Queen Christina of Sweden in the years 1652 and 1656, respectively two and six years after his recorded death.

Apart from the difficulty – again worth repeating – that there was almost certainly no formal Rosicrucian movement as such, the claim that Descartes was himself a Rosicrucian, or at least sympathetic to Rosicrucian ideas, is exceedingly doubtful. Only consider his Jesuit connections and loyalties and, more importantly, the fact that his thought, so crucial for the scientific and philosophical developments of the time, is fundamentally opposed to anything that smacks of 'magia, cabala, alchymia'.

And consider also the fact that his friend and helper Marin Mersenne, also educated by the Jesuits at La Flèche, was so vehement an opponent of Rosicrucianism. Mersenne was convinced that a Rosicrucian cabal really existed, that its members practised magic, and that they spread evil ideas while moving invisibly from one country to another. By his tireless attacks on everything to do with 'magia, cabala, alchymia' and 'macro-microcosmical magical philosophy' he helped clear the way for the new science and philosophy of which his friend Descartes was one of the founders.[17]

It is true that there remain superficial similarities between Rosicrucian rules and Descartes' rules about living 'hidden from view', applying his medical knowledge for free, and seeking ways to lengthen life; and also his intense desire to find a single method to unlock all knowledge, and his interest in mathematics and the investigation of nature. But these latter ambitions were not restricted to Rosicrucians alone, unless the mere interest in science and philosophy makes someone a Rosicrucian – which it does not.

What, then, is one to make of this? The clincher has to be Descartes' Jesuit connections. All his life he was loyal to the Jesuits, and not only painfully careful to avoid offending them but actively keen to have their approval, most especially of his writings, which he wished them to adopt as textbooks in their schools.[18] If he was indeed working in the Jesuit interest as an agent commissioned to enquire into Rosicrucian activity and to monitor it, he would only have been one of many employed by them to do so. So to describe him as a Jesuit spy, wandering Europe in search of information about occult societies, is neither so dramatic nor so surprising – for all that it sounds both – given the circumstances of the time. Only scholars, soldiers and aristocrats travelled, and only scholars and aristocrats knew languages, especially Latin; and only scholars had the right entrée to the kinds of circles where Rosicrucians might be expected to gather; so if the Jesuits knew a clever fellow with both interests and skills in many of the same things as the Rosicrucians professed, they might very well employ him. I think it quite plausible that they thus employed Descartes – again: as one of many – and that his wanderings in Europe between 1619 and 1625, about which we know so little, are explained thereby. Add to this Descartes' use of pseudonyms, such remarkable coincidences as his turning up in Ulm where Johann Faulhaber lived, his appearance in Bohemia at the time of the Palatinate crisis, his arrival in Paris at the same time as the Rosicrucian scare, and the rumours of his association with Rosicrucians, and the plot thickens. Then consider that, although he had been left a small farm in Poitou, he was not a rich man, and that his years of travel required money. His travelling might have been both required and funded by such work.

And there is one final large clue, the full details of which appear in their proper place below. In 1628 Descartes was invited to a private interview with one of the King of France's chief ministers. It took place just at the time that Jesuit influence in France was again being opposed by the French government, in parallel with renewed diplomatic support – together with the possibility of military support – from France for the Protestant cause in the Thirty Years War. Immediately after that interview Descartes went into self-imposed (self-imposed?) exile in the United Provinces, and did not return to France for a dozen years, when the people present and the circumstances obtaining at the time of his departure had both long vanished.

That interview, I suggest, might have been a sticky one, in which Descartes was told that his former association with Jesuit activities in favour of the Habsburg interest was known to France's authorities, and that he would do well to leave the country.

What the story of the Rosicrucian furore shows, when one surveys it for its larger lessons, is that once enquiry had burst open the lid of orthodoxy that had hitherto constrained it – this was the achievement of the Renaissance but especially of the Reformation – the first result was the springing up of a luxuriance of weeds, among them the shoots that, with later more assiduous tending, become the seed crops of science and philosophy. Thus from the anarchy of ideas represented by 'magia, cabala and alchymia' and the mystical employment of number, strangely but headily admixed with astrology and forms of Protestant zeal, came the steadier growth of responsible science. If one were pressed to put dates on the flow of this tide, one would say 'magia, cabala and alchymia' reached its height in the period between 1550 and 1620, with responsible science growing from among its excitements in the later part of same period, and becoming increasingly vigorous from the early years of the seventeenth century onwards, but especially from the 1620s.

As an added complication, the rejection of Scholastic

thought, with its roots in Aristotelian physics and metaphysics, was a premise for some practitioners of the new occultism as well as for those who were bringing responsible science to birth. Given this, together with the fact that the new furore of ideas was contemporaneous with bitter religious divides and the threat to order – both religious and temporal – that these divides represented, it is easy to see why orthodox religion on both sides of the Catholic–Protestant quarrel were made anxious by what was happening. It was hard enough for practitioners of the new sciences and pseudo-sciences alike to grasp the difference between the fanciful and fruitful among them, so observers were at a double disadvantage: they were threatened in their orthodoxy and confused by the Babel of ideas assaulting it. No doubt more astute minds, even in the major religious movements, could tell the difference between a Galileo and a Dr Dee, but because both kinds of thought were hostile to the interests of orthodoxy, both kinds of thought had therefore to be proscribed. Giordano Bruno (on the 'magia, cabala and alchymia' side of things) was burned at the stake in 1600, and Galileo (on the science side of things) was put under house arrest in 1632, showing that to be a votary of unorthodoxy, whether nonsensical as with alchemy or responsible as with science, could be a very dangerous occupation.

4

Nine Years of Travel

According to his own testimony in the *Discourse*, Descartes followed his spell in Duke Maximilian's army with 'nine years of travel' before settling down to systematic work on science and philosophy. These itinerant years were 1620 to 1628 inclusive. They were far from years of idleness; apart from the endeavours that the preceding chapter suggests he was engaged in, Descartes attempted in this period to draft at least two works, the *Exercises in Good Sense*, now lost, and *Rules for the Direction of the Mind*. Both were efforts to state the insights about method that had come to him in the seminal years 1618 and 1619, but evidently the task proved much more difficult than he expected at first.

He was also at work on mathematics and science, for by the time he came to wider public notice in Paris in the years between 1625 and 1628 he already had a reputation among cognoscenti in both spheres, based not on publications but on personal contacts and correspondence. This reputation burgeoned from 1625 onwards, largely as a result of the indefatigable news-spreading activities of Marin Mersenne, who for many years acted as a one-man science newsletter and correspondence centre for Europe, and who told his wide circle of acquaintances about Descartes.

When Descartes and Mersenne first became properly acquainted in the early 1620s the latter was engaged in editing a large compendium of mathematics, the *Synopsis Mathematica*, which appeared in 1626. Their shared interest in mathematics created an immediate bond. They had been pupils at La Flèche at the same time, but Mersenne was eight years older than Descartes and had entered the college two years earlier than he, so it is unlikely that they knew one another there (though Mersenne probably remembered Descartes' older brother Pierre). Between 1609 and 1611 Mersenne studied theology at the Sorbonne, and then joined the order of Minim Friars. From the early 1620s his lodgings in Paris were a meeting place for the best mathematicians of the day, including Fermat, Gassendi, Roberval, Beaugrand, Descartes himself and, later, Pascal.

Mersenne was a powerful ally for Descartes because his attacks on alchemy, astrology and the Rosicrucians made him an unimpeachable arbiter of orthodoxy. This gave weight to his later defence of Descartes against charges of heterodoxy. Later still, Mersenne defended Galileo in the same way, and even more importantly was the first to make Galileo's work widely known outside Italy, by translating and commenting on it. One of his own main contributions was to the investigation of prime numbers, one type of which is still known as a 'Mersenne prime'.

Through Mersenne, Descartes also came to know Claude Mydorge, a wealthy man and an enthusiast for physics and mathematics whose independent means enabled him to indulge his passion fully. Mydorge worked on geometry and optics, wrote a book on conic sections, and invented mathematical recreations and puzzles as a sideline, and is remembered for his accurate measurement of the latitude of Paris. The association between him and Descartes proved important later because of their joint labours on optics. Mydorge made Descartes a number of optical instruments for experimental use, with significant results for the understanding of vision.

Descartes' Paris visit of 1623 was therefore a useful one, full of promise for the development of his mathematical work. But he did not stay long. In a letter to his father and brother written on 21 March of that year Descartes announced his intention of setting off to Italy the very next day. The letter appears to have an apologetic tone; he is going, he says, to gather experience of the world, to form better habits, to grow more able even if he does not in the process grow richer. He also had to settle the affairs of a family connection (in fact his godmother's son) who had recently died in Italy, having held the post of commissary general for food supplies to French troops in the Alps. There is a hint in the letter that he might have considered purchasing the deceased man's post. Some biographers conclude from this letter that Descartes' family thought him a wastrel for travelling about rather than settling down to the family avocations of law and prosperity. But it is also possible that he needed to offer an explanation for an Italian journey which would seem plausible to them or whoever enquired, given that going without any explanation would otherwise have appeared arbitrary or capricious.

Adam observes that the itinerary Baillet gives of Descartes' route was largely drawn from Montaigne's account of his Italian journey, published in 1581 and remembered now for its amusing account of how, in the interests of becoming a Roman Citizen for the fun of it, Montaigne had to kiss the toe of the Pope's velvet slipper – devout lips being guided to the correct point on the slipper by a cross inked there – after progressing towards the papal throne by going down on alternate knees, zigzag fashion. Using Montaigne as a guide, Baillet gave Descartes' route as Basle, Innsbruck, the Brenner Pass, and thence to Venice through the Val Telline. Once again the impressive innocence of Baillet's account is matched by the later biographers who quote him. For assuming that Descartes indeed travelled via the Val Telline – the highly important and politically significant Val Telline – rather than an alternative route (and there were some safer and easier ones), it takes only a brief acquaintance with historical geography and the circumstances of the time to find the choice very interesting. For, yet again, Descartes' doings tie in with the fraught politics of the day.

With Frederick expelled from the Palatinate and Bohemia, and with Protestant rebellion in the latter kingdom quelled, the Habsburg cause must have seemed in fine shape. But France's earlier policy of containing the Habsburgs, begun by Henri IV and interrupted during the regency of his widow Marie de Medici, was at that very point being revived by Louis XIII. Henri IV had seen that the only way to contain Habsburg power was to interfere with the cordon of Spanish possessions strung round France's frontiers, from the Pyrenees through Milan, and up the 'Spanish Road' to the coast of Flanders. When Louis XIII was at last able to pay sufficient attention to foreign policy matters – he was distracted at home by renewed Huguenot troubles, largely of his own making – he saw that although the Spanish cordon could not be broken without all-out war, it could be weakened by pressure at strategic points. In particular, he saw that interference with the lines of communication between Spain's Italian possessions and the Spanish Netherlands would be most serviceable to French interests. And the early 1620s was a suitable moment for interference, given that hostilities between Spain and the United Provinces had latterly resumed, and the Spanish Road was in heavy use.

Spain had two routes northwards from Milan to its territories in the Netherlands. One led through Savoy to Franche Comte, the other passed through the Adda valley, the Val Telline north-east of Lake Como, and thence into the Tyrol. Because Charles Emmanuel, Duke of Savoy, was an unreliable ally, and because the Savoy route was vulnerable to French attack from Lyons, the Spanish were cautious about using it. This made the Val Telline an absolutely essential lifeline for supplying the Spanish Netherlands. Louis XIII, therefore, made the Val Telline the jugular on which he proposed to press his finger.

The people of the Val Telline were Catholics, but control of the pass lay with an association of Protestant landlords known as the Grisons (the Grey Leagues or Graubunden) who administered the Val Telline as a vassal province, leasing its offices to whoever would pay most. Because of its acute strategic importance it was coveted by the Spanish in Lombardy, by France, and by Venice. For decades before the outbreak of the Thirty Years War these great powers had vied over it, each seeking to make treaties with the Grisons for its exclusive use. Early in the seventeenth century the Spanish Habsburgs, impatient with the insecurity of their communications, built a fortress at the Val Telline's mouth, and put the Catholics of the pass into their pay, thus gaining an important advantage in the competition for control of it. When the Bohemian troubles were in full spate in 1620, the Catholics of the Val Telline rose against the Grey Leagues and the Spanish sent troops to help them, with the result that the Val Telline fell completely into Habsburg hands. The English ambassador at Venice, Sir Henry Wotton, wrote to London: 'The Spaniards are now able to walk (while they keep a foot in the Lower Palatinate) from Milan to Dunkirk upon their own inheritances and purchases, a connexion of terrible moment in my opinion.' His fears proved justified when in 1623 a large Spanish force marched through the Val Telline and on towards the Spanish Netherlands.

France, Savoy and Venice unreservedly shared Sir Henry's anxieties. In February 1623 they signed the League of Lyons, pledging to get the Habsburgs out of the Grisons' lands (while incidentally announcing the intention of helping themselves to some choice Habsburg possessions in north Italy too). Alarmed, the Habsburgs tried to neutralise the threat by ceding control of the Val Telline to the Pope, who sent his own army to guard it. But this was not good enough for the Lyons League, for of course it meant that the Habsburgs still had untrammelled use of the pass. So Louis XIII sent an army to occupy all the Grison territory, and backed the Grisons themselves in capturing Tirano at the pass's eastern end.

This success plunged the Habsburgs in general and Spain in particular into a terrible fix. The latter could not resupply her troops in the Netherlands, her line of communication to the Austrian Habsburgs was cut, and her hold on Milan was now vulnerable to attack from Savoy.

At this moment of triumph over the Habsburgs, French policy was subverted by political difficulties at home, in which a renewed Huguenot rebellion played a major part, making it necessary to recall France's troops from Italy and Switzerland.[1] Thus a crucial moment passed, and another opportunity to shorten the great European war went with it. From France's point of view the circumstances were not altogether bleak: the political instability in Paris brought Richelieu to power, so that for the next eighteen years the country had a single continuous administration with a highly able minister at its helm. But that was no consolation on the immediate foreign policy front.

So Descartes travelled through the Val Telline in the spring of 1623, shortly after the League of Lyons was signed with the express purpose of prising that sensitive region from Habsburg control. Apart from the uneasy military situation in the Val Telline, which might itself have discouraged a solitary traveller, it must have seemed strange for a Frenchman to pass through crucial Habsburg-held (and thus enemy) territory at a time of such high tension – unless of course he had a purpose, contacts, and safe conduct arrangements in hand.

Recall again the fact that Jesuit interests were not France's interests, but emphatically Habsburg ones: and leave the circumstances – granting yet again that they might have been innocent, and yet again entirely and purely coincidental – to suggest what they may. It is mightily frustrating, though, that given the possibility that Descartes' visit to the Val Telline was indeed somehow linked to the momentous events of the day, that his own later silence, and the profound secrecy cloaking the frantic espionage of those tumultuous times, means that we can only note the repeated and speaking coincidences in this part of Descartes' life, and leave them at that.

★　　★　　★

From the militarily tense and dangerous Val Telline Descartes went to Venice, no great distance once the mighty Alps had been left behind. Baillet tells us that he there saw the festivities in which the Doge's marriage to the sea is celebrated. Since this ceremony takes place on Ascension Day, which fell on 16 May that year, the circumstance dates Descartes' visit accurately.

From Venice Descartes might have gone to Loretto, having promised himself to make a pilgrimage there after his extraordinary insights and dreams of 10 November 1619. If he did so he was again following in Montaigne's footsteps. And if he did so in earnest – that is, as a devout Catholic believing in the shrine's spiritual importance – the action demonstrates a deeper and less questioning faith than is fully consistent with the attitude of rational enquiry expected of a philosopher. For Loretto is the supposed site on which angels deposited the house of the Holy Family after carrying it thither from its original site in Nazareth. Loretto was for many centuries one of the chief pilgrimage destinations in Europe; in addition to the Holy Family's cottage it contains a fragment of the manger (brought equally miraculously from the stable in Bethlehem?), which would explain the degree of hyperbole bestowed on it much later by Pope John Paul II, who called it 'the holiest place on earth'.

Did Descartes sincerely believe any of this? At that very time he was writing, or at least meditating, what became his *Rules for the Direction of the Mind*. Rule 2 states, 'We must occupy ourselves only with those objects that our intellectual powers appear competent to know certainly and indubitably.' Although he claimed to be able to show, in his *Meditations,* that the existence of a deity can be known with certainty, it is a long distance from there to the truth of the traditions of a given faith, such as the one about angels carrying the Holy Family house to Loretto. Indeed it is arguably impossible for anyone to feel 'competent to know certainly and indubitably' that the shrine was the Holy Family's house, thus miraculously transported across the eastern Mediterranean (with a temporary lie-over, the tradition adds, in the Balkans). In characteristic fashion – politic or pusillanimous: the question is open – Descartes says nothing of the matter.

Although Descartes' next known stop was Florence, and although he was in Italy for two years and therefore must have remained in all these major centres for several months at a time, he made no effort to meet Galileo.[2] If he had wondered beforehand whether Italy might be a place to settle, given the legacy of scientific enquiry there and the bright afterglow of Renaissance arts, he had by this time made up his mind against it. Later he suggested that his reasons turned on the climate – he regarded it as too hot – and the prevalence of crime.[3] Another reason he could have given was that the attitude of the Inquisition to science, never friendly and growing yet more inimical, was a major disincentive.

Indeed, the Inquisition was at that very time bringing Italy's lead in science to an end. Large straws had been in the wind since Giordano Bruno was burned at the stake in Rome's Campo dei Fiori on 17 February 1600. The Church claimed that Bruno was put to death for his errors in saying that Jesus was not the son of God but a skilful magician, and moreover that God's mercy would ensure that even the devil would be saved at last; but most people knew that he was condemned also for his defence of the Copernican system, and for his doctrine of the plurality of inhabited worlds. Descartes doubtless also recognised that it was something of all four.

Moreover, this was the Italy in which the Carmelite friar Paolo Antonio Foscarini had received a famous and chillingly polite letter from Cardinal Bellarmine in 1615, thanking him for his memorandum showing that Copernicus's theory was not inconsistent with Scripture, but pointing out that, 'If there were a real proof that the Sun is in the center of the universe, that the Earth is in the third heaven, and that the Sun does not go round the Earth but the Earth round the Sun, then we should have to proceed with great circumspection in explaining passages of Scripture which appear to teach the contrary.'

But the sheathed irony of this remark was blunted by the fact that Bellarmine had already reminded Foscarini of how matters stood: 'As you are aware, the Council of Trent forbids the interpretation of the Scriptures in a way contrary to the common opinion of the holy Fathers. Now if your Reverence will read, not merely the Fathers, but modern commentators on Genesis, the Psalms, Ecclesiastes, and Joshua, you will discover that all agree in interpreting them literally as teaching that the Sun is in the heavens and revolves round the Earth with immense speed, and that the Earth is very distant from the heavens, at the center of the universe, and motionless. Consider, then, in your prudence, whether the Church can tolerate that the Scriptures should be interpreted in a manner contrary to that of the holy Fathers and of all modern commentators, both Latin and Greek.'

Descartes, in his prudence, saw these straws in the wind well enough. In 1625, when he left Italy after his two-year visit, the condemnation of Galileo was only eight years away, and already it was clear that the country held no future for a thinker.

★　　★　　★

Descartes left Italy in the early summer of 1625, travelling through Piedmont and entering France via the Mount Cenis pass, observing avalanches as he did so.[4] By June he was at his family home of Chatellerault, where he did a most interesting thing: he tried to get a job, and of exactly the kind that his father and brother would strongly have approved. Indeed it was the very job his distinguished great-uncle and godfather Michel Ferrand had held while Descartes was being brought up in his house: lieutenant-general of Chatellerault .

This uncharacteristic turn of events richly prompts speculation. Suppose the hypothesis about Descartes' intelligence work is true: his seeking a permanent post in family territory and in the family trade — that is, as a local legal dignitary — suggests that for one reason or another his spying life had come to an end. The lieutenant-generalship was at that moment for sale; perhaps Descartes' family had alerted him to its availability, and he had returned to investigate. The asking price was 16,000 crowns, and Descartes had 10,000 to hand. Baillet says that a friend offered to lend him at least some of the extra money required at no interest, and in July Descartes sold some more parcels of family land, doubtless to finish putting the required capital together.

But matters were not plain sailing. Money could not have been the only consideration, for when Descartes wrote to his father, then in Paris, to discuss the matter, he mentioned that his lack of legal experience was an impediment, and suggested spending some time in a more junior position to learn the ropes. No paternal reply is extant, and the immediate next steps in the venture are lost from view. But evidently the intention of finding a settled and prestigious post was a serious one, because in the following year Descartes returned to the area on the same errand, this time in company with his father's highly distinguished friend Vasseur d'Etoiles, receiver-general of the royal finances. So powerful a supporter implies that at this point Descartes was in earnest.

Despite the help of the king's receiver-general, however, Descartes did not get an official post. Willingly or otherwise, he abandoned the idea not only of the lieutenant-generalship but of any career in law or administration.

Perhaps the disappointment was not too great. After the first job-seeking visit in 1625 Descartes settled in Paris, where he spent almost all of the next three years, not leaving again until 1628. There was a good reason for this: the second half of the 1620s was a delirious time to be in Paris, which was experiencing the height of the 'libertine era', with new and radical ideas everywhere. Descartes was right in the middle of the excitement, which obviously made the prospect of legal life in the provinces pale by comparison.

The 'libertine' episode in Paris during the 1620s was not, as the term doubtless suggests at first, a matter of wine, women and song, but of intellectual liberty. It was a moment of en-lightenment and healthy scepticism, one of the first flowerings of the European mind beyond the foetid post-Reformation conflicts of religious traditions and doctrines.

The term 'libertine' has an interesting history. It was first applied in the mid-sixteenth century to a sect of Protestants in the Netherlands and northern France who, with impeccable logic, concluded that since the deity had ordained all things, nothing could be sinful. They duly acted on this principle. Neither their delightful view nor what they did on the basis of it met with approval from any other sect, whether Catholic at one extreme or Calvinist at the other, and so the libertines became a byword for sensuality, debauchery, depravity and general 'Epicureanism'. This of course gave rise to the standard and now most familiar sense of 'libertine'. By association, however, the term also came to apply to anyone suspected, as a result of having advanced views, of rejecting the principles of religion, and especially (given the time and date) Christianity. For a time in the seventeenth century this was indeed the word's chief meaning, and anyone to whom it was applied would thereby have been understood to have an interest in science and philosophy – and therefore to be unorthodox at least, and usually suspect, in matters of religion. As a blanket term it was of course inaccurate, for by no means all of the leading scientists and philosophers of the time were atheists or agnostics, and indeed very few of them publicly avowed being either. Indeed, some of them were sincere believers, or at very least believed that outward adherence to, and profession of, the faith was a necessity – not just for their personal safety (one could be burned at the stake otherwise), but for the good order of society. Such people were in good company: Plato had long before argued that the generality of people should be encouraged to believe in gods so that they would behave well, and would be more prepared to die in battle. Rational self-interest might suggest the wisdom of taking Plato's hint and supporting *hoi polloi* in their credulities.

The reason for the seventeenth-century application of the term 'libertine' to people with intellectual interests (whether they were atheists or not) was that conservatives assumed that advanced thinking must lead to dissolute morals. This non-sequitur was so established in the public mind by the early eighteenth century that in order to preserve a distinction between people of lax morals and people of advanced views, 'libertine' was reserved to the former and the latter came to be called 'free thinkers' or 'philosophes' instead. While this cluster of terms was in transition, writers like Pierre Bayle attempted to keep the distinction between moral and intellectual libertinage by describing votaries of the latter as 'libertines of the mind' (*libertins d'esprit*) as opposed to 'libertines of the body'. But in the early seventeenth century a 'libertine' was a 'philosophe', not (or not necessarily also) a seducer and drunkard; and it is this intellectual sense that is conveyed by the term here.

It happens that the age of Louis XIV in France was one in which morals and language were equally free – the censorious would say coarse and degraded – so that those who were libertines in our intellectual sense might quite well have kept several simultaneous mistresses, visited bordellos, and inter-larded their speech with streams of profanities, all in a way then perfectly acceptable to everyone other than the orthodox and pious among their contemporaries. But moral 'laxity' is a thing of fashion, and the succession of ages has seen 'laxity' and 'puritanism' come and go cyclically, as when Victorian prudery replaced Regency loucheness only to be replaced by the era of Freud in its turn. So this aspect of the Sun King's France is not a consequence but an adjunct of the dawning of modern science and philosophy, both by their own routes stem-ming from the liberation of the mind from the straitjacket of orthodoxy. But this came later; in Descartes' day the 'libertines of the mind' were just beginning.

The 1620s are important to the libertine story – some historians describe what happened in the 1620s as the 'libertine crisis' – because they constitute a crucial moment in the process of the modern world's tearing itself away from the old world. Of course this parturition took much bloody and painful struggle over a far longer period, starting with Luther's nailed theses in 1517 and ending only with the Treaty of Westphalia in 1648; but when looked at through the lens of the history of thought, the 1620s take on a pivotal significance. In that decade one sees the last major effort of the old world to repress the new; and in it some of the most significant founding ideas of the new world – among the very foremost of them those of Descartes himself – were forged and first expressed.

The 'libertine crisis' began when, in 1619 at Toulouse, an itinerant teacher of philosophy and medicine, one Giulio Cesare Vanini, was burned at the stake. His crime was 'atheism' (but also, by circuitous implication, homosexuality). His name became a byword throughout Europe for atheism and the 'naturalism' that accompanied it – that is, the view that nature is the ultimate reality and source of all things. Until Pierre Bayle defended Vanini later in the seventeenth century, most writers aped the virulent attack launched by a Jesuit apologist called Francois Garasse who stigmatised Vanini as a paradigmatically dangerous threat to religion and therefore the safety of society. The story is of more than passing interest in connection with Descartes for, in the controversies that surrounded him in the 1640s, he found himself being likened to Vanini – a charge he angrily, even violently, resented and rejected.

Vanini had begun his career as a Carmelite monk, studying theology and medicine in Naples, Rome and Padua before travelling throughout Europe, occasionally serving as a tutor or secretary in noble households. Later critics asserted that he had got into trouble for being a homosexual, and that he had killed a man in a fight, this latter being his reason for emigrating for a time to England, where he abjured his

Catholicism. On returning to France he travelled under the pseudonym 'Pompeio Usiglio', keeping mainly to the south of the country (to avoid Paris and the reach of central government), and supporting himself by giving private lessons. In Toulouse, a city famous for its ardent persecution of heterodoxy, one of his pupils denounced him for 'mocking at sacred things, vilifying the Incarnation, refusing God, attributing everything to fate, adoring nature as the bounteous mother and source of all being . . . he had fallen into impiety and sacrilege and disgraced his priest's habit by the publication of a book called *The Secrets of Nature*.'[5] Toulouse's city fathers chose to act against him because 'the unfailing attraction of novelty for the young brought him many disciples, especially from amongst the young men fresh from school.'[6] Given that Vanini asserted that men had no souls but died as other animals did, and that the Virgin Mary was a woman like any other and needed to have sexual relations to get pregnant, his views were certainly outrageous for their time. While being led to the stake in Toulouse's Place du Salin he cried out in his native Italian, 'I die cheerfully, as befits a philosopher!'

Legend adds that when ordered by the attendant priests to ask God's mercy, Vanini replied that if there were a God he would ask him to blast with lightning the unjust Parlement of Toulouse, and if there were a devil he would ask him to submerge the Parlement in hell; but that since neither existed, he could pray to neither. That this is legend is attested by the fact that a reading of Vanini's work (and few of his many virulent detractors then and during the remaining decades of the seventeenth century bothered to do so) shows that he was not in fact an atheist, but held that there must be a Necessary Being as the ground of existence for contingent beings, and that this being must further be an Absolute Being capable of resolving all contradictions within itself, since the universe is full of contradictions requiring resolution. Such views might not satisfy orthodox notions derived from revealed religion, but they certainly do not constitute atheism.[7]

The wild chorus of condemnation, vilification and horror that rose around Vanini's name took its cue from the violent assault mounted by Garasse, whose criticisms were entirely ad hominem and not at all concerned with Vanini's ideas. A more considered engagement with those ideas came shortly afterwards from a more considered pen: that of Descartes' friend and colleague Marin Mersenne, in his *L'Impiété des Déistes*.[8] But Mersenne's response to the anxieties prompted by intellectual radicalism was not heeded as much as the frantic propaganda exemplified by Garasse.

As a result of the Vanini affair, a mood set in which well expressed the fear of the old world at what the dawning new world was doing to established certainties. Vanini's execution was the first step; it was followed by several high profile and much discussed further attacks on heterodoxy. One was the 1622 execution in Paris of Jean Fontanier, an occultist who taught mystic doctrines he had learned while travelling in the East. In 1623 the poet Théophile de Viau was accused of atheism. He was tortured and condemned to death, but in 1625 his sentence was commuted to banishment, no doubt because he was well-connected and much admired among Paris's cognoscenti. He died a year later, aged only thirty-six.

The fact that the proximate cause of de Viau's arrest and trial was the 'obscene' poetry he had published in *Le Parnasse satirique*, together with suspicions of homosexuality, should not be taken to suggest that charges of atheism were polite masks for attacks on obscenity and homosexuality. Rather, the latter were taken to be expressive of atheism, or identical with it. For how – so the reasoning went – could anyone soil his hands with either if he were a person of orthodox faith? 'Atheism', remember, was a capacious term, in effect meaning heterodoxy in avowed beliefs, or noticeable practice, or both. As always, silence and discretion were safeguards, though not infallible ones; and Descartes, as repeatedly noted here, was assiduous in maintaining both when it came to tricky matters, but vociferous in proclaiming his orthodoxy when opportunity offered.

The event that most closely touched Descartes, however, was the celebrated banning by the Parlement of Paris of a debate about Aristotelianism. Three of the city's leading 'erudite sceptics', Antoine Villon, Jean Bitauld and Etienne de Claves, proposed to debate fourteen atomistic theses and, in the course of doing so, to refute Aristotelianism not merely by argument but by the demonstration of chemical experiments. Since 'Aristotelianism' meant the old world, orthodoxy, established dogma, indeed everything to which the new philosophy was opposed both in substance and method, the challenge was a bold one.

The meeting, scheduled for August 1624, stirred enormous interest, and an audience of nearly a thousand was expected at the demonstration. But the Paris Parlement banned the meeting, and its three organisers were banished from the city on pain of death. A few weeks later, on 4 September 1624, the Parlement issued a decree, having taken advice from the Sorbonne's Faculty of Theology, outlawing under penalty of death the teaching of any views 'contrary to the ancient approved authors, and from holding any public debates other than those approved by the Doctors of the Theology Faculty.'[9]

This event was associated in the minds both of the public and the authorities with the Rosicrucian scare recently in full spate, and with the contemporaneous publication of Robert Fludd's works in Paris. Fludd was an English physician and alchemist who wrote prolifically, advancing a theory of the creation which started with an account of the macrocosm's emergence from the abyss and the emergence, in turn, of man as microcosm – man in his own turn being macrocosm to the microcosms of his own body's constituent cells, each of which is in turn a macrocosm to a yet smaller microcosm – and so on until the cycles of creation have reached their completion. His works were dedicated to the Brothers of the Rosy Cross, and his closest associate was Michael Meier, who explicitly claimed to be a Rosicrucian. Naturally enough, the works of this famous Hermetic master, regarded with awe and not a little suspicion in his own native England, caused an anxious stir in France, which is why Mersenne undertook to write against them.

Mersenne charged Fludd with heresy, atheism, and the practice of magic. He did not castigate Fludd for alchemical investigations, but argued that these should be confined to the domain of science and kept strictly separate from theology – a particularly interesting view, given what Descartes' philosophy later made possible: namely, the legitimation of scientific enquiry by allowing the safe separation of science from theology, thereby doing much – indeed, single-handedly the most done by any seventeenth-century thinker – to free science from theological interference.

Mersenne had many other worries about Fludd's views. For one thing, he thought they implied a demotion of Christ to the angelic world, and for another he especially disliked Fludd's

123

concept of the 'anima mundi', the world soul, and the notion that individual souls 'whether of man or brutes' are sparks struck from it. Fludd replied to Mersenne in print, and a debate unfolded between them which for years riveted the attention of all literate Europe.[10]

For present purposes the interest of Mersenne's wrestling match with Fludd is that it represented a subtle defence of serious enquiry, not only from the fanciful extremes of 'magia, cabala, alchymia' but also from the reactionary attitudes of authority and orthodox religion. The danger was that if 'magia, cabala, alchymia' provoked too great a crackdown from the temporal and ecclesiastical powers, each equally threatened by the fearful implications of unorthodoxy, then legitimate science would suffer too; so it was necessary to keep a space open for the latter, and to protect its credentials from being tainted by the former. Mersenne and his contemporaries in the serious sciences were performing a delicate balancing act, fending off opposing threats while trying to protect their own work from attracting the wrong kind of attention from a nervous Parlement, court and church.

This endeavour was largely successful. The 'erudite sceptics' succeeded in effecting the break with tradition that was required for enquiry in the new sciences to blossom. Many of the leading lights were materialists, atomists, deists or even atheists, but some had high connections at court and most were sensible enough to keep their opinions quiet outside the elite intellectual circle of *libertinage erudite* that they collectively formed.

Descartes was not a sceptic in the way that Gabriel Naude and La Mothe Le Vayer were, but he was certainly erudite, and because Mersenne and Mydorge had advertised his intellectual virtues to their circle before he returned to Paris, he was soon a member of it and much sought after – as he tells his brother in a letter (now lost but quoted by Baillet) written in July 1626. That reputation was built on what Mersenne and Mydorge had learned of Descartes' work and views since their acquaintance with him began properly in 1623. At about that time he had been busy putting together a book discussing the geometry of solid figures, among other things exploring the problem of how to extend the treatment of plane (two-dimensional) figures to three-dimensional ones. By 1625 he had begun to turn his attention to other mathematical problems and to optics, again clearly in ways that excited the admiration of Mersenne and the 'erudites'. And rightly so; for at about this time Descartes made an important scientific breakthrough: he discovered the law of refraction.

This is the law that gives a geometrical description of the behaviour of rays of light as they pass through the interface between one optical medium and another. In fact, the law had twice been discovered earlier: in 1601 by the English astronomer and mathematician Thomas Harriot, and in 1621 by Willibrord Snell, professor of mathematics at the University of Leiden. Harriot and Snell did not publish their respective discoveries; Harriot's work has only recently come to be appreciated from a study of his manuscripts, while Snell had better fortune in having his priority over Descartes recognised by Huygens in the 1690s. The law of refraction is now known as Snell's Law as a result. But it was Descartes who, apart from discovering it independently, first gave it a published mathematical description. That publication had to wait more than ten years, however; it did not see print until Descartes included it in the 'Dioptric' essay in his *Discourse on Method* in 1637.

Descartes' discovery of the law resulted from the intensive experimental work he did with Mydorge, Villebressieu, and an instrument-maker called Guillaume Ferrier, in the mid-1620s in Paris. One of their chief interests concerned how to shape a lens so that it would collect parallel rays of light into a single focus, thus overcoming the vexing problems of distortion suffered by refracting telescopes. Scholars attempting to understand how Descartes arrived at the law of refraction are puzzled by the fact that in his 1637 publication of it, his demonstration is inadequate, so they have sought to identify some other route by which he derived it.[11]

Even more significantly for his later thought, Descartes returned at this time to the subject that had preoccupied him following his 'day of discoveries and night of dreams' in 1619, namely, the question of method – and in particular, the identification and statement of rules for conducting effective enquiry. He did not finish the book; and the portion of it that he wrote down was not published until thirty-four years after his death, appearing in Dutch in 1684, and in Latin (the medium for reaching a far wider readership) only in 1701. The book, incomplete and brief, came to be called *Rules for the Direction of the Mind (Regulae ad Directionem Ingenii).*[12]

Descartes' aim in the *Rules* was to give clear and useful directions for achieving success in the search for truth. The original plan was for a work in three parts, each containing twelve rules. In the event, only the first set of twelve rules was completed; the second set stops at rule eighteen, with just the headings for rules nineteen to twenty-one to follow; and there is no third set. The second set deals chiefly with mathematical enquiry, and the projected third set was planned to deal with the empirical sciences. The first set concerns cognition in general, starting from the premise that the aim of study should be to arrive at truth, and proceeding to state how that is to be done.

We should, Descartes says, investigate only those objects that we certainly and indubitably grasp, and moreover grasp for ourselves; and we must accept that we need a proper method for doing so, one which involves ordering and arranging our objects of study carefully, reducing complicated matters to their simplest parts, and beginning our enquiries from these latter in a clear step-by-step manner. This allows us to see everything in a single sweep of thought, grasping all the relevant connections, and keeping it all under constant review. We must stop when we reach difficulties, which will not be the result of our inadequacies (if we have followed the preceding rules properly), but will be intrinsic to the subject itself. Locating the point at which a particular problem becomes unsolvable is itself an important discovery. Concentrating on the easiest matters will give us the habit of seeing the truth clearly and distinctly; methodically reviewing the discoveries of others will exercise our intelligence; continually reviewing what we have learned will make our knowledge more certain and will greatly increase our mental capacity. And finally, we must make use of all the aids provided by reason, imagination, sensory perception, and memory, so that we grasp simple propositions distinctly, bring what we already know into the correct relation with what we are investigating, and identify what must be compared with what, so that we make the best use of our intellectual powers.[13]

That is what the first twelve rules say in sum, and it has to be confessed that although they constitute good advice, and in the process raise a number of philosophically interesting points which closer study of Descartes' philosophy brings out, they are hardly an infallible recipe for the discovery of truth – which is what Descartes was specifically eager to provide. Without doubt they were rules he found personally useful, as a way of disciplining his enquiries and reminding him always to work incrementally from one simple and clear proposition to the next, limiting each advance to small steps, leaving nothing out and constantly reviewing every stage, thus placing reliance only on what he was sure was right. But this characterisation of right method is highly general, and is limited even in its theoretical use.

Descartes was of course hoping to contribute to one of the greatest concerns of his time, which was the discovery of methods of enquiry that would exclude nonsense and guarantee genuine knowledge as their outcome. He and Francis Bacon (the latter in his *Novum Organon* and *The Advancement of Learning*) stand out as theorists of method because their other work keeps their methodological theories alive; but they were not alone in the quest for this grail. Hermeticists and Rosicrucians shared the desire to discover methods that would unify all knowledge and enable a practitioner to discover anything and everything, moving from discoveries in one region of thought to discoveries in another by infallible means. This was what Descartes and Bacon sought too. But they hoped to arrive at responsible knowledge of the world – a grasp of truth – rather than mystical insights and magical powers.

In the background of Descartes' thinking about method was an emerging general philosophy of nature which owed much to the influence of his friend Mersenne. In the mid-1620s Mersenne published two books setting out his philosophical and scientific views, the *Questiones celeberrimae* and the *Observationes et emendationes*. In them he sought to carry out the task described in connection with his controversy with Fludd: to show how to uphold orthodox Catholicism while at the same time defending a mechanistic conception of nature in opposition to the threats both of scepticism and Renaissance occultism. Scepticism denied the possibility of secure knowledge; Renaissance occultism claimed to attain it by magic and arcane practices. As noted, religious orthodoxy was affronted and alarmed by both these challenges, and was too ready to lump both of them together as menaces, and to classify responsible scientific enquiry along with them. That is why Mersenne further sought to show that religious orthodoxy was not called into question by treating the realm of nature as a mechanism whose laws could be discovered by experiment and described by mathematics. This was to be done by distinguishing between what must properly be understood in supernatural terms – the things that pertain to religion – and those that must be understood in natural terms – the things that pertain to the sublunary world. One of the faults he diagnosed in Renaissance occultism was precisely that it attempted to explain the natural world in terms of supernatural properties and powers that were other than those that belonged to God.

Mersenne wrote copiously on mathematics, mechanics, music, acoustics and optics, and offered genuine insights into all of them. If he had done nothing else, he would figure in the history of science for these contributions alone. But his greatest contribution was as the conduit of philosophical and scientific exchanges in his day, by keeping thinkers in touch with one another or at least with one another's ideas. He was a one-man post-office, abetting the cross-fertilisation of ideas in a period rich in discovery and debate.

In Descartes' case Mersenne's influence was direct. The work Descartes was soon to embark upon shows the marks of Mersenne's recipe for protecting religious orthodoxy while making scientific investigation of the world acceptable. The assumption that Descartes starts from in his own mature work – that the natural world can be described as if it is a mechanism operating according to quantifiable laws – was already implicit in the discussions he had had with Beeckman some years earlier, but Mersenne's statement of it, coupled with his views about method and how to use sceptical doubt as the starting point for attaining certainty, provided the foundation for Descartes' later work, and almost certainly prompted him to begin writing the large and ambitious book he entitled *The World* (*Le Monde*) in the late 1620s.

The rich intellectual life of 1620s Paris, despite the anxieties of the orthodox and occasional persecutions by the authorities, might seem to have been the perfect environment for embarking on a large project such as Descartes had in mind. Yet suddenly – abruptly, unexpectedly – in late 1628 Descartes left Paris and went to the United Provinces of the free Netherlands. He lived there for almost all the rest of his life; and moreover, he did so in circumstances of partial secrecy, only reluctantly letting his home address be known, and changing his place of residence often. The standard reasons given by the biographers for his quitting Paris and his subsequent puzzling behaviour are, first, that he had come to find social life in Paris too distracting, and desired peace so that he could think and write, and secondly, that he had been encouraged to do so by a great man, Cardinal Berulle, who urged him to delay no

longer in writing down his important ideas for the benefit of an
expectant world.

The first reason doubtless might have a measure of truth in
it; Descartes is himself on record saying as much, despite
the fact that his first choice of place and occupation in the
Netherlands suggests otherwise – for he registered to study
at Franeker University and then, after a stay in the bustling
city of Amsterdam, at Leiden University. But it is interesting
to note that events in the larger world suggest an additional, or
perhaps the real, reason for Descartes' leaving France. Most
biographers assume that when he settled in the Netherlands in
1629, he had decided to do so permanently; but his registering
as a student at Franeker and Leiden universities suggests that at
first he planned to spend only a couple of years there, attached
to intellectual communities while he wrote, and waiting on
events in France to see whether a return might be feasible.
It proved not to be, and as a result Descartes spent all but six
months of the rest of his life there – the next twenty years: the
most productive years of his life, as they proved.

The accepted story of Descartes' removal to the Netherlands
is of course based on Baillet's account, itself pieced together
from anecdotes told by Descartes' friend Clerselier and his
earliest biographer Pierre Borel. It goes as follows. In the
autumn of 1628 Descartes went with a number of friends,
among them Mersenne and Villebressieu, to hear a talk given
by a chemist called Chandoux at the home of the Papal Nuncio
to Paris, Guido Bagni. Chandoux's talk was aimed principally
at refuting Aristotelianism, and it attracted much applause –
from everyone (says Baillet) other than Descartes. Present at the
talk was the great Cardinal Berulle, founder of the Oratorians
and minister of the Crown, who noticed Descartes' reticence

and asked him to state his opinion. This Descartes did. According to Baillet, Descartes praised Chandoux's eloquence and his rejection of Aristotelianism, but said that it was not right to accept that mere probability is good enough when truth should be the aim. 'He added,' says Baillet, 'that in the presence of people happy enough to accept probabilities, as with the illustrious company he was honoured to address, it was easy to pass off what is false for what is true, and conversely to make the truth seem to be falsehood.' Descartes proceeded to demonstrate this, asking anyone in the audience to propose what he took to be an evident truth, which he then showed by probable steps to be false, and vice versa for a supposed evident falsehood. 'The assembled company was astonished by the power and extent of genius displayed by M. Descartes in his reasoning; but they were even more surprised to find how easily their minds could be duped by probability.'[14]

Rendered anxious by this demonstration, the company appealed to Descartes to say whether there was a method that would insure against falling prey to such sophisms, and Descartes of course replied that indeed there was: his own method. And he added that here was a small number of clear and certain principles in terms of which all nature could be understood, contrary not only to the Scholastic philosophy derived from Aristotle, but from what Chandoux offered in its stead – which anyway was, Descartes argued, really much the same as Aristotelianism.

And now comes the story's denouement. Cardinal Berulle was so impressed by Descartes, according to Baillet, that he asked him 'to talk to him again another time privately on the same subject. M. Descartes, conscious of the honour he had received from such an obliging proposal, visited the Cardinal a few days afterwards, and explained to him about his first philosophical ideas, on the basis of which he perceived the futility of the way philosophy is commonly treated. He showed the Cardinal what the applications of his ideas would be, if well conducted, and how useful they would be to the public if applied to medicine and mechanics, from the former recovering and conserving health, and from the latter lessening and lightening man's labours.'[15]

In response, Baillet continues, Berulle 'used the authority he had over Descartes' mind' to encourage him to proceed without delay in this important work. 'He even made it an obligation of conscience for Descartes to use his God-given power and penetration of mind for illuminating nature, a gift He had not vouchsafed to others.' This adjuration, together with the encouragement given by his friends, finally made up Descartes' mind to leave the bustle and distraction of Paris, and the heat of its climate, and to seek 'perfect solitude in a moderately cold land where no one would know him.'[16]

Thus Baillet's version; and even if it were not the case that he had demonstrably constructed it out of Borel, Clerselier and bits of Descartes' own published works, it smacks heartily of fiction. Descartes' latest biographers agree in suspecting as much, Watson chief among them; as he puts it, 'This long story is what Clerselier, Baillet and Lipstorp think *should* have happened. Descartes did go away from France more or less forever – and wrote all his published works in the United Provinces – and this is difficult to explain for anyone who wants to write a panegyric about *France's* greatest philosopher. So there must have been a strong impetus coming from very high up. If not from God, then from Cardinal Berulle, who was known to talk to God every day.'[17]

The larger events of the time, however, suggest that although Cardinal Berulle might well have provided the impetus for Descartes to leave France, it was not in quite the way Baillet would have us believe. To see what they are, a few steps back are necessary.

In 1628, the year Descartes decided to quit his native country, the government of France in the capable, not to say ruthless, hands of Cardinal Richelieu was just turning its attention from home affairs to foreign affairs. It will be remembered that France's intervention in the matter of the Val Telline had been interrupted by Huguenot problems at home, requiring the return of the French army. In 1624 Richelieu had astutely written, 'Physicians hold it for an aphorism that an internal weakness, however small in itself, is more to be feared than an external injury, however large and painful. From this we learn that we must abandon what is to be done abroad until we have done what must be done at home.' In 1624 what needed to be done was restoration of government control over all France, then in fractious mood, rather than confrontation with Habsburg power elsewhere in Europe. But by 1628 that necessary task had been completed to Richelieu's satisfaction, and he was turning his attention to the Habsburgs again – and this time in a strong position to do so.

Opportunity offered in the form of a crisis over Mantua, important not for itself but because its dukes controlled two strategic frontier towns between Milan and Savoy, namely Casale and Montferrat. The duchy of Mantua had fallen vacant and been claimed by a Frenchman, the duc de Nevers. The prospect of a Frenchman having control of geographically sensitive towns alarmed the Habsburgs, for the usual reason that it threatened connections between the various reaches of their domains. Accordingly, Emperor Ferdinand II sent an army to seize Mantua while his Spanish cousin laid siege to Casale. Richelieu, after seeing to it that the German states would not actively support Ferdinand II, took an army into Savoy to relieve Casale, and then proceeded to occupy another crucial frontier town, Pinerlo. By the time that the Treaty of Cherasco was signed in 1631, Richelieu had gained Mantua for the French duke and Pinerlo for France itself – a most satisfactory outcome.

Moreover, while preparing these actions against the Habsburgs in their northern Italian backyard, Richelieu laid the ground for another formidable constraint on Habsburg ambitions. He did this by encouraging the German princes, including the redoubtable Maximilian, to be more robust in resisting Imperial policies. And he also made an alliance with Gustavus Adolphus II of Sweden, just then about to make himself a powerful factor in northern Europe and the eastern and southern Baltic. In the end this proved a less successful ploy from Richelieu's point of view, because Gustavus's successful invasion of northern Europe prompted the German princes to temporise their opposition to the Emperor in case they needed his help. Still, Richelieu's aim of weakening Habsburg power proved largely successful from 1628 onwards, and that year and the next were the crucial periods when his plans for doing so were laid.

Richelieu was a protégé of Cardinal Berulle, who had been instrumental in bringing him into court circles early in his career. Although in 1628 Berulle had only a year of life left, he was still a major figure in French life and government. Two decades beforehand he had been a counsellor to Henri IV, and more importantly still he was the founder of the Oratory,

which he had set up specifically to be an alternative to the
Jesuits as a source of religious and educational inspiration;
for Oratorian schools educated the children of the French
ruling class, which was always at odds with the Jesuits both in
internal and foreign affairs. Further, Berulle was the spiritual
teacher of St Vincent de Paul, and he was hotly opposed to
the Huguenots. As a senior religious figure in the French
establishment, close to the Crown, and opposed to Habsburg
and Jesuit interests, he therefore makes an interesting figure for
Descartes to have a private interview with, just as France was
about to resume active opposition to Habsburg power. For if it
is true that Descartes was involved in some way with pro-
Habsburg Jesuit interests, or until a couple of years beforehand
had been so involved, the fact that he was interviewed by
Cardinal Berulle and immediately afterwards emigrated permanently to the Netherlands, comes to have an altogether
different significance. These thoughts prompt the surmise –
no more than that – that the story of Descartes' departure
for the Netherlands has more to do with the troubled state
of affairs in Europe than what is claimed in the unlikely tale
told by Baillet.

Just how doubtful these matters are, though, is illustrated
by the fact that some commentators take a different view of
Berulle's place in French political life at the time, suggesting
that as advisor and confessor to Louis XIII's mother Marie de
Medici, he was in fact opposed to Richelieu's anti-Habsburg
policy. The line of thought goes as follows: Marie de Medici
was in perennial opposition to her son, sympathising instead
with the Habsburg interest. When in September 1629 the
court debated Richelieu's plans for a campaign in Italy over the
Mantuan question, Berulle opposed them in line with Marie's

preferences. A few weeks later he was dead – poisoned, say the conspiracy theorists, by Richelieu, although official history says that he died of a stroke while saying mass.[18]

The problem with this story is that Berulle and Richelieu were too like-minded on matters of policy. In 1625 Berulle went to London to arrange the marriage of Louis XIII's sister Henrietta to Charles I of England, cementing an alliance much desired by Richelieu, who hoped – unsuccessfully, as it transpired – to prevent England from aiding the Huguenot cause. (Always a strong opponent of Protestantism, Berulle had to leave England early because he was suspected of conspiring in favour of the Catholic interest there.) The fact that Berulle disagreed with some aspects of policy does not signify hostility to the point of assassination; the councils of all kings and governments obviously see debate, differences of view, and the offering of alternatives, as a matter of course. Moreover, Berulle had in effect been in government with Richelieu – his protégé, remember – since the early 1620s when the first chapter of Richelieu's anti-Habsburg policy was being written, and he was still with him in government when he died in 1629. Of course, alliances and friendships often change; but in this case we would need evidence that it had changed to the point where Richelieu had to murder Berulle.

A clincher in this argument is the unity of view that bound Richelieu and Berulle over the Huguenot question. Both detested the Huguenots, though when Richelieu was appointed Louis XIII's chief minister in 1624 he was initially prepared to tolerate them. They were, however, difficult to tolerate, at least from the court's point of view, because they had their own army and they controlled eight 'circles' in southern France, in effect constituting a state within a state. When

Richelieu was occupied with contesting Habsburg tenure of the Val Telline, the Huguenots sought to profit by strengthening their position in La Rochelle, the coastal town that was their de facto capital. Richelieu brought his army home to dissuade them, and the Treaty of La Rochelle was signed (with English prompting) to defuse the situation. But the treaty only gave the Huguenots time to strengthen in preparation for outright rebellion, which erupted in 1627. England gave them help, but not for long; Richelieu quickly expelled the forces sent by Charles I under the Duke of Buckingham, and the infamous siege of La Rochelle began. By blocking the town's harbour Richelieu starved to death 20,000 of the 25,000 population, and then (in a *coup de théatre*) on 28 October 1628 sent Louis XIII into the town at the army's head to 'capture' the remnant of its dazed and enfeebled defenders.

Berulle was an enthusiastic supporter of this policy. He received his cardinal's hat in 1627 because of his credentials as a champion of the Church and the Catholic cause, a fact that Richelieu and Louis XIII consciously exploited. In his last years, coinciding with these events, Berulle wrote works on Mary Magdalene and the life of Jesus, maintaining his reputation as one of the leading 'devots' of Catholicism in France. This was a significant help to the legitimacy of Richelieu's domestic policy in the eyes of Catholic France itself. Berulle may have been Marie de Medici's confessor, but it is hard to see him as an opposition figure in the France of the day. If he interviewed Descartes on matters other than philosophical method, it was certainly not to encourage him to help damage French interests by aiding the Habsburg cause.

★   ★   ★

One thing that Baillet's tale tells us, though, is how Descartes was viewed by the intellectuals of 1620s Paris, and here there is little reason to doubt him. We know already that he was valued and admired by Mersenne, informally the president of the circle of savants gathered in that city. He was at the centre of Mersenne's group, and it is very likely that its members indeed urged him, as Baillet tells us, to commit more of his ideas to paper, though they assuredly saw some of his mathematical work in manuscript – and perhaps drafts of his *Rules*. In 1628 Descartes was aged thirty-two, feeling his powers in philosophy, though probably with most of his mathematical discoveries behind him, at very least in germ – for mathematics is on the whole a youthful sport of the intellect – and ready to settle to further study and endeavour. One way or another, Cardinal Berulle did him a favour; his life after leaving Paris and settling in the Netherlands was an immensely productive one.

There is little personal detail available about Descartes in his Paris period apart from these general hints, save for one rumour: that he fought a duel over a lady. But he also said at about this time that he had never met a woman who could compete in beauty with the truth. If ever he did meet such a woman, it was in his new home in the sea-pressed, windmill-bedecked marshes occupied by the energetic and flourishing free Dutch, then enjoying their Golden Age.

5

Animals on the Moon

Descartes was in the Netherlands by the beginning of 1629, and there he remained for the next twenty years which, as noted, means in effect the rest of his life — save for its last few months, when he travelled to Sweden at the bidding of its queen, and where, in that northern chilly darkness, he caught the disease that killed him.

By leaving France for permanent residence in the Netherlands, Descartes was stepping out of the history of Europe and into the history of ideas. The bitter tumult of the Thirty Years War continued for virtually the whole time that he lived in the Netherlands, but almost exclusively in the German territories and northern Italy, and Descartes played no further part in it of the kind hypothesised here — and indeed was scarcely affected by it in any other way either.[1] He had chosen his place of refuge wisely, for despite continuing theological disputes and sometimes lively internal politics, the United Provinces of the Netherlands were largely peaceful, tolerant, and growing rapidly richer by the year. But things were very different in the great central swathe of German Europe. There the long war's effects were very terrible; estimates are hard to make, but some historians put the death toll from conflict, starvation, displacement of populations, disease and general calamity, in many millions. The German centre of Europe was devastated, and did not recover for a hundred and fifty years afterwards.

Ultimately the war was a defeat for the Habsburg interest, but for that ensuing century and a half it seemed like a Pyrrhic victory for central Europe itself. And consider also the then powerful kingdom of Sweden under its great king Gustavus, who took his people into the war on the Protestant side and dreamed of a Baltic empire, and consider likewise the once powerful kingdom of Spain, even by then living on past glory alone. For both these great kingdoms the bloody conflict was their final scene in starring roles, for neither has since stood at front stage in world history.

But the history into which Descartes now fully stepped – the history of science and philosophy – was an equally potent matter, for this was the point at which the modern mind was being shaped, and Descartes' part in the process was a major one. Gifted, combative and proud, he by now fully had a sense of his intellectual powers, and felt ready to respond to the repeated requests of his friends and acquaintances to commit his discoveries and theories to paper.

In his twenty Dutch years Descartes wrote the works that immortalised his name. This suggests that at last, after the excitements and travels in the years since he had left Poitiers University, he had settled down and found the tranquillity and stillness commonly believed necessary for intellectual work. But this was not the case. For some of the time, it is true, he found tranquillity, but he also found controversy; and as if in proof of the questionable reasons he had for quitting France, he kept changing his address, begging Mersenne in a letter to tell no one where he lived.[2] His other biographers and commentators attribute this secrecy to his desire to work undisturbed, and without paradox they attribute his frequent changes of residence to the same motive, even though few things are more disturbing than often changing residence. But other anxieties might have weighed with Descartes; it is striking that his need for secrecy diminished after some years, and indeed for the last part of his Dutch sojourn his whereabouts were no secret to anyone.

Descartes' choice of a place to go, given the necessity of leaving France, was not a hard one. The unsettled state of the warring German lands, the heat and disorganisation of Italy, and by contrast the flourishing, wealthy, populous and relatively liberal atmosphere of the Netherlands in its seventeenth-century glory, settled the matter for him by itself. Moreover, he knew the Netherlands already from his Breda period, could speak the language to some extent, and had his friend Beeckman there. A yet further inducement was that, as the country had grown rich following its post-Reformation liberation from Spain, many schools and universities had sprung up in its rapidly expanding towns, and in them Descartes saw an opportunity for furthering his work. Long before this time he had made up his mind to try to replace Aristotelian orthodoxy in matters of science and philosophy with his own views, and that meant getting them accepted into the curricula of academies. His great ambition was to have the Jesuits adopt them, but as a step towards that end he wanted to persuade some of the new Dutch schools to adopt them first. When he arrived in the Netherlands it was with the aim of writing out his ideas in a treatise, and promoting its acceptance as a textbook. The first four Dutch years were devoted to that task.

For our purposes, a happy feature of Descartes' long sojourn in the Netherlands is that because he was separated from Mersenne and others who mattered to him, he was obliged to write letters, and accordingly wrote many. In the second of the two decades – the 1640s – his fame brought him to the attention of two socially distinguished women: Princess Elizabeth, daughter of the ill-fated Winter King and Queen of Bohemia, and Queen Christina of Sweden. Both, but especially the first, prompted him to write about subjects he might not otherwise have investigated, which added to his oeuvre and yet further to his celebrity. It is an irony that he should have had such a warm and consequential epistolary friendship with the Princess Elizabeth of Bohemia, given that he had been pitted against her parents' side of the argument at the opening of the Thirty Years War, nearly a quarter of a century before their correspondence began.

In his first months in the Netherlands, probably starting in late 1628, Descartes was in Dordrecht with Beeckman, the only person, so Descartes told him, with whom he could discuss science properly. Their friendship immediately renewed itself, but only temporarily; it was to receive a serious setback some months later. From Dordrecht Descartes went to Amsterdam, staying long enough to begin an acquaintance with Henry Reneri, a scholar who was later to be important to the dissemination of his ideas. These were just visits; he had not yet reached the place where he wanted to settle for the time being, which was Franeker, a small town (it is so still) in Friesland in the north of the Netherlands. Franeker was at that time an important regional centre for education, having had its university since 1585 (it lasted until 1811) – one of the Reformation institutions which sprang up, and in the 1630s were still springing up, all over that vigorous country.

Descartes arrived in Franeker in the spring and registered at the university as 'René Des Cartes, French philosopher' in an entry dated 16 April 1629. Registration was free and there was no religious test for entry, so this was an easy and attractive way for Descartes to make contact with people who might be intellectually stimulating. He attended the lectures of the university's professor of mathematics, Adrien Metius, author of a treatise on practical geometry and arithmetic, and brother of Jacques Metius, who had some claim to be one of the first improvers of the telescope. Descartes profited from the opportunity to widen his knowledge of astronomy and anatomy.

Franeker was the home, for her first nineteen years, of an exceedingly brilliant girl called Anna Maria van Schurman, whose knowledge of the classical tongues had inspired admiration among the learned before she was a teenager, and who had been praised by such poets as Anna Roemers Visscher and Jacob Cats for her literary knowledge in Hebrew, Greek, Latin and French. Schurman and her widowed mother left Franeker for Utrecht only a year before Descartes' arrival. In 1635 Utrecht acquired its own university, and Schurman – still in her twenties – was invited to write the celebratory ode for its opening. She was also permitted to study there, closeted in solitude behind a screen with a grille. Henry Reneri was appointed to a professorship at Utrecht, and soon afterwards – for by that time Descartes had published some of his ideas in his *Discourse on Method* – began to teach Cartesian philosophy to its students, Schurman among them. At about that time Descartes and Schurman met; she was 'the star of Utrecht' for a number of years, and published several of her works while there, including *De ingenii mulieribus ad doctrinam, et meliores litteras aptitudine* (On the aptitude of the female mind for science and letters). Their lives touch again indirectly in that both were patronised by Princess Elizabeth – in Schurman's case, when Elizabeth sheltered a primitive Christian sect Schurman joined in her later years (to the bitter disappointment of her many humanist admirers). But the personal acquaintance between Descartes and Schurman ceased as a result of their taking different sides in an acrimonious personal dispute that broke out between Descartes and the rector of Utrecht University, Gisbert Voetius, whom Schurman liked.

The point of mentioning Anna Maria van Schurman is that it illustrates the importance attached to learning in the Netherlands at that time. For all its mercantile interests and emphatically bourgeois society, the Netherlands was then Europe's leading country for the arts and sciences. Elsewhere in Europe a prodigy like Anna Maria van Schurman might have gone unrecognised and uncelebrated – might indeed have been regarded with a certain repugnance as having proclivities unbecoming a girl (though acceptable in queens like Elizabeth of England or Christina of Sweden, or a princess like Elizabeth of Bohemia; royalty was granted license) – but seventeenth-century Franeker was proud of Schurman, as was Utrecht. Into such an environment Descartes came in the spring of 1629, and he found it very congenial. The letters he wrote at this period show that he was thinking about metaphysics – in particular, the existence of God and the immortality of the soul, and about music – in particular, the effects of music on the mind;

and most of all about optics and optical illusions, in particular the problem of how to make lenses that would be free of the aberrations which then afflicted all available lenses.

In June Descartes wrote to Jean Ferrier in Paris inviting him to come to the Netherlands so that they could work together on a machine for cutting hyperbolic lenses, which Descartes had worked out would give a sharper focus than the spherical lenses everyone else produced.[4] Ferrier was a gifted maker of scientific and optical instruments, and Descartes was convinced that with his designs and Ferrier's skills they could make lenses that would, as he said in a letter to Ferrier, give such clear magnification that they would be able 'to see whether there are animals on the moon.' His idea was that he and Ferrier would live and work together 'like brothers', with Descartes bearing all costs.[5]

Ferrier was at that very point being offered a job by no less a personage than Gaston, brother of King Louis XIII of France, which would involve living in apartments in the Louvre as one if its resident craftsmen. While waiting for this mouth-watering appointment to be confirmed Ferrier prevaricated, to the extent that Descartes eventually became irritated, and wrote him an angry letter. While still trying to persuade him to come, though, Descartes was cautious about revealing his where-abouts; he told Ferrier that he should travel to Dordrecht, where Beeckman would give him instructions about the next stage of his journey, and money for undertaking it. The secrecy cannot have added to the invitation's attractions.

If Ferrier had joined Descartes in Franeker and they had worked on lenses together, it is possible that the errors in Descartes' design might have become evident to him. As it was, decades later Robert Hooke of the Royal Society in

London attempted to construct Descartes' hyperbolic-lens-making machine, and found – as he had predicted – that it would not work. But an examination of the correspondence between Descartes and Ferrier about the theory underlying the machine makes it clear that Descartes had discovered an important law in thinking about hyperbolic lenses: the sine law of the refraction of light.

Ferrier was not the only person Descartes quarrelled with, nor the most significant. Following the renewal of contact between Descartes and Beeckman, a major rift opened between them because of Descartes' occasional aptness for Luciferian pride. In a letter to Mersenne, Beeckman said that he had taught Descartes about harmony ('the sweetness of consonances' in music) when the two were collaborating ten years earlier. Mersenne told Descartes what Beeckman had said, and Descartes, taking this to be an imputation either of plagiarism on his part, or of Beeckman's priority in the discovery about harmony, grew very angry. 'I am most obliged to you for informing me of my friend's ingratitude,' he wrote to Mersenne. 'I think I have dazzled him by bestowing on him the honour of writing to him, and he thought that you would think even better of him if he told you that he had been my teacher ten years ago. But he is utterly wrong.'[6]

Evidently, Mersenne had asked Descartes not to tell Beeckman that he, Mersenne, had passed on Beeckman's remarks, so at first Descartes said nothing about the matter to Beeckman – until Mersenne visited the Netherlands in 1630, and learned from reading Beeckman's journals the extent to which the young Descartes of 1619 had indeed been indebted to the Dutchman for both the manner and matter of a number of his early speculations. Although Descartes had so far said nothing, he had asked Beeckman for the return of his little *Treatise on Music*, and thereafter ceased to write to him. When Mersenne realised that Descartes had been more than a little unfair to Beeckman he taxed him with it, and Descartes exploded – against Beeckman. 'Last year I took back my *Music* from you not because I needed it but because someone told me you'd spoken of it as if I had learned it from you,' he wrote to him in a rage. 'Now that I have established that you prefer stupid boasting to friendship and truth, I say to you in two words that even if you had indeed taught something to someone, it would be hateful of you to say so, and even more hateful if it were false. But it is worst of all when you have learned from the person yourself . . . I warn you not to show those who know me my letters to prove this because they know I am accustomed to learn even from ants and worms.'[7] When Beeckman wrote back in conciliatory terms suggesting that they meet to talk things over, Descartes replied in even more violent language. 'You claim great praise for teaching me about the hyperbola. If I did not pity you for being sick I would certainly not be able to keep from laughing, because you don't even know what a hyperbola is.' And then, 'I'd never have suspected that your stupidity and self-ignorance is so great that you really believe I have learned more from you than I am accustomed to learn from other natural things . . . it is obvious to me from your letter that you sin not from malice but insanity.'[8]

It is instructive to be reminded of what Descartes had written to Beeckman as he travelled in Germany a decade before: 'I shall honour you as the first mover of my studies and their first author. For you, truly, have roused me from idleness, and rewoken in me a science I had almost forgotten. You have brought me back again to serious endeavours, and have improved a mind that had been separated from them. If therefore I produce anything that is not contemptible, you have a right to claim it as yours.'[9] As Beeckman's journal shows, not only did he not claim anything of Descartes' as his own, but he was frankly generous about everything he learned from others, including his school pupils; and he even rejoiced in Galileo's published successes, despite having privately anticipated several of them in his own work.

The episode does Descartes no personal credit. A reconciliation of sorts was effected, but the old cordiality had gone, and when Beeckman died a few years later Descartes showed little regret.[10] The incident demonstrates how much his intellectual confidence had grown in the ten years since his previous sojourn in the Netherlands, and with it his conviction that he had much of value to offer. He was beginning work on an ambitious project – nothing less than a new system of the universe; a comprehensive natural philosophy which he confidently intended should replace Aristotelianism – and as all thinkers have done in modern times, particularly in mathematics and science, he was determined to get the credit for his discoveries by being acknowledged as the first to make them. That explains his rage at Beeckman, whom he unjustly suspected of trying to steal his thunder. It also, to add to the gracelessness of the incident, explains his refusal to acknowledge what Beeckman had indeed taught him.

Doubtless Descartes chose Franeker as his place of resort because it combined a certain remoteness – located in Friesland, the Netherlands' north – with a university; but a few months' stay seems to have been enough to persuade him to move closer to the centre of things. In fact he went right to the centre, moving in October 1629 to Amsterdam. This gives the lie to previous biographers and commentators when they say that Descartes left France for the Netherlands to escape people and to enjoy the peace and quiet needed for his work; for Amsterdam in this rich and ebullient period of the Netherlands' history was scarcely a place of peace and quiet. It was one of the great cities of the world, populous, busy, a crossroads for trade and travel, the commercial capital of what was arguably the most successful international economy then in existence.[11] Descartes lived in the city for considerable stretches over the next six years, starting in Kalverstraat before moving to the Dam (this latter the city's busiest thoroughfare, located right at the city's heart), and later to Westerkirkstraat.

But his residence in Amsterdam was not continuous. In the summer of 1630 he went to Leiden, registering at the town's university as a student of mathematics on 27 June. The *Album Studiosorum* also gives his address: he lodged at the house of Cornelis Heymeszoon van Dam, who lived with his wife and five children at the Verwelfde Voldersgracht. (Five children? More peace and quiet, evidently.) Whereas registration had been free at Franeker, Descartes had to pay at Leiden; the *Album Studiosorum* differentiated between those who attended with and without fee, and his name appears among the former. The principal attraction for him at Leiden's university was the presence of the brilliant polymath Jacob Golius, who was not only professor of Arabic and author of a celebrated Arabic dictionary, but also professor of mathematics.[12]

At the university Descartes renewed his acquaintance with Henry Reneri, and their association now blossomed into an important friendship. Reneri subsequently moved to Deventer to take up an appointment at the École Illustre, and Descartes visited him there for long periods in 1632 and 1633. They discussed Descartes' views in detail, and Reneri read his un-published manuscripts. In 1635 Reneri became professor at the newly-founded university of Utrecht and began to lecture on Descartes' theories, the first significant step in the dissemination of Cartesian thought apart from personal correspondence.

Descartes attended not only Golius's lectures on mathematics but also those on astronomy by Martin Hortensius. Given that he was engaged in writing about these subjects in his new 'system of the world' it must have been a stimulus – even if he disagreed with what he heard, a negative stimulus – to his labours. But by far the most important event for Descartes in 1630 was his meeting with Constantijn Huygens, a large figure in the Netherlands' history, and a crucial patron and protector for Descartes thereafter.

Constantijn Huygens was the same age as Descartes, but had already distinguished himself in the diplomatic service of his country on missions to Venice and London, and was the first secretary to the Prince of Orange in his office as Stadhouder of the United Provinces. In a long career (he died aged ninety in 1687) he served three princes of Orange in their office of Stadhouder: Prince Maurice, Prince Frederick-Henry, and Henry III. In addition to his government work he acquired distinction as a poet, was knowledgeable about the sciences, and was a patron of Rembrandt. His father had also been chief advisor to a Stadhouder, and his son Christiaan Huygens – aged just one when Descartes and Constantijn Huygens first met – was to acquire fame as a scientist, later becoming a Fellow of the Royal Society of London. Constantijn himself had been knighted by James I in 1622 for services which, also later performed by his son Christiaan, were not greatly different from those hypothesised here for Descartes: the transmission of intelligence, and other secret helps.

Descartes said of Constantijn Huygens: 'I could not believe that a single mind could occupy itself with so many things, and equip itself so well in all of them.' This was high praise from one so jealous of his own abilities. Huygens recognised Descartes' qualities in return, and his support, as the sequel will show, was unstinting. One of the earliest results of their acquaintanceship was that Huygen's brother-in-law became Descartes' banker.

This was a flourishing period for Descartes. He was happy; he wrote to his Paris friend, the writer Jean-Louis Guez de Balzac, 'I sleep ten hours a night here, without a care to wake me.' Amsterdam was a mere half-day's journey from Leiden, so in the late autumn of 1630 he moved back to the great city, and in the following spring again wrote to de Balzac, rejoicing in the anonymity of walking among crowds busy with their own affairs, a fascinated spectator of the life of a bustling entre-pôt. 'There is no one here other than me who does not engage in commerce,' he told de Balzac. 'Each is so wrapped up in his own affairs that I could live here my whole life long without being noticed by anyone. I walk every day through the tumult of a great people with as much freedom and ease as you enjoy in your country paths; and I pay no more heed to the people I see than I would to the trees in your woods or the animals that live there. Even the noise of their doings does not disturb my reveries more than would the babbling of a stream. Reflecting on their activities gives me as much pleasure as you get from watching the peasants in your fields, because I see that

153

everything they do enhances the place where I live, so that I shall want for nothing. You are given pleasure by seeing how your fruits and vines flourish, and you enjoy their abundance; that is how I feel when I see the ships coming into port here, bringing all the produce of the Indies and everything rare in Europe.'[13]

It is not difficult to see why Descartes was in such a positive frame of mind. He had devoted himself to intellectual labours, and there are few things as satisfying as developing ideas and writing about them. The work he was engaged on was his book *Le Monde*, the aim and contents of which was to give a systematic description of the natural world and man. 'But just as painters, not being able to represent all the different sides of a body equally well on a flat canvas, choose one of the main ones and set it facing the light, and shade the others so as to make them stand out only when viewed from the perspective of the chosen side,' he wrote, 'so too, fearing that I could not put everything I had in mind in my discourse, I undertook to expound fully only what I knew about light. Then, as the opportunity arose, I added something about the sun and the fixed stars, because almost all of it comes from them; the heavens, because they transmit it; the planets, comets, and the earth, because they reflect light; and especially bodies on the earth, because they are coloured, or transparent, or luminous; and finally about man, because he observes these bodies.'[14] In other words, Descartes arranged his account of the natural universe (of everything other than the spiritual realities of God and the supernatural) by employing the idea of light as the connecting thread; light itself, then its sources, its medium, the things that reflect it, and the thing – man – that observes it.

Le Monde was finished, but never published (the reasons why are revealed below). At least, it was never published in its original form. But Descartes excerpted parts of the manuscript for publication a few years later, and the book's two chief components appeared after his death as *Traité de la Lumière* and *Traité de l'homme*. Most of the writing of *Le Monde* was done at Henry Reneri's home in Deventer in 1632; he wrote from there to Mersenne in June of that year to report progress.[15] Prior to this Descartes was busy researching – and not only in astronomy and mathematics, as his university studies show, but also anatomy, so that he could better understand the way animal and human bodies function. In April 1630 he wrote to Mersenne, 'my work is going slowly, because I take much more pleasure in acquiring knowledge than in putting into writing the little that I know . . . I am now studying chemistry and anatomy simultaneously . . . the problems in physics that I told you I am addressing are all so connected and mutually dependent that it is not possible for me to solve one of them without solving all of them, and I cannot do that more quickly or briefly than in the treatise I am writing.'[16] In Amsterdam one of his lodgings was on a street of butchers (doubtless Kalverstraat), and he reported going every day to watch the butchers slaughter animals and to collect anatomical specimens from them to take home and study.

The pleasure Descartes took in the process of researching and writing *Le Monde* is evident in his letters, which (apart from those addressed to Beeckman during the contretemps) are rich in ideas and technicalities of a mathematical and scientific kind. He showed the mathematical part of his work to Golius, who responded positively, eliciting from Descartes a characteristic reply: 'I am very much obliged to you for your favourable judgement on my analysis, for I know very well that the greater part of it is due to your good manners. I have a somewhat better opinion of myself all the same, because I see that you have made a full examination of the facts before passing final judgement on it.'[17]

From the point of view of the history of thought, the deeply significant thing about Descartes' *Le Monde* is the assumption on which it rests: that the natural world can be examined and understood as a system of matter in motion obeying natural laws, without the need for any invocation of supernatural forces or agencies. This way of thinking about the universe was the seventeenth century's great revolutionary departure, because it premises the idea that even if one believes that the world is created by a deity, nature can be regarded as functioning independently according to its own laws. Just as a watch works by itself once it has been set going by a watchmaker, so the world, once begun, thereafter operates according to mechanical principles without needing the constant supervision and intervention of an external agency. When Descartes put this idea to Mersenne by saying that once the metaphysical question of God's existence and creative agency is settled, the world itself can be treated as a purely material realm, he cautiously added that, of course, this must be treated as a fable, an 'as if'; for he did not wish to impugn the theological doctrine that the existence of a deity is necessary to the world, nor that the account of creation in Genesis is literally true.[18] This rider rings hollow, of course, since if the material realm requires only natural laws, the introduction of (literally) a *deus ex machina* to invent it and get it going is superfluous; but Descartes was anxious that his sincerity in this belief should be taken as unquestionable, and he never wavered in his efforts to soothe religious sensibilities in his letters to Mersenne and others, nor in later

156

trying to get the Jesuits to approve and even adopt his works.

But in the works themselves there is much to make the religiously orthodox uneasy. Once God had given his initiating push to the universe, according to Descartes' principles in *Le Monde*, the mechanism can run itself for eternity. Stars and planets, and the earth itself, would form from the interactions of swirling matter, and everything else would naturally follow as an outcome of the same laws, even to the emergence of humankind itself. 'The laws of nature are sufficient to cause the parts of the chaos [of matter] to disentangle themselves and arrange themselves in such good order that they will have the form of a quite perfect world,' Descartes wrote, 'a world in which we shall be able to see not only light but also all other things, general as well as particular.'[19] This of course must be understood, Descartes repeatedly wrote, 'as if' God had decided to create matter and its laws and to allow the latter to operate uninterruptedly on the former; but this of course is just an imaginary and illustrative supposition; 'allow your thought to wander beyond this world to view another world,' he wrote, 'a wholly new one which I shall bring into being before your mind in imaginary spaces . . . we are taking the liberty of fashioning this matter as we fancy . . . let us expressly suppose . . .'[20]

But if this was intended to mollify the scrutinising officers of the Inquisition, two things Descartes then said would quickly have altered their view. First, he pointed out that his description of how the universe could form according to natural laws is both clear and consistent – the implication being that this was indeed no 'as if' at all. 'Were I to put into this new world the least thing that is obscure, this obscurity might conceal some hidden contradiction I had not perceived, and hence, without thinking, I might be supposing something impossible. Instead, since everything I propose here can be distinctly imagined, it is certain that even if there were nothing of this sort in the old world, God can nevertheless create it in a new one. For it is certain that he can create everything we can imagine.'[21]

Secondly he insisted that the description is entirely naturalistic, that is, based on scientific principles alone: 'Note that by "nature" I do not mean some goddess or any other sort of imaginary power. Rather, I am using this word to signify matter itself, in so far as I am considering it taken together with all the other qualities I have attributed to it.'[22]

And so Descartes proceeded, describing the 'imaginary' world, its laws, its phenomena, and the presence in it of human beings – considered, according to the 'imaginary' hypothesis, as a composition of body and soul, in which the body is 'nothing but a statue or machine made of earth.'[23] He gives a full account of the workings of the body – the digestion, the circulation of blood, respiration, the workings of the 'animal spirits' which flow through the 'cavities of the brain' and the nerves to work the muscles. He draws an analogy with the moving, music-playing and even speaking water-powered statues in the royal gardens of St Germain in Paris: 'Similarly you may have observed in the grottoes and fountains in the royal gardens that the mere force with which the water is driven as it emerges from its source is sufficient to move various machines, and even to make them play certain instruments or utter certain words depending on the various arrangements of the pipes through which the water is conducted.'[24]

'Indeed,' he continues, 'one may compare the nerves of the machine I am describing [i.e. the human body] with the pipes in the works in these fountains ... When a *rational soul* is present in this machine it will have its principal seat in the brain, and reside there like a fountain-keeper who must be stationed at the tanks to which the fountain's pipes return if he wants to produce, or prevent, or change their movements in some way.'[25]

This part of Descartes' account was based on close anatomical studies. Only human beings have souls, in his view, so it follows that non-human animal bodies are *merely* machines, devoid of emotion and sensation, and operating simply by stimulus and response. Accordingly, his anatomical studies included vivisection. 'If you cut off the end of the heart of a living dog,' he wrote, 'and insert your finger through the incision into one of the concavities, you will clearly feel that every time the heart shortens, it presses your finger, and stops pressing it every time it lengthens.'[26] He had what he took to be empirical grounds for thinking that animals were simply stimulus-response mechanisms; in what is the first known observation of the conditioned reflex, he told Mersenne that if you whip a dog repeatedly when a violin is playing, after half a dozen or so times the dog will whimper and cower merely at the sound of the violin.[27]

There is no point in denying that Descartes' vivisection and ill-treatment of animals is disgraceful. If this smacks of hindsight, courtesy of our more sensitive and sentimental contemporary attitudes to animals, then so be it. It is hard to understand how any intelligent person could fail to recognise the vivid presence of emotion and sensation in animals, especially the dogs and horses they had most dealings with, or to ask themselves what the point would be for animals to display exact behavioural analogues of human pain and emotion if they lacked the conscious qualia of these things within. Famously, the 'argument from analogy' which says that we can infer the presence of conscious experience in another creature (human or animal) when its outward behaviour resembles our own when we have just such conscious experience, is vulnerable to sceptical challenge; for an actor can seem to bleed and weep while feeling no pain, and there are creatures which suffer from a condition that makes them wholly insensate, despite being outwardly normal.[28] But the supposition that all creatures other than oneself lack conscious experience, emotion and sensation, despite the intimate similarity of anatomy, environment and behaviour, is irrational; and it was frankly irrational of Descartes and his contemporaries to think in these terms about animals.

Of course, their real reason for doing so was theological; the thought that dogs and horses might have souls (and might accordingly go to heaven, or a canine or equestrian version of heaven), seemed to them preposterous, given that they had accepted the (equally preposterous?) premise that there are such things as souls in the first place. And what use is a soul in a body unless it is to give it reason and experience, emotion and feeling? It follows that in lacking souls, dogs and other animals lack all that appertains to souls – and so could be cut open and experimented upon with impunity. One legend has it that, while living in Leiden, Descartes threw a cat out of a first floor window to demonstrate its lack of emotion and sensation (how defenestration was supposed to establish this is unclear), and I have seen the window in question, for it is still pointed out by the managers of an hotel located directly opposite the house, from which it is separated by a canal.

If nothing else, these aspects of Descartes' thought establish his bona fides on the theological front. The fact that he inserted

(Nicolas Etienne Edelinck, Bridgeman Art Library)

1. Adrien Baillet (1649–1706), Descartes' first major biographer.

(Reymond, Mary Evans Picture Library)

2. Descartes' birth-place in La Haye, now called Descartes.

3. King Henri IV of France, reigned 1589–1610, founder of La Flèche school.

(akg-images)

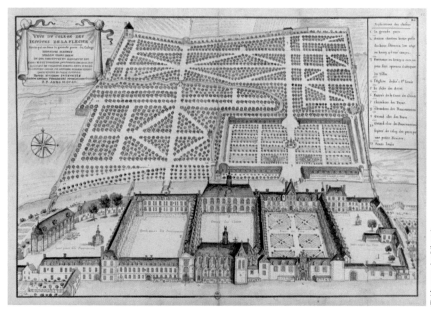

(Bridgeman Art Library)

4. The famous Jesuit College of La Flèche where Descartes was educated.

5. Portrait of the young René Descartes,
aged about twenty, artist unknown.

(Frans de Momper, Bridgeman Art Library)

6. View of Breda in the United Provinces, where Descartes briefly served in the army of Prince Maurice of Nassau, and where he met Isaac Beeckman.

(Johann Andreas Thiele, Bridgeman Art Library)

7. Prince Maurice of Nassau (1567–1625), Stadhouder of the United Provinces.

(Wolfgang Kilian, Bridgeman Art Library)

8. The warlike Duke Maximilian of Bavaria (1581–1662) in whose army Descartes served at the Battle of the White Mountain outside Prague on 8 November 1620.

9. A stove-heated room with a portrait bust of Descartes, recalling the famous day of discoveries and night of dreams, 10 November 1619.

10. A Rosicrucian allegory, engraved by Johann Theodore de Bry in the early sixteenth century. The Latin superscription reads, 'the rose gives honey to the bees' – that is: the secrets of the rosy cross are open to those who work hard at discovering them.

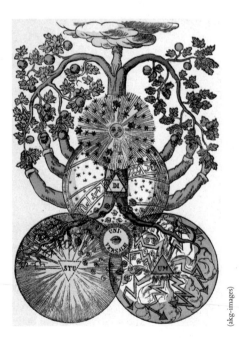

11. The Rosicrucian 'Tree of the Awareness of Good and Evil' in a coloured woodcut from *Geheime Figuren der Rosenkreuzer*, 1785.

12. The Rosicrucian Parnassus of knowledge ('mons philosophorum'). The difficulties to be encountered on the way up its steep paths are represented by, among other things, an unfriendly lion. (Also from *Geheime Figuren der Rosenkreuzer*, 1785.)

13. The ill-fated Winter King and Queen – Elector Palatine Frederick V with his wife, Elizabeth Stuart, daughter of James I and VI of England and Scotland. This picture depicts their wedding in 1613.

14. Ferdinand II, Holy Roman Emperor 1617–1637. The large forward-thrusting jaw was an hereditary feature among the Habsburgs, so severe in some cases that members of the family could not eat properly.

15. Christian of Anhalt (1568–1630), Elector Frederick V's chief minister, defeated at the Battle of the White Mountain in 1620.

Chriſtianus Princeps Anhald

16. The Battle of the White Mountain, 8 November 1620, at which Duke Maximilian, on behalf of the Emperor Ferdinand II, defeated Elector Frederick V. This battle marks the opening of the Thirty Years War.

17. Marin Mersenne (1588–1648) Descartes' friend, and the centre of a Europe-wide nexus of scientific and philosophical correspondence.

Le V. et tres pieux P. F. MARIN MERSENNE, Theologien, Philosophe, et Mathematicien, de l'ordre des Minimes de S.t François de Paule, Tres célèbre par toute l'Europe, Né a Oyse au Mayne le 8. Septembre 1588, et decedé a Paris le 1. Septembre 1648.
B. Moncornet excudit avec privilege du Roy

18. The city of Leiden, 'the Dutch Athens'. The free Netherlands became Descartes' home from 1628 onwards.

Academia Lugdunensis

19. The University of Leiden, where Descartes' theories were the subject of bitter battles between his supporters and opponents.

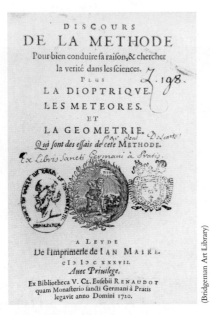

21. The first page of Descartes'
Discourse de la Methode.

20. The frontispiece of
Descartes' *Discourse de la Methode*
(1637) in an edition of 1710.

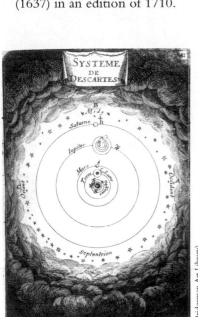

22. An engraved representation of
Descartes' theory of the universe, by
Alain Manesson Maillet in 1683.

23. An illustration from 'La
Dioptrique' in the *Discourse de la
Methode*.

24. The numerous family of Elector Frederick of the
Palatinate, among them – as a young girl – the brilliant Princess
Elizabeth with whom Descartes corresponded.

Tom. 2 Pag. 139.

Pascal trouvant la 32.ᵉ proposition d'Euclide.

25. The infant genius of Blaise Pascal (1623–1662) prompted him to do mathematics wherever and whenever he could.

26. Pierre de Fermat (1601–1665), Descartes' great – and greater – rival as a mathematician.

27. Amsterdam in the seventeenth century, the Dutch Golden Age. For most of his time in the Netherlands Descartes lived within easy travelling distance of the city.

FOSSA DOMINICA; LUGDUNENSEM VIAM | De *HEERE-GRACHT*, komende van de *LEIDSCHE-*
Deferenti. | *STRAAT; rondo naar den SPIEGEL en VYSEL-*
P. Schenck exc: Amst: C.Priv: | *STRAAT.*

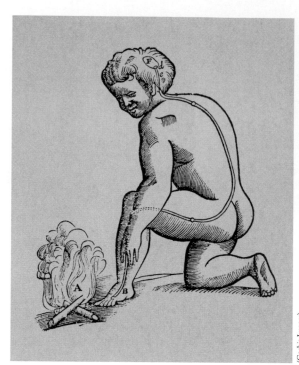

28. An illustration from Descartes' *Treatise on Man* showing transmission of sensory input by nerves to the brain.

(Corbis Images)

mée qui fortiroit d'vn fourneau, flotteroit inceffam-
ment çà & là, felon que les diuerfes parties de cette fu-
mée agiroient contre luy diuerfement; Ainfi les peti-
tes parties de ces Efprits, qui fouleuent & foutiennent
cette glande eftans prefque toufiours differentes en
quelque chofe, ne manquent pas de l'agiter & faire
pancher tantoft d'vn cofté tantoft d'vn autre, comme

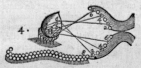

4.

vous la voyez en cette figure 41, où non feulement fon
centre H eft vn peu éloigné du centre du cerueau mar-
qué o, mais auffi les extremitez des arteres qui la foutiennent, font courbées en telle forte, que prefque tous
les Efprits qu'elles luy apportent, prennent leur cours
par l'endroit de fa fuperficie a, b, c, vers les petits tuyaux 2, 4, 6, ouurans par ce moyen ceux de fes pores qui
regardent vers là, beaucoup dauantage que les autres.

LXXVI.
Quel eft le
principal
effet des ef-
prits qui
fortent de
la glande.

Or le principal effet qui fuit de cecy, confifte, en ce
que les Efprits fortans ainfi plus particulierement de
quelques endroits de la fuperficie de cette glande, que
des autres, peuuent auoir la force de tourner les petits
tuyaux de la fuperficie interieure du cerueau dans lef-
quels ils fe vont rendre, vers les endroits d'où ils fortent,
s'ils ne les y trouuent defia tout tournez; & par ce moyen

29. A page from Descartes' 'De Homine Figure'.

(Bridgeman Art Library)

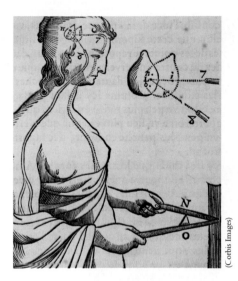

30. An illustration from the
Treatise on Man.

(Corbis Images)

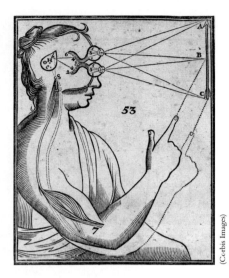

31. Descartes' theory of vision
graphically represented in the
Treatise on Man.

(Corbis Images)

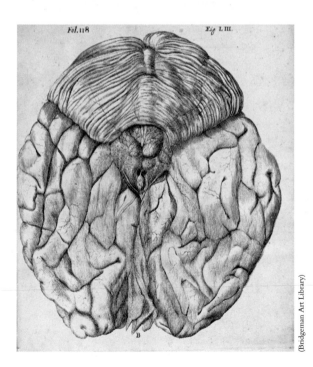

(Bridgeman Art Library)

32. The anatomy of the brain in an illustration
from Descartes' 'De Homine Figure.'

33. Queen Christina of Sweden.

34. Descartes explaining something from one of his books to
Queen Christina at the Court in Stockholm.

35. The best-known portrait of
Descartes, by Frans Hals. It hangs in
the Louvre in Paris.

36. A less well known and much kinder portrait of Descartes, by
Sebastian Bourdon. Unless it is a posthumous evocation of Descartes based
on other portraits, it was probably done in the mid or late 1640s.

37. A fanciful mid-nineteenth century depiction of Descartes musing in Amsterdam, by Felix Philippoteaux.

38. The genius as hero: Descartes in marble.

his finger into the heart of a dying dog, having first sliced off the heart's apex, shows that he really held the standard view, or something very like it, about souls and their exclusivity to human beings.

Descartes' work on *Le Monde* was nothing if not up to date. In 1629 and again in 1630 a Jesuit astronomer called (rather appropriately) Christopher Scheiner had observed at Rome the phenomenon of parhelia – this being the appearance of 'sundogs' or mock suns beside the real sun, caused by refraction of sunlight through ice crystals in the earth's atmosphere when the sun is near the horizon. Descartes wrote to Mersenne to get full details of Scheiner's account, and to ask for the latest observations and theories on comets. 'For the last two or three months I have been quite caught up in the heavens. I have discovered their nature and the nature of the stars we see there and many other things which a few years ago I would not even have dared to hope to discover,' he wrote, displaying nothing if not magnificent confidence in his work.[29]

All through 1632 and into the summer of 1633 Descartes worked apace at *Le Monde*, much of the time at Henry Reneri's home in Deventer, writing often to Mersenne for information and to keep him up to date with progress. In July 1633 he told Mersenne that the book was nearly finished, and promised to send him a copy of the manuscript before the end of the year. Galileo's *Dialogue Concerning the Two Chief World Systems* had been published just recently, in 1632, and Descartes asked Mersenne to tell him what Galileo had to say about such matters as the speed of falling bodies and the ebb and flow of tides. As this shows, Descartes had not been able to get hold of a copy of Galileo's book, which nevertheless was making a stir in scientific circles.

And not only in scientific circles; for the book had stirred theological circles also, and to no good end. In the summer of 1633 Galileo was arrested and condemned by the Inquisition, and all copies of his *Dialogue Concerning the Two Chief World Systems* available in Rome were burned. This was a terrible shock to Descartes. He immediately abandoned his plans to publish *Le Monde*, and wrote in trepidation to Mersenne:

I had intended to send you my *World* as a New Year gift, and only two weeks ago I was quite determined to send you at least part of it, if the whole work could not be copied in time. But I have to say that in the meantime I took the trouble to enquire in Leiden and Amsterdam whether Galileo's *World System* was available, for I thought I had heard that it was published in Italy last year. I was told that it had indeed been published but that all the copies had immediately been burned at Rome, and that Galileo had been convicted and fined. I was so astonished at this that I almost decided to burn all my papers or at least to let no one see them. For I could not imagine that he – an Italian, and as I understand in the good graces of the Pope – could have been made a criminal for any other reason than that he tried, as he no doubt did, to establish that the earth moves. I know that some Cardinals had already censured this view, but I thought I had heard it said that all the same it was being taught publicly even in Rome. I must admit that if the view is false, so too are the entire foundations of my philosophy, for it can be demonstrated from them quite clearly. And it is so closely interwoven in every part of my treatise that I could not remove it without rendering the whole work defective. But for all the world I did not want to publish a discourse in which a single word could be found that the Church would have disapproved of; so I preferred to suppress it rather than to publish it in a mutilated form.[30]

Under the impact of the shock about Galileo, and presumably for public consumption, given that much of the content of his letters to Mersenne was communicated to others – Mersenne being such a tireless epistolary clearing-house for communication among savants – Descartes' remarks about assiduously avoiding theological offence were evidently intended as an insurance policy, in case he somehow got into trouble. In this pusillanimous and frankly unconvincing vein, given his obvious ambition, he continued: 'I have never had the inclination to produce books, and would never have completed it if I had not been bound by a promise to you and some other of my friends; it was my desire to keep my word to you that constrained me all the more to work at it. But after all I am sure you will not send a bailiff to force me to discharge my debt, and you will perhaps be quite glad to be relieved of the trouble of reading wicked doctrines. There are already so many views on philosophy which are merely plausible and which can be maintained in debate, that if my views are no more certain and cannot be approved of without controversy, I have no desire ever to publish them.'[31]

But after all these protestations, the manuscript that Descartes was going to burn, then keep secret, and which he hoped would not offend the Church, and which might contain wicked doctrines, and which he never wanted to write – this manuscript would after all be sent to Mersenne: 'Yet, after

having promised you the whole work for so long,' he disin-
genuously continued, 'it would be bad faith on my part if I
tried to satisfy you with trifling pieces; so as soon as I can I shall
let you see what I have composed after all, but I ask you to be
so kind as to allow me a year's grace so that I can revise and
polish it. You drew my attention to Horace's saying, "Keep
back your work for nine years," and it is only three years since
I began the treatise which I intend to send to you.' And then,
suddenly anxious again, he adds, 'I ask you also to tell me what
you know about the Galileo affair.'[32]

The Galileo affair is a significant one, not only for the story
of Galileo himself but because it marks the last major throw of
the dice for the Church in its Canute-like effort to stop the tide
of science. What was at issue was the Copernican model in
which the earth goes round the sun, and its direct conflict with
scripture. In the beautiful words of the King James version of
Psalm 104, the text cited by the Church states:

> O Lord my God, thou art very great; thou art clothed with
>   honour and majesty.
> Who coverest thyself with light as with a garment: who
>   stretchest out the heavens like a curtain:
> Who layeth the beams of his chambers in the waters: who
>   maketh the clouds his chariot:
> Who walketh upon the wings of the wind:
> Who maketh his angels spirits; his ministers a flaming fire:
> *Who laid the foundation of the earth, that it should not be removed*
>   *for ever.*

The crucial passage is of course this last, italicised, line. For the
faithful its import is reinforced by the minatory implications

of God's question to Job out of the whirlwind: 'Where were you when I laid the foundation of the earth?' On the authority of Psalm 104 the Church announced that Copernicus, Galileo and science had to be wrong. Eighteen years beforehand, in 1616, Cardinal Bellarmine and the Inquisition had censured Galileo for premising that the earth moves. He had not taken heed, and now the Inquisition was trying to suppress the absurdity of the doctrine that the earth swings through space; for not only does divinely-inspired scripture tell us the contrary, but so does the evidence of one's own eyes – for, when one looks out of the Vatican windows at the pilgrims on their knees in St Peter's Square, one sees the world standing still and firm, with the heavens circling quietly and steadily above.

The prosecution of Galileo did not come out of nowhere. For two decades Galileo's discoveries had been a thorn in doctrinal flesh. It began with his perfection of the telescope and his use of it to make epoch-changing discoveries. In 1609 he received reports of a powerful 'spyglass' made by a Dutchman, and set about perfecting one for himself, using his wonderful skills as a craftsman and mathematician and basing his endeavours, as he put it, on the 'doctrine of refraction'. He made a number of telescopes, using existing techniques to produce instruments with a magnification of about four, but quickly learning how to grind and polish lenses more effectively so that he could attain magnifications of eight or nine. He saw the immense commercial, military and marine potential of what he had done – and for a handsome increase in salary gave the rights for the manufacture of telescopes to the Senate of Venice. But he also saw its scientific value. He had a fine instrument available by the end of 1609, which he called a 'perspicillum'. He it put to his eye and gazed through it at the heavens – and in the two months of December and January 1609–10 transformed history. He saw the mountains on the moon, he saw that the Milky Way consisted of innumerable individual stars, and he saw the satellites of Jupiter. He promptly named them 'the Medicean stars' and along with an announcement of this flattering appellation he sent a good telescope to the Medici prince in question, the Grand Duke of Tuscany, who thereupon appointed him 'Ducal Mathematician and Philosopher' at an excellent wage. This was timely; the Venetian Senate had just woken to the fact that their 'rights' to the manufacture of telescopes was worthless, since Galileo had not invented the instrument, and anyway Venice could not hope to control the manufacture of telescopes elsewhere in the world. They froze Galileo's salary, but by then he was on his way to Tuscany.

Galileo published his telescopic discoveries in a little book called *Sidereus Nuncius* (the Starry Messenger). But in the next couple of years he made more accurate observations of the moons of Jupiter and, while puzzling over inconsistencies in his data, realised he had to take into account variables in his own position relative to the motions he was observing – specifically, variables which had to be caused by the motion of the earth round the sun, thus showing that Copernicus's model was not, as Copernicus himself had taken it, merely a convenience for simplifying calculations of the motions of heavenly bodies, but actually correct. Galileo had in fact known this for a long time; in a 1598 letter to Kepler he acknowledged that he was a Copernican. But he did not make an issue of his convictions in this respect, and for the time being kept them private. He was feted in Rome for his telescopic discoveries, and elected to fellowship of the Accademia dei Lincei, which gave him great satisfaction.

What brought the Copernican question to the fore was the public pronouncements of Galileo's former pupil Castelli, by then professor of mathematics at Pisa. Castelli was asked by the Grand Duke of Tuscany, Cosimo II, and his mother the Grand Duchess Christina of Lorraine, to explain the discrepancy between scripture and the Copernican model. In complying he defended the Copernican model, and wrote to Galileo to show off to his former teacher about how successful he had been in making the Copernican case. In his reply Galileo asserted his view that the Bible should always be interpreted according to what science had discovered, and not vice versa. Copies of this letter were shown by Galileo's enemies to the Inquisition, which, however, at that point did nothing – they were biding their time. Then, in 1616, Galileo wrote directly to the Grand Duchess iterating his conviction that scripture should not be taken literally if it is inconsistent with what mathematically-based science reveals about the world. In the process of arguing for this view he made it clear that he took the Copernican theory to be literally true. 'I hold that the Sun is located at the centre of the revolutions of the heavenly orbs and does not change place, and that the Earth rotates on itself and moves around it,' he wrote. 'I confirm this view not only by refuting Ptolemy's and Aristotle's arguments, but also by producing many on the other side, especially some pertaining to physical effects whose causes perhaps cannot be determined in any other way, and other astronomical discoveries; these discoveries clearly confute the Ptolemaic system, and they agree admirably with the Copernican position and confirm it.'[33]

This was a provocation that the Church could not ignore. Pope Paul V instructed Cardinal Bellarmine to have the

Copernican theory examined by the Sacred Congregation of the Index, as the Inquisition was officially known. On 24 February 1616 the Cardinals of the Inquisition took submissions from theological experts – note this – and concluded that the Copernican theory must be condemned. Cardinal Bellarmine informed Galileo, who had taken no part in the enquiry, that he was henceforth forbidden to hold Copernican views, and certainly forbidden to teach or promote them.

The proscription kept Galileo quiet for a time, but when Cardinal Matteo Barberini became Pope as Urban VIII in 1623 he felt less constrained, for Barberini had long been an admirer of his work. Galileo promptly dedicated his new book, just about to published, to Urban VIII. This was *Il Saggiatore* (*The Assayer*), setting out Galileo's ideas about scientific method, and containing the following celebrated passage: 'Philosophy is written in this grand book, the universe, which stands continually open to our gaze. But the book cannot be understood unless one first learns to comprehend the language and read the characters in which it is written. It is written in the language of mathematics, and its characters are triangles, circles, and other geometric figures without which it is humanly impossible to understand a single word of it; without these one is wandering in a dark labyrinth.'

Urban VIII invited Galileo to papal audiences on six separate occasions, and by these and other means made Galileo feel that there would be no danger in promoting the Copernican view when he came to write out his complete system of the world, the *Dialogue Concerning the Two Chief World Systems*. Ill health made work on this magnum opus proceed slowly, and Galileo did not complete it until 1630. He tried to get permission to have it published in Rome, and failed; eventually he secured permission for publication in Florence, where it appeared in 1632. The outcome was the trial and condemnation by the Inquisition, and a life sentence of house imprisonment under a guard of officers appointed by the Inquisition.

Five years after the *Dialogue* was banned it was published at Leiden under the title *Discorsi e dimostrazioni matematiche intorno a due nuove scienze attenenti alla meccanica*. Descartes' years in Italy, together with his knowledge of Latin, would have made it an easily accessible read. But he had already read it by then. It did nothing to abate his alarm about the dangers involved in holding the Copernican view. In February 1634 he wrote to Mersenne announcing that, after all, he was not going to send *Le Monde*, but was going to keep it entirely to himself: 'I have decided wholly to suppress the treatise I have written and to forfeit almost all my work of the last four years in order to give my obedience to the Church, since it has proscribed the view that the earth moves. All the same, since I have not yet seen that the proscription has been ratified by the Pope or the Council [it was made by the Congregation of Cardinals set up for the censorship of books], I should be very glad to know what the view in France is on this matter, and whether their authority is enough to make the proscription an article of faith.'[34]

There was an added worry; the very people he most wished to placate and even to enlist on his side were clearly on the side of the Congregation of the Index in this matter. Referring to a book by Scheiner called *Rosa Ursina* Descartes continued:

If I may say so, the Jesuits have helped to get Galileo convicted: Father Scheiner's entire book shows they are no friends of Galileo's. Besides, the observations which the book contains provide so much proof to dispossess the sun of the motion attributed to it that I cannot believe that Father Scheiner himself does not share the Copernican view in his heart of hearts; and I find this so astonishing that I dare not write down my feelings on the matter.

As for myself, I seek only repose and peace of mind . . . I am hardly capable of instructing others and especially those who, if the truth were known, would perhaps be afraid of losing the reputation which they have acquired through views that are false.[35]

Descartes' disquiet did not stop there. Two months later he was writing to Mersenne again, still in anxious confusion about the Galileo affair, because he thought that his previous letter had gone astray, and that Mersenne would still be in doubt about his attitude – and especially his acute apprehension that he too might fall foul of the Inquisition. In this next letter he shows that he had been debating with himself and others whether the condemnation of Galileo amounted to a statement that the fixity of the earth had been pronounced an article of faith, for, if not, Descartes still had a slim hope of being able to publish his views without fear of censure. But his timidity in the matter proved overwhelming:

From your last I learn that my last letter to you has been lost . . . [in it] I told you at length the reason why I did not send you my treatise. I am sure you will find it so just that, far from blaming me for resolving never to show it anyone, you would be the first to exhort me to do so, if I were not already fully so resolved.

Doubtless you know that Galileo was recently censured by the Inquisitors of the Faith, and that his views about the movement of the earth were condemned as heretical. I must tell you that all the things I explained in my treatise, which included the doctrine of the movement of the earth, were so interdependent that it is enough to discover that one of them is false to know that all the arguments I was using are unsound. Though I thought they were based on very certain and evident proofs, I would not wish, for anything in the world, to maintain them against the authority of the Church. I know that it might be said that not everything which the Roman Inquisitors decide is automatically an article of faith, but must first be approved by a General Council. But I am not so fond of my own opinions as to want to use such quibbles to be able to maintain them. I desire to live in peace and to continue the life I have begun under the motto 'to live well you must live unseen' . . .

As for what it is that causes a stone one has thrown to stop moving, that is quite clear: it is air resistance, something one can easily feel. But the reason why a bent bow springs back is more difficult, and I cannot explain it without referring to the principles of my philosophy, which I think I must keep quiet about from now on . . .[36]

Unable to let the matter rest, after discussing some other matters Descartes returned to the troubling theme of Galileo's condemnation, this time in a state of deep disquiet over the fact that his own endeavour to disguise his views by representing them as being about an imaginary world in which purely mechanical laws govern, seemed doomed to fail:

As for the result you tell me of Galileo's experiments, I deny them all; but I do not conclude the motion of the earth to be any less probable ... I am astonished that an ecclesiastic should dare to write about the motion of the earth, whatever excuses he may have. For I have seen letters patent about Galileo's condemnation, printed at Liege on 20 September 1633, which contained the words 'though he pretended to put forward his view only hypothetically'; thus they seem to forbid even the use of this hypothesis in astronomy. For this reason I do not dare to tell [a certain correspondent] any of my thoughts on the topic. Moreover I do not see that this censure has been endorsed by the Pope or any Council, but only by a single congregation of the Cardinals of the Inquisition; so I do not altogether lose hope that the case may turn out like that of the Antipodes, which were similarly condemned long ago. So in time my *World* may yet see the light of day; and in that case I will need my own arguments to use myself.[37]

The to-and-fro of Descartes' unhappy thoughts about the affair are here obvious to see. He is going to keep his thoughts forever secret; he does not want to offend the Church; how can the Church dare to pronounce on such matters; they do not even allow the hypothesis to be advanced as a merely explanatory device; yet ... after all ... it is only the Inquisition, not the Pope or Council which has condemned the Copernican view, so maybe one day his own views will see the light of day ... Back and forth Descartes went, fearing and hoping, desiring Mersenne's advice, reassurance, help, protection and sympathy.

Months later, in August, he was still harping on the matter.

By this time he had seen a copy of Galileo's book, brought to him by Beeckman – now on restored terms – though Descartes only had thirty hours to leaf through it, because Beeckman was en route to Dordrecht. He disagreed with parts, and found that other parts agreed with his own views. To Mersenne he said, 'I must admit, however, that I have come across some of my own thoughts in his book.'

Although Descartes' initial scare quietened somewhat, enough to excerpt parts of *Le Monde* and put them together with his writings on method to constitute the celebrated *Discourse on Method*, issued in 1637 as his first published work, in 1640 he was still nervous that the Church would discover that he harboured Copernican views, and persecute him for it. In December of that year he iterated all his anxieties to Mersenne, and all his customary protestations about being 'zealous for the Catholic religion' and keen not to 'hazard its censure, because believing very firmly in the infallibility of the Church'[38] – but by then, as we shall see, he was considering publishing an account of his scientific views anyway, for reasons that were becoming stronger than his fear of censure.

What makes Descartes' reaction to Galileo's condemnation the more surprising and, one has to say, unedifying, is that other savants, among them Gassendi and Mersenne himself, went ahead and published pro-Copernican works in the years immediately after the Inquisition's judgement. In 1634, even as Descartes wrote one after another frightened letter to him, Mersenne published Galileo's *Mechanics* and – *mirabile dictu* – a summary of the *Dialogue* itself.[39]

6

Francine

Descartes was without question a man of scientific bent. On Sunday 15 October 1634 he wrote in the flyleaf of a book that on that day he had conceived a child with the serving maid Helena Jans in the room he rented in the house of an Englishman called Thomas Sargent in Amsterdam's Westerkirkstraat. The confidence of this announcement – it proved true – is striking. Baillet was in a dilemma, having thus to report his hero's commission of the sin of fornication with a maidservant, and not just that but the subsequent production of a bastard child; so he ascribed the aberration – as he thus implied it to be – to Descartes' scientific interest in anatomy.

In the register of baptisms in the Reformed Church at Deventer (no Catholic church being available), on 7 August 1635, the arrival was recorded of Francine, daughter to Helena Jans and 'Rener Jochems' (Rener son of Jochems). There is no evidence, documentary or circumstantial, that Descartes married Helena Jans, but later enemies who were Catholics accused him of apostasy because he had married a Calvinist in a Protestant church, the claim doubtless being a fabrication from the fact that he had his child baptised in such a church.

And as it happens, Francine was not an illegitimate child despite the fact that Descartes did not marry her mother, for the law of the United Provinces stated that it was enough for children to be legitimate that their fathers acknowledged them.

Helena Jans was not the only servant in whom Descartes took an interest. Quite differently, he became fond of a manservant called Jean Gillot, and taught him mathematics so well that Gillot eventually became the head of an engineering college in Leiden.

At this point in the story another figure enters, whom it becomes necessary to introduce because he is the man Descartes himself described as 'at once my translator, my apologist, and my mediator'. The man is Claude Clerselier, one of the chief sources of our information about Descartes' life. Clerselier was an ardent admirer of Descartes, and as Descartes' remark implies, he played a significant role in disseminating Cartesian ideas during Descartes' lifetime – but even more so after his death, by editing and publishing his letters, seeing unpublished works into print, and collecting and making available materials for use by the earliest biographers, not least among them Baillet.

Clerselier had made a good marriage, for his wife Ann de Virlorieux brought him a handsome dowry. It was a family-arranged marriage; he was sixteen and she twenty-two when it took place, but it proved happy, and they had thirteen children. He was a counsellor in the Parlement of Paris, and later served as proxy treasurer-general of the Auvergne when the official holder of that office, Pierre Chanut, went as France's ambassador to Sweden. Chanut figures large in Descartes' story too, for it was he who arranged for Descartes to go to Sweden as a guest of its monarch, Queen Christina, in 1649. Both Clerselier and

Chanut knew Descartes from his Paris years, and thereafter Mersenne kept them in touch with his work. When Clerselier became involved in translating and editing Descartes' work he thereby became closer to it and to Descartes than Mersenne had ever been.

The significance of Clerselier to the story of Descartes' excursion into paternity is that he left a record of a conversation he and Descartes had about the matter. As reported by Baillet (who, remember, was concerned to present Descartes in the best light, at a time when fathering children out of wedlock was frowned upon) the purport of the conversation was as follows: 'The mistake [Descartes] made once in his life contrary to the honour of his celibacy . . . is less proof of an inclination to women than of weakness. God quickly raised him above it, so that the recollection of his fall could be the source of constant reproof to him, and so that his repentance would be a healthful remedy, elevating to his soul. By this glorious restitution he could return to a perfectly Christian philosophy [and] innocence of life.'[1]

Whatever the real source of this pious exclamation – and Clerselier was a pious man quite capable of lacquering his hero's character to protect it in the eyes of posterity; that is a common phenomenon; all keepers-of-the-flame do it – it does not quite sit with Descartes' proud and independent character, nor his public acknowledgement in the baptismal register of Deventer that he had fathered a child. Nor does it square with the fact that he delighted in Francine, and loved her, as events proved.

It is humanly improbable that Descartes only ever had sexual intercourse once, though his flyleaf entry about Francine's conception is possible evidence to that effect – though how he knew that successful conception had taken place is anyone's guess. As Watson tellingly observes, as a scientist Descartes would most likely have wished to repeat any experiment he undertook, and several times at that, to see whether the results were uniform.[2] I agree.

Glimpses of Descartes as family man are few but tantalising, and in respect of Helena Jans a little ambiguous. In a letter written in August 1637 he set out arrangements for Helena and Francine to join him in new lodgings. His hostess was, he wrote, perfectly happy to have the little girl (Descartes referred to her as 'my niece') to come and live with him, 'and that we would easily agree on the price because it was indifferent to her whether she had one child more or less to take care of.'[3] As Descartes' hostess was in need of a servant he also suggested that Helena hasten to leave her present employment 'before St Victor's Day', this being the traditional date for hiring and firing servants, and to come to work where he was lodging.

What this suggests is that Descartes and Helena did not live as a couple, although they liked to be together if they could, and that he was fond of his little daughter and wished to have her with him. If Helena worked as a maid in the house where Descartes and his 'niece' lived, Helena could be near her daughter and she and Descartes could continue to engage, *pace* Clerselier's pieties, in anatomical experiments, without marrying or openly living in sin.

The evidence of affection between Descartes and Helena, apart from the fact that they shared a daughter, lies in a remark, touching in its implications, that occurs at the end of the letter just quoted. Descartes concludes it by saying, 'the letter I have written to Helena is not urgent, and I would prefer that rather than giving it to your servant to take to her, you keep it until she comes to find you, which I believe she will do at the end of this week to give you the letters she has written to me.'[4] This shows that she was literate, and wrote him letters (plural), and that he wrote to her; and this, note, is three years after Francine's birth; evidence of a settled domestic tie.

In a letter written a year later, in August 1638, Descartes described to Mersenne a scene of domestic pleasure, which strongly appealed to Watson's lively imagination: a father with his small daughter on his knee, clapping his hands to make an echo bounce back from a corner of a garden filled with tall weeds. The little girl runs to see what is there, but of course finds nothing; she runs back; herself tries unsuccessfully to provoke the echo; and laughs with delight when her father repeats the trick.[5] By this time Descartes was living in the country near Santpoort, and had a garden where just such scenes doubtless often occurred. The pleasure his daughter gave him must have been enhanced by signs of intelligence, because Descartes had ambitious plans for Francine; he had by then begun to make arrangements for her to be educated in France with a Madame du Tronchet, whom Baillet says was a distant relation of Descartes and a highly respectable lady ('the mother,' Baillet breathlessly assures his readers, 'of an ecclesiastic.')

On the first of September 1640 Descartes was in Leiden, engaged in discussions with his publisher, when a messenger arrived post-haste from Santpoort saying that Francine was dangerously ill. He rushed home as fast as he could, to find her covered in a rash with a raging temperature. It was scarlet fever.[6] This illness, caused by streptococcal bacteria in the throat, is now easily curable but was then a desperately serious childhood disease. With its short incubation period of just one to two days it struck quickly and violently, first with fever and a sore throat, then with a sandpapery rash that started on the neck and chest and spread to the whole body. Descartes had long nourished an amateur interest in medicine, hoping that his infallible method for acquiring knowledge would eventually reveal to him the secret of longevity. But as he had told Mersenne in a letter written in February 1639, he had never been able to cure a fever.

And so it proved again. After three days of illness, on 7 September 1640, Francine died. She was aged just five. A few months later, in a letter to Alphonse Pollot, Descartes wrote that he was not the kind of philosopher who thinks that men should not cry, and added that he knew what he was speaking about, because he had just lost two of the people who had been dearest to him.[7] Baillet said that Francine's death was 'the greatest sorrow that Descartes ever experienced in his life,'[8] and one can well believe it.

'Two people': might Helena also have succumbed to the fevers that, as Descartes reported to Mersenne, raged in the late summer of 1640? After this time there is no more mention of her in his correspondence, or in any other sources; she vanishes from view. Descartes' father had also recently died; so had his sister; and he might have meant either of them by this remark. But he had seen neither of them for years, and had maintained little contact with either. The possibility that he meant Helena is a real one, and deepens the tragedy.[9]

Descartes' letter to Pollot, written in January 1641, was occasioned by the fact that Pollot had himself just suffered a bereavement – his brother had died – and Descartes' aim was consolation.

I have just learned the sad news of your loss, and though I do not undertake to say anything in this letter which could have any great power to soften your pain, I still cannot refrain from trying, so as to let you know at least that I share what you feel. I am not one of those who think that tears and sadness are appropriate only for women, and that to appear a stout-hearted man one must force oneself to put on a calm expression at all times. Not long ago I suffered the loss of two people who were very close to me, and I found that those who wanted to shield me from sadness only increased it, whereas I was consoled by the kindness of those who I saw to be touched by my grief. So I am sure that you will listen to me better if I do not try to check your tears than if I tried to steer you away from a feeling which I consider quite justified.[10]

But Descartes also believed that consolation should be accompanied by encouragement to fortitude, for life goes on. It is clear, from the letters he wrote to Mersenne and others after the grief of the previous September, that he found his best consolation in work, and had returned to it after some weeks with gratitude for the relief it gave him.

Nevertheless [he therefore continued] there should be moderation in your feelings, and while it would be barbaric not to be distressed at all when one has due cause, it would also be dishonourable to abandon oneself completely to grief; we do ourselves no credit if we do not strive with all our might to free ourselves from such a troublesome passion . . . Now I certainly do not want to advise you to use all your powers of determination and steadfastness to check the internal agitation you feel straight away – for this would perhaps be a cure more troublesome than the original sickness. But equally I do not advise you to wait until time alone heals you, still less to sustain and prolong your suffering by your own thoughts. I ask you merely to try to alleviate the pain little by little, by looking at what has happened to you from whatever perspective can make it appear more bearable, while at the same time taking your mind off it as much as you can by other activities. I am well aware that I am telling you nothing new here. But we should not despise good remedies just because they are in common use; and since I have myself made successful use of this one, I felt myself bound to include it in this letter.[11]

'Since I have myself made successful use of this one': writing four months after the worst sadness of his life, Descartes was showing the spirit of the philosopher in its most redoubtable form.

7

The Shape of Snow

The six short years that elapsed between the conception and the tragic death of Francine Descartes – 1634 to 1640 – were seminal ones for Descartes in other respects too. The Galileo debacle of 1633 had left him temporarily silenced and constrained despite four years of concentrated work, but although the anxieties thus provoked lasted all of Francine's short lifetime, his silence did not. On the contrary, within a couple of years Descartes had decided to use some of the work that went into *Le Monde* for a book that would set out his stall without being theologically controversial, and which he hoped might pave the way for the eventual acceptance of his ideas by serving as a textbook for schools.

In the immediate aftermath of the Galileo affair Descartes continued with his studies in anatomy, medicine, astronomy and optics; his letters to Mersenne and others are full of technical detail on all these subjects. But the prospect of the founding of a new university in Utrecht, at which Descartes' friend and disciple Henry Reneri had been invited to take a professorship, offered a fresh opportunity to get the results of his work more widely known. Reneri was determined to put Descartes' ideas into the public domain by means of his lectures. He knew those ideas well; he had discussed them with Descartes over several years, and had read the manuscript of *Le Monde* as it was being written. But although a university platform promised a substantial advance in the direction of Descartes' aims, it was by no means the same as having his ideas available in print. In any case, as both he and Reneri saw, there had to be a book setting out some at least of Descartes' key conceptions to accompany the lectures. And he was very keen that merely verbal reports – even worse, misreports – of his views should not get into circulation, especially to avoid offence to the Church. Ambitious as ever, Descartes accordingly set to work with the plan of a book different in scope from *Le Monde*.

The new university of Utrecht was officially opened at a ceremony on 26 March 1636. Reneri began to lecture on Descartes' ideas immediately, and they were enthusiastically received. The promised book was still not ready, but by then preparations for it were well advanced. It appeared at last in June 1637, printed by Jean le Maire of Leiden. It was Descartes' first published work; he was forty-one, so it had been a long time coming. Although few people, even among savants, realised it at the time, its appearance was a major event in the history of thought. Some scholars now regard it as one of the two seminal texts of the modern world (the other being Newton's *Principia*). The book was, of course, the celebrated treatise now called the *Discourse on the Method and Essays*.

Descartes found organising the material for the book a relatively smooth matter, for most of it was already written. The process of publication was less smooth. At first the firm of Elzevir – already at that time a famous publishing house – told

Descartes that they wished to be his publishers, but when he visited Leiden to start the complex process of seeing the book into print they began to make difficulties. Descartes did not specify what they were when telling Mersenne about them, but anyway he took the manuscript elsewhere. Mersenne offered to arrange for its publication in Paris, and Descartes was tempted by the offer; but in replying he said, 'my manuscript is no better written than this letter; the spelling and punctuation are equally careless and the diagrams are drawn by me, that is to say, very badly. So if you cannot make out from the text how to explain them to an engraver, it would be impossible for him to understand them.'[1] It was clearly an advantage for an author to be present during the publication process for the reasons Descartes suggests, but Mersenne's offer was attractive enough for Descartes to consider accepting it, and he told Mersenne that he wished to have the work printed in 'a handsome fount on handsome paper', with two hundred copies for himself to distribute.

In the same letter Descartes described the contents of the book – and its title, which, though hardly snappy, well describes what he sought to offer in it: 'The Plan of a Universal Science, which is capable of raising our Nature to its Highest Degree of Perfection, together with the Optics, the Meteorology and the Geometry, in which the Author, in order to give proof of his universal Science, explains the most abstruse Topics he could choose, and does so in such a way that even persons who have never studied can understand them.[2]

'In this *Plan* [he wrote to Mersenne] I explain part of my method. I try to prove the existence of God and of the soul apart from the body, and I add many other things which I imagine will not displease the reader. In the *Optics*, besides treating of refraction and the manufacture of lenses, I give detailed descriptions of the eye, of light, of vision, and of everything belonging to catoptrics and optics. In the *Meteorology* I dwell principally on the nature of salt, the causes of winds and thunder, the shapes of snowflakes, the colours of the rainbow – here I try also to demonstrate what is the nature of each colour – and the coronas or haloes and the mock suns or parhelia like those which appeared at Rome six or seven years ago. Finally, in the *Geometry* I try to give a general method of solving all the problems that have never yet been solved. All this I think will make a volume no bigger than fifty or sixty sheets. I do not want to put my name to it, as I resolved long ago; please do not say anything about it to anybody unless you judge it proper to mention it to some publishers . . .'[3]

The *Meteorology* is the most textbook-like part of the book, and was doubtless intended by Descartes to be so. The *Optics* is in essence a practical treatise on the manufacture of optical instruments, and Descartes went so far as to aim it at the 'uneducated craftsman' on whom the production of such instruments most depended. In *Le Monde* Descartes' account of light had been tightly embedded in his overall physical theory, but here that theory is wholly absent.

Between them, the *Meteorology* and the *Optics* covered most of two out of the four main areas of Descartes' concerns, the other two being mathematics and metaphysics. At an early stage of planning the book Descartes was uncertain whether to include his mathematical work, and it was only later, when the *Meteorology* was already at the printers, that he decided to do so. Gaukroger plausibly conjectures that the reason for Descartes' indecision was that his active interest in mathematics had ceased some years before, and that his discoveries had been rediscovered, or anyway shared, by others since, among them Pierre de Fermat (with whom he was soon to have a bitter controversy).[4]

But the most important part of the book is its first part, the *Discourse on Method* itself. It is the first statement of Descartes' developing metaphysical ideas, and its great significance lies in its being a response to the urgent situation created by Galileo's condemnation. As Descartes recognised, the Church's censure of Galileo raised in acute form the problem of how natural science could be pursued at all, given the danger of conflict between the results of scientific investigation and the Church's teachings. He wanted to show that there is no conflict; and moreover, he wanted to prove this in the context of also showing how science could proceed without having to disguise itself as 'hypotheses' about imagined worlds.

The *Discourse* is less fluent than the rest of the work, because it is patched together from a number of texts Descartes had written at various times over the preceding years, although he only put it into its final version after the companion essays were finished. Its most immediately striking feature is that it is written in the first person singular as if it were an essay in auto-biography, all the while informally addressing the reader as 'you'. No doubt this form came naturally to Descartes, and he anyway had a number of explicitly autobiographical points to put in support of his 'method' of enquiry; but it also served the purpose of making his reasonings easy and agreeable to follow, like listening to someone reminisce. 'I have never presumed my mind to be in any way more perfect than that of the ordin-ary man,' he rather over-modestly claims near the beginning; 'indeed I have often wished to have as quick a wit, or as sharp and distinct an imagination, or as ample or prompt a memory as some others.' And yet, he continues, the method he has discovered will infallibly help all who follow it to increase their knowledge and raise it incrementally to the highest point of which their minds are capable.[5]

The first three sections of the *Discourse* are in fact purely auto-biographical, describing Descartes' education and the journey of his mind to the point where he realised that, despite his excellent education at La Flèche, he needed to rethink the basis of enquiry so that he could be sure to arrive at truth. He therefore devised a set of rules to think by, enjoining the use of careful and responsible small steps always, and a set of moral principles to live by while he was seeking knowledge with the help of those rules. 'In fact, I venture to say that by strictly observing the few rules I had chosen, I became very adept at unravelling ... questions,' he claimed – here he expressly meant mathematical questions, but the implication is that his method is universally efficacious.[6]

The fourth section anticipates, in briefer and more direct form, the famous arguments which open the most widely studied of Descartes' philosophical works, the *Meditations on First Philosophy*. Since two of its paragraphs encapsulate his position very succinctly and clearly, they are worth quoting in full. The first states his celebrated dictum 'I think therefore I am,' and the supporting argument for it:

For a long time I had observed that in practical life it is sometimes necessary to act upon opinions which one knows to be quite uncertain just as if they were indubitable. But since I now wished to devote myself solely to the search for truth, I thought it necessary to do the very opposite and reject as if absolutely false everything in which I could imagine the least doubt, in order to see if I was left believing anything that was entirely indubitable. Thus, because our senses sometimes deceive us, I decided to suppose that nothing was such as they led us to imagine. And since there are men who make mistakes in reasoning, committing logical fallacies concerning the simplest questions in geometry, and because I judged that I was as prone to error as anyone else, I rejected as unsound all the arguments I had previously taken as demonstrative proofs. Lastly, considering that the very thoughts we have while awake may also occur while we sleep without any of them being at that time true, I resolved to pretend that all the things that had ever entered my mind were no more true than the illusions of my dreams. But immediately I noticed that while I was trying thus to think everything false, it was necessary that I, who was thinking this, was something. And observing that this truth *I am thinking, therefore I exist* was so firm and sure that all the most extravagant suppositions of the sceptics were incapable of shaking it, I decided that I could accept it without scruple as the first principle of the philosophy I was seeking.[7]

This deceptively simple and apparently irresistible argument has been a rich subject of debate in the philosophical tradition ever since. No one does, because no one can, doubt the truth of 'I think therefore I exist'; but no one has yet given a definitive account of what kind of truth it is. If this seems surprising, note that by the terms of Descartes' own argument, one cannot treat the claim 'I think therefore I exist' as – despite appearances – a simple deduction of the conclusion, 'I exist,' from the premise, 'I think', because that would only work if there were a further premise available, a hidden major premise to the effect that 'Everything that thinks, exists'. But this is ruled out by the working hypothesis that all previous beliefs are false.[8] Moreover, if one goes with a toothcomb over the argument, as academic philosophers do, the first problem one encounters is whether Descartes can legitimately employ the kind of sceptical doubt he uses to see whether there are any indubitable beliefs left over when he has doubted everything possible.[9]

The sceptical considerations Descartes invokes at the outset of his quest for certainty – the fallibility of our senses, the liability to error of our reasoning powers, the hypothesis that all experience might be illusory, a mere dream – had been recognised and discussed by philosophers in classical antiquity from Plato onwards; but his selection and use of them in this sharply-focused manner revived debate about them in a way that dominated philosophy for the next three centuries and more.

So did Descartes' statement of the point that occurs in the very next paragraph, where he commits himself to 'dualism', that is, the theory that mind and matter are two distinct substances:

Next I examined attentively what I was. I saw that while I could pretend that I had no body and that there was no world and no place for me to be in, I could not for all that pretend that I did not exist. I saw on the contrary that from the mere fact that I thought of doubting the truth of other things, it followed quite evidently and certainly that I existed; whereas if I had merely ceased thinking, even if everything else I had ever imagined had been true, I should have had no reason to believe that I existed. From this I knew that I was a substance whose whole essence or nature is simply to think, and which does not require any place, or depend on any material thing, in order to exist. Accordingly this 'I' – that is, the soul by which I am what I am – is entirely distinct from the body, and indeed is easier to know than the body, and would not fail to be whatever it is, even if the body did not exist.[10]

This famous statement of 'Cartesian dualism' was the other great legacy for debate that Descartes bequeathed to philosophy. Again, the simplicity and plausibility of the argument is striking; but unlike the 'I think therefore I exist' statement, which is true, the claim that minds exist independently of bodies is at least highly improbable, according to the powerful testament of our best science and our most persuasive philosophy. Whereas mental objects and events (thoughts, memories, visual experience, and the like) have no physical properties as such – for example: weight, position in space, colour, scent – all evidence suggests that they are in some sense the products of brains, and cannot exist without them.

The idea that mental life is fundamentally neurological and takes place as activity in brain structures is now the standard view. It is exceedingly well supported by all the empirical evidence, even though the problem of 'qualia' (the subjective character of experience – the colours we see, the sounds we hear, the aromas we smell in the private inner world of sensation and feeling) is unsolved; for we still do not know how qualia arise in consciousness from the complex interactions of brain cells. That they do so arise is of course unquestionable; and we know a great deal about the computational activity of the brain – how it deals with information passed to it from the outside world by the senses, and how it effects its millions of finely adjusted and rapid responses to that information, most of it never apparent to our conscious minds. Optimists say that one day we will indeed understand how brains give rise to qualia in conscious experience. Pessimists think that we will never be clever enough to understand our own brains. (Happily, the pessimists have not stopped the effort to understand.)

The problem for Descartes and his immediate successors in philosophy was: how can two such utterly different things – mind and body – interact? How can a thought cause my physical arms and legs to move? How can a pin dividing my flesh cause the sensation of pain in consciousness? One can illustrate the point by analogy with a homelier question: how can one hit a baseball with a swirl of mist? Descartes at first suggested that mind and matter interact through the pineal gland in the brain – until he realised that this was merely a way of hiding the problem inside a small intercranial organ.[11] He ended by saying that mind–matter interaction is a mystery that only God understands.

How difficult the problem is for anyone who accepts the basic dualistic premise – that the universe contains two utterly different substances – is well illustrated by the heroic solutions proposed by two of Descartes' successors in the philosophical tradition, Malebranche and Leibniz. They both settled for the idea that mind and matter are indeed too different to interact, and therefore do not do so, but only *seem* to from the viewpoint of our finite and inadequate understandings. What happens, said Malebranche, is that when God sees that something in the material realm requires a mental correlate, and vice versa, he acts to provide it; so, when your stomach is empty he causes a feeling of hunger in your mind, and a desire for a sandwich; whereupon he then causes your arms and legs to carry you to the kitchen cupboard, to remove the bread and jam, and to eat it; whereupon he next causes you to have pleasant taste sensations, and a feeling of satiety – and so on. Note that the central tenet of this view is that God is the only causal agent in the universe. Critics observe that the drawback with this is that, even for an omnipotent and omnipresent deity, the very large number of mind-body correlations re-quired every moment of the average day makes for hard work; God must be an exceedingly busy being. Moreover it also requires him to be involved in the causation of a great deal of wickedness. Defenders of Malebranche reply that God is too clever to commit himself to too much hard work, and somehow arranges matters to avoid it. But as to the wicked-ness problem: well, here Malebranche has to attempt a delicate argument indeed, based on the idea that sin is an 'intermission in activity' and therefore not the result of God's causal agency at all. This argument has not been very influential.

Leibniz's more restful (from God's point of view) solution is to say that the mental and material realms are as two clocks which have been set going in exact harmony, so that when one shows the time on its dial, the other strikes the time with its bell, making observers believe them to be connected. The drawback with this theory, however, is that it requires strict determinism in the history of the universe; everything must happen as an absolutely invariable outcome of the first setting-going by God at the beginning of time; and this means there is no free will, which in turn means that morality is an empty notion because no-one can do other than as he or she does. Furthermore, it means that the wickedness in the world was preordained too, and that God must be held responsible for it.

Malebranche's theory is known as 'Occasionalism' because God acts to provide mental and material correlates on each occasion required. Leibniz's theory is known as 'pre-established harmony' or 'Parallelism', for self-explanatory reasons. The interest of these theories lies chiefly in illustrating the impasse bequeathed by Descartes to anyone who accepted his dualistic premise – which, of course, was scarcely deniable in an age where religion dominated, thus making it impossible for any-one to deny the existence of immaterial souls, a thesis which, anyway, Descartes sincerely believed.

The real solution to the mind-body mystery, however, as our best scientific investigations now tell us, is that mind and matter are not two different things at all, because there is only physical stuff in the world; which solves the interaction problem. But it does not solve the problem of consciousness.[12]

Descartes' *Discourse and Essays*, and the suppressed *Le Monde* which preceded it, between them have in germ all of his philosophy and science. His next two great works, published in the 1640s – the *Meditations* and the *Principles of Philosophy* (in the main, a scientific textbook) – set out the same views in more detail and with additional matter, but with no change of doctrine. So from what has thus far been said about Descartes' intellectual outlook one can see the point of his claims that 'the end of all study ought to be to guide the mind to form true and sound judgements on everything that may be presented to it,' and that 'the sciences in their totality are but the intelligence of man; and all the details of knowledge have no value save as they strengthen the understanding.' The express implication is that the purpose of philosophy – understood to mean enquiry in its most general sense – is not the mere accumulation of facts and information, not mere erudition, but the attainment of understanding, which is a thing greater than knowledge. The route to it, said Descartes, is his method.

Descartes' method was suggested to him by his early studies in geometry and arithmetic, and in particular by the fact that although he saw that these two sciences offered many truths, and gave much material for deducing further truths, they did not explain themselves sufficiently – that is, show why their truths were true. He had in mind the fact that the discoveries of the ancient mathematicians were, by and large, peculiar to the problems they dealt with; there was no sense among the ancients of the general principles that explained any relationship between the different discoveries they made. In almost all cases, the discoveries of ancient geometry and arithmetic were triumphs of self-standing ingenuity. A way of connecting different aspects of geometry to each other, and of expressing them in a common notation which would enable discoveries to be generalised, was needed.

The means to this began to be provided at last by the mathematicians of the sixteenth century, chief among them Francois Viete, who in effect invented algebra, thus furnishing the tools for the task of generalising geometry, while at the same time savants such as Luca Pacioli, Geronimo Cardano and Niccola Tartaglia used geometrical means to solve various equations. But notation was still clumsy and unsettled, and the very names used in mathematics differed from one school or country to another. Part of Descartes' contribution was to induce some order into this confusion. He invented the now standard way of representing powers as superscript numbers (as in 10^2) – without a systematic way of denoting the homogeneity of successive powers the binomial theorem could not have been expressed. It is now standard to denote unknown quantities by means of lower case letters from late in the alphabet (x, y, z . . .) and known quantities from early in the alphabet (a, b, c . . .); this convention was established by Descartes.[13]

Good notational innovations are a powerful help to progress in a subject such as mathematics; by their means Descartes was able to make his own contributions, and to facilitate that of others. And his own contributions were substantial. He is one of the independent founders of analytical geometry, he helped lay the foundations for differential calculus, he set out methods for solving equations up to the fourth degree (he believed his method would apply to higher degrees) – and more besides. Not all that he hoped for his mathematical work stood the test of subsequent examination; but these are substantial claims on posterity's notice nevertheless.

I dwell on Descartes' mathematical achievements because they illustrate the method he placed so much weight upon, and set out in detail in his *Rules for the Direction of the Mind*.[14] His view was that anything we wish to know about can be grasped by starting with the simplest elements, and then proceeding by small and careful steps from each element to the next, each step explaining the next. The simplest elements are distinguishable by their intuitive character, and can therefore be 'clearly and distinctly' perceived. Truth in general requires a clear and distinct perception of its object; therefore given that the objects of knowledge constitute a series in which each can be understood in terms of the one before it, it is obvious – so

Descartes argued – that enquiry must begin at the simplest first element and thence proceed carefully through the series, each connection being fully grasped.

The 'I think therefore I am' seemed to Descartes a paradigm case of a clear, distinct and directly intuitable starting truth of just the kind required as the first step in metaphysical enquiry. And this led to what he saw as the next truth: that he was essentially a 'thinking thing' – a mind or soul – whose existence is independent of body. In geometry he solved the problem of giving a general treatment of curves by reducing them to straight lines, and of giving the locus of a point by determining its distance from two given straight lines (the axes of co-ordination – legend has it that the idea for this came to him as he watched a fly crawling on his ceiling; it was a moving point mappable from the straight edges of the ceiling where they met the supporting walls). In the case of physics, the prime idea is that the material universe can be exhaustively understood in terms of spatial extension and movement alone.

But the 'I think therefore I am', or indeed any of the clear and distinct perceptions from which enquiry can proceed according to this method, is not by itself enough. A crucial element is missing: and that is the existence of a good God who will not allow us to be led astray in our reasonings if we use our intellectual powers responsibly and carefully. It is not merely the existence but the *goodness* of God which is crucial here; his goodness is what ensures that the right use of our minds will lead to truth, providing that we guard against our natural and sinful human propensity to error. In the *Discourse* Descartes merely invokes the idea of God's goodness as a guarantor of enquiry; it was a few years later, in the *Meditations*, that he set out this aspect of his case more fully.

At the end of the *Discourse* Descartes explains that he wrote it in French instead of the more usual Latin because 'I expect that those who use only their natural reason in all its purity will be better judges of my opinions than those who give credence only to the writings of the ancients.'[15] In sending a copy to one of the teachers at La Flèche he said that he had written in such a way that 'even women might understand me.'[16] This is a little odd; in the seventeenth century Latin was the universal language of the literate and scholarly, and if Descartes wished to be understood everywhere, from England to Italy as well as in the Netherlands and the German states (at least those in which anyone was still reading, overwhelmed as they were by war and rapine during all these years), he would have done better to write in Latin. Yet he chose French, thus limiting his audience to his native land and those among the upper classes in other countries for whom French was a natural second language.

He sent copies of his book to King Louis XIII, Cardinal Richelieu, and the French ambassador to the Hague. Of course he did not expect any of them to read it. The remaining 197 copies – as indicated in his letter to Mersenne, he was determined to have 200 free copies from his publisher for his own use – were widely distributed. He sent three copies to La Flèche, as noted, hoping that the book would be adopted as a textbook, at least for the *Meteorology* section. He wrote to Etienne Noel, 'There is no one, I think, who has a greater interest in examining the contents of this book than [the Jesuits] . . . I do not know how they will be able to teach these subjects from now on as they are taught year by year in most of their colleges, unless they either disprove what I have written or follow it.'[17]

He sent a copy to Cardinal De Bagni, whom he had met in Paris in the late 1620s when De Bagni was Papal Nuncio there, and to Cardinal Barberini, nephew of Pope Urban VIII. These were intended to 'test the waters', as he put it – not to see if his views were theologically acceptable, but to see if they were congenial; which is to say, he hoped for the Church's support, not merely its sufferance. A bookshop in Rome ordered a dozen copies from Jean le Maire in Leiden on condition that it said nothing about the movement of the earth; and since it happily did not, one can assume it was displayed and sold in the eternal city to French-reading persons of an enquiring turn.[18]

The book excited great attention, both positive and negative. Dozens of scholarly readers wrote responses to, and criticisms of, various parts of it. The most contentious part was the *Discourse* itself, for it touched (somewhat too lightly) on so many matters of philosophical importance that it was bound to provoke questions and disagreement. But each of the essays stimulated its quota of reactions, and Descartes replied to a number of his critics, even to those whose complaints were like the one from Libertus Fromondus of Louvain University, who said that Descartes' theory of vision must be wrong because 'noble actions like sight cannot result from so ignoble and brutish a cause as heat' – this being a paradigm of the kind of thinking that had hampered science since Aristotle.

But the adverse criticisms Descartes received from the Paris mathematicians to his *Geometry* and aspects of his *Optics* brought out his worst side – the same bitter and vituperative sentiments that he had displayed against Beeckman. Indeed, so angry was his response that it prompts a question about his relations with these mathematicians when he was in Paris; there is the flavour of bad history in it. Part of the problem was that Descartes did not fully work out the problems he presented in the *Geometry*: he skipped certain steps, and in some cases merely threw down a gauntlet to his readers to prove something for themselves if they could. But in Paris there were mathematicians of outstanding ability, not least among them Pierre de Fermat, and they understood Descartes' work very well – too well, as it happened, for there were aspects of the *Geometry* that invited criticism.

The problem began when Descartes sent a manuscript of the *Discourse and Essays* to Mersenne for the latter to secure a licence – a *privilege* – from Louis XIII for the book to be published in France. The government official responsible for sifting such applications was none other than Jean Beaugrand, a mathematician with a special interest in efforts to develop algebra, who had recently edited a new edition of the works of Francois Viete, and who was familiar with the work of the English mathematician Thomas Harriot, whose *Artis Analyticae Praxis* had appeared just six years before. Viete and Harriot were the two mathematicians principally responsible for developing algebra in the early modern period before Descartes. When he read the *Discourse and Essays,* Beaugrand noted Descartes' claim that he had constructed his mathematics wholly from his own resources, and disbelieved him, for he thought he saw a reliance on the work of both Viete and Harriot. He wrote to Mersenne accordingly, and published two pamphlets pursuing the allegations. Descartes denied them vigorously, but the imputation of unacknowledged borrowing – more bluntly, of plagiarism – was not good for Descartes' reputation, and it interfered with a proper assessment of his mathematical contribution.[19]

To add to this, one of the geometrical techniques devised by Descartes was shown by Beaugrand to be less good than one already developed by Fermat (he was Fermat's patron and encourager). Descartes was chagrined by this; but he later quietly accepted an aspect of Fermat's technique in place of his own, for Fermat's method was indeed superior. But at the time the attack of the Paris mathematicians made him see red: he wrote a fulminating letter on the first day of March 1638, in response to three letters from Mersenne bringing news of the attacks by Beaugrand and others, together with what he thought was evidence of Beaugrand having misused his manuscript, failing to return it to Mersenne, and deliberately delaying the granting of a *privilege*:

I must first thank you very carefully [so Descartes' bitter reply to Mersenne begins] for scrupulously drawing to my attention many things which it is important that I should know. I can assure you that so far from being bothered by the bad things that are said about me, I rather revel in it; indeed, the more extravagant and outrageous it is, the more I consider it to my advantage, the more it pleases me and the less troubled I am by it. I know that these spiteful people would not go to such lengths to speak ill of me if others did not speak well of me. Besides, truth sometimes needs to be contradicted in order to be better recognised. But those who speak without reason or justification deserve nothing but scorn.

As for M. Beaugrand, I am amazed that you condescend to speak of him, after the way he treated you . . . As for the discourses written by him and those of his ilk, please treat them with contempt, and make it clear to them that I have nothing but contempt for them. Above all, please do not agree to send on to me any writing, either of his or anyone else's, unless those who offer it to you add a note to the effect that they agree to my publishing it along with my reply ... after seeing M. de Fermat's last letter, which he says he does not want published, I expressly asked you not to send me any more letters of that sort. Of course if a Jesuit or a priest of the Oratory, or anyone else who was incontestably honest and level-headed, wishes to send me something, we would have to be more cautious. I shall make myself freely available to people such as these, but not to those spiteful characters whose aim is anything but truth.[20]

Given that Fermat was the greatest mathematician of the day, and the Jesuits and priests of the Oratory did not always merit description as 'incontestably honest', this reads oddly today. But there was more. Descartes refused to read one of Fermat's treatises, returning it unopened with the remark that everything it contained would already be found in his own work; and – not entirely consistently, given that he had just claimed that Fermat's insights aped his own – he described Fermat's work as 'dung'. In the same scatological vein, he described Beaugrand's letters as fit only for use as lavatory paper.[21] Indeed, Beaugrand excited Descartes' special animus: his work was 'so impertinent, so ridiculous, and so despicable' and the man himself 'has as much impudence and effrontery as ignorance.'[22] No doubt the temperature of Descartes' remarks is explained by the fact that Beaugrand called him 'the methodical impertinent', playing on the title of the book.[23] Descartes dismissed other mathematicians who criticised his work as 'flies'; he described Gilles Roberval as 'less than a rational animal' and Pierre Petit as a 'little dog who barks after me in the street.' The great Thomas Hobbes, as posterity knows him to be, appeared to Descartes 'extremely contemptible'. Still smarting three years later when he wrote the Preface to his *Meditations on First Philosophy*, Descartes described his critics as 'silly and weak', as holding 'false and irrational' views, and as being 'arrogant'.[24]

Roberval was the professor of mathematics at the College de France, and one reason for his opposition to Descartes was the offence he understandably therefore took, as the country's top academic mathematician, at not being sent a copy of the *Discourse,* nor even of the separately printed pamphlet version of the *Geometry.* Whether this was an intended slight by Descartes, or (as Watson suggests) Mersenne's way of fostering controversy and dispute, the result was the same: Roberval attacked Descartes' work at every opportunity, and all Descartes' efforts to placate him, flatter him into compliance, and eventually insult him, could not avert the stream of hostility. Descartes ended by telling Mersenne that Roberval was as vain as a girl, had a head like a dwarf, and behaved like the fool in an Italian farce who 'continues bragging and remains always victorious and invincible even after having his ears boxed and his face slapped with a slipper.'[25]

In the light of Descartes' negative reaction to criticism of the *Discourse,* the motive for his endeavour in the later *Meditations* to work out his philosophical arguments in more detail – especially his arguments for the existence of God – becomes palpably clearer. In its Preface he provides an excuse for the shortcomings of the *Discourse*: 'My purpose there was not to provide a full treatment,' he now says, 'but merely to offer a sample, and learn from my readers how I should handle these topics at a later date.' And he adds that he thought it would not be helpful 'to give a full account' of his views in a book written for the general reader in French, 'in case weaker intellects might believe that they ought to set out on the same path.'[26]

Even when the dispute between Descartes and a critic was friendly, as it was with another professor at the College de France called Jean-Baptiste Morin, any differences of opinion made Descartes eventually retreat from the field, asking Mersenne not to send him any more of the disputant's queries and comments. Morin was particularly flattering to Descartes; he described him as having 'one of the most subtle and fertile minds of the century,' a mind 'capable of leaving something rare and excellent for posterity.'[27] Objections and questions from Morin went via Mersenne to Descartes, who collected them and replied by the same route; but eventually Descartes told Mersenne, 'I will make no more reply to M. Morin . . . just between us, it seems to me that his thoughts are even more distant from mine than they were at the beginning, such that we could never come to an agreement.'[28]

In sharp contrast to Descartes' bitter view of the mathematicians who attacked him was his reaction to those whose attitude was favourable. Girard Desargue and Florimond Debeaune liked his book, praised it, and in return bathed in his smiles. He told Mersenne that he thoroughly liked Desargue's 'good mind' and the 'curiosity and clarity of his language.'[29] Desargue helped Mersenne urge the granting of the *privilege* for the book, and on reading the essay on *Optics* immediately wished to have lenses ground according to its prescription. Debeaune proved helpful in another direction: he studied

Descartes' book so thoroughly that he was able to point out a tiny error in the measurements of refraction, for which Descartes wrote in admiration to thank him. Debeaune saw that Descartes had deliberately obscured some of the workings in the *Geometry* in order not to reveal the principles underlying them, and argued that it would have been better for everyone if he had done otherwise. Remarkably, Debeaune had studied the *Geometry* in such depth that, he said, he could write it out from memory if ever the book were wholly lost, complete with all the necessary workings that Descartes had omitted. Soon afterwards Debeaune did indeed write out all the suppressed workings, and sent them to Descartes under the title 'Notes sur la Geometrie'. These notes were eventually translated into Latin and published as a supplement to the Latin version of the *Geometry* in 1649.[30]

The great interest generated by the *Discourse* persuaded Descartes of two things: that he must now leave mathematics behind him, and that he must write a more careful and thorough account of his philosophy than he had given in the *Discourse*. This latter task – the writing of the *Meditations on First Philosophy* – now began to occupy him. And he made a strategic decision: that he would circulate the *Meditations* before publication, soliciting objections; and that he would publish the objections, together with his replies, along with the text of the *Meditations* itself, thus avoiding the messy sequel of correspondence that had attended the *Discourse*'s appearance.

A final word on Descartes' mathematical contributions is in order, and properly belongs to the historians of the subject. 'In terms of mathematical ability Descartes probably was the most able thinker of his day,' says Carl Boyer, after describing the ideas in the *Geometry*, 'but he was at heart not really a mathematician. His geometry was only an episode in a life devoted to science and philosophy.'[31] This is true; but it was a significant enough episode. Speaking of Descartes' contribution, E. T. Bell is more emphatic: 'This one thing [analytic geometry] is of the highest order of excellence, marked by the sensuous simplicity of the half dozen or so greatest contributions of all time to mathematics. Descartes remade geometry and made modern geometry possible.'[32] As Boyer points out, most of the uses to which Cartesian co-ordinate geometry is now put were not anticipated by Descartes; he was working purely theoretically; his achievement was 'a triumph of impractical theory as was the *Conics* of Apollonius in antiquity, despite the inordinately useful role that both were ultimately destined to play.'[33] But this is not of course a criticism; quite the contrary.

8

Descartes Contra Voetius

In the years following the publication of the *Discourse*, and despite the acrimonious feelings generated in him by some of his critics, Descartes was in good health, and enjoying respite from public quarrels past and to come in the company of his daughter. This was the period of Francine's brief lifetime, when he had both her and Helena with him at his seaside home at Santpoort near Harlem, under the immense open skies of the North Sea coast, with Amsterdam not far away, and nothing but a long stretch of grey water between him and Lowestoft in England. The Harlem coast consists of rolling sand dunes covered with tough, deep-green grass that undulates like the sea itself in the wind; a bracing, pleasing, peaceful conjunction of sea, sky and earth.

Two of Descartes' biographers – Vrooman and Gaukroger – comment on the more contented tone of his correspondence in these years, and even 'a certain enthusiasm and exuberance'; and they note that he was trying to find a scientific method for reversing the greyness which was 'coming with a rush' in his hair. He told Huygens that he was taking such good care of himself that he thought he might live another hundred years.[1] Indeed he was engaged then, as intermittently he often was, on aspects of medicine, especially such as would prolong life. When Huygens once asked him for a few pages of explanation of mechanics, Descartes replied that he was too busy conducting research of importance for the 'life and preservation of the human race'.[2] He proposed to write a treatise on medicine, aimed at 'exempting [humankind] from an infinite number of illnesses of the body and the mind, and even perhaps the weaknesses of old age, if we had enough knowledge of its causes and of all the remedies that nature has provided us.' He even, he claimed, planned to devote the whole of the rest of his life to this crucial enquiry.[3] It is a tragic irony that his ambition in this direction so shortly preceded the death of Francine.

He made friends with two Catholic parish priests in Harlem, who served as a *post restante* for his mail, and he had occasional visits from other friends, including Reneri and Huygens, the latter sometimes bringing other people with him. One of Descartes' visitors reported to Mersenne that he had just spent 'half a day talking about music with our hero Descartes', but he might equally well have spent half a day in Descartes' herb garden, or watching him dissect (and vivisect) animals. Descartes once gestured towards some fish and rabbits he was dissecting and said, 'this is my library.' Despite his reply to Huygens about mechanics, his restless curiosity kept him busy thinking about the principles of cogs, levers and screws, and writing about them to Mersenne.

But the principal occupation of Descartes in these years was writing, and eventually publishing, the *Meditations on First*

Philosophy. On 9 January 1639 he wrote to Mersenne to reassure him about his health, because 'you and some other excellent people are very concerned on my behalf when two weeks pass without your receiving a letter from me . . . [but] I have acquired some little knowledge of medicine, and I feel very well, and look after myself with as much care as a rich man with gout.'[4] And then he told Mersenne that he had in mind a project for the rest of the winter which would brook no distraction, and therefore Mersenne must please not write again until Easter, unless there were an emergency; that he must not worry if he had no news from Santpoort, but must accept that Descartes was healthily and excitedly working on philosophy.

Descartes wrote the *Meditations* in Latin – in that language the main title is *Meditationes de Prima Philosophiae* – and finished it in April 1640. It was published the following year in Paris by Michel Soly. The subtitle of the first edition ran: 'in which are demonstrated the existence of God and the immortality of the soul.' But because the book does not directly address the question of the soul's immortality, Descartes rewrote the subtitle into a more accurate version for the second edition: 'in which are demonstrated the existence of God and the distinction between the human soul and the body'. The second edition was published in Amsterdam by the Elzevir company – Elzevir by this time evidently chastened as a result of losing Descartes' first book to a rival. In 1647 the *Meditations* appeared in French, in a version approved by Descartes himself, translated by a young aristocrat, the duc de Luynes.

The title page of the first edition carried the words: 'with the approval of the learned doctors.' Descartes dedicated the book to the Dean and Doctors of the Faculty of Theology at the

Sorbonne, and his dedicatory epistle to them drips with earnest sanctimony. Ever anxious to avoid offending the Church, and eager to have its approval, he thought by this means to secure both aims. Despite the title-page claim that their approval had been secured, however, the doctors of the Sorbonne had not given it, and despite Descartes' endeavours to steer clear of theological controversy, he was already in the middle of it long before the book was published. Perhaps, indeed, the dedication to the Sorbonne had the additional motive of getting the moral support of their approval in a battle he was fighting in the Netherlands with a new enemy: Gisbert Voetius.

Voetius was the professor of theology at Utrecht, and within a few years was to become the university's rector. He was a figure of great influence in Church affairs in the Netherlands, and had a history of engaging with relish in theological controversy. Famous, learned and powerful, he was a formidable opponent, and he did not like either Descartes or his ideas. Trouble began when Descartes' friend and champion, Henry Reneri, died in March 1639. Two events consequent on his death fanned Voetius' animosity. One was the funeral oration delivered at Utrecht university by Reneri's friend Anton Aemelius, who praised Reneri's advocacy of Descartes' philosophy and Descartes as 'the Archimedes of our century . . . the confidant of nature.' The oration was published, which made it seem like an official approval of Cartesian ideas. This angered the traditional professors whose views were controverted by the new-fangled philosophy.

Then Henry Regius, the recently appointed professor of medicine at Utrecht, took up the baton laid down by Reneri, and began to lecture on Descartes' views. He was a highly popular teacher, and an extrovert who was not in the slightest troubled by controversy. He even indeed courted it on Descartes' behalf, for they had become close – as a master and disciple are close – and remained so for a time, Regius helping Descartes to prepare the manuscript of the *Meditations*, and giving him an easy first set of 'Objections' to be answered.

In June 1640 Regius offered a set of Cartesian theses for public debate at the university, the better to advertise them. Voetius saw this as his chance to combat Descartes' growing influence in the university, and accepted the challenge. He proposed not only to demolish Cartesian philosophy, but Descartes himself.

The stage was thus set for a struggle that lasted five years. Its opening salvos were complicated for Descartes by the fact that Francine died just three months later, while he was also in the midst of arranging the publication of the *Meditations*, which involved writing replies to the objections he had solicited, through Mersenne, from the leading thinkers of the day. The worst aspect of the controversy was the obstacle it represented to his hopes of eventual Church approval for his ideas. The seaside idyll of Santpoort seems to have vanished in a single season.

Voetius' hostility to Descartes did not come out of the blue, but was a chapter in a longer-running saga of concerns stemming from the controversy that had wracked the Netherlands over Arminianism. In fact, the Arminian problem was not merely a religious but a political one – if questions of religion and politics can meaningfully be separated in that age – for it affected the question of the unity of the United Provinces. This matter was touched upon in an earlier chapter, but its role in Voetius' attack on Descartes justifies a closer look.

In essence, the Arminian controversy turned on the question

of free will. Orthodox Calvinists held to Calvin's view of strict predestination – the thesis that God had, at the beginning of time, selected a fixed number of people for salvation, all the rest being condemned independently of merit. The injustice and irrationality of this view was repugnant to reflective minds, not least among them that of Jacobus Arminius (Jakob Herman-zoon, 1560–1609), professor at the University of Leiden, who began as an orthodox Calvinist preacher and teacher, but soon came to reject the *decretum horribile* of Calvin about absolute predestination, and was regarded as the leader of the 'Remonstrants' who rejected this aspect of Calvin's doctrines. Arminius died in 1609, but the controversy generated by his opposition to predestination waxed, until the great Synod of Dort in 1618–19 emphatically rejected his views and reasserted orthodox Calvinism. Nevertheless, sympathies for the Arminian position remained, and since it was in this respect close to the Catholic doctrine of free will, aspects of Cartesian thought later came to be associated with it. This was chief among Voetius' motives for attacking Descartes.

At the outset Regius's pro-Descartes lectures were confined to certain questions in physiology, and chiefly focused on the circulation of the blood. Had he listened to Descartes, or been a closer disciple of Descartes' views, he would not have laid himself open to the counter-attack that Voetius mounted. But Regius did not conceal his adherence to the Copernican view of the universe, and he also held that the soul and body are only accidentally united; if they were substantially connected, so the argument went, the body would be required to accompany the soul to heaven. Voetius saw this as heretical; in response Descartes told Regius to charge Voetius with holding that the soul is material. The charge and counter-charge took the form of pamphlets, Regius's reply to Voetius being published on 16 February 1642. Descartes wrote to Regius, 'As far as I hear from my friends, everyone who has read your reply to Voetius praises it highly – and very many have read it.' Voetius used his influence to get the magistrates of Utrecht to ban Regius's pamphlet, which prompted Descartes to add, 'Everyone is laughing at Voetius and says he has lost hope for his cause, seeing that he has had to call on the assistance of the magistrates for its defence.'⁵

The brouhaha surrounding the battle between Regius and Voetius was so great – it even involved student riots and much hurling of furniture – that the Senate of Utrecht University forbade Regius to teach physics, telling him to restrict himself to medicine. Descartes consoled him by writing, 'You should not be upset that you have been forbidden to lecture on problems in physics; indeed I would prefer it if you had been forbidden even to give private instruction. All this will redound to your honour and the shame of your adversaries.'⁶ But the university senate went further, and banned the teaching of Cartesian philosophy completely. This outraged Descartes. In the second edition of the *Meditations* he included a document, disguised as a letter to the French Jesuit priest Jacques Dinet, attacking Voetius bitterly, calling him quarrelsome, envious, foolish, a stupid pedant, a hypocrite, an enemy to truth, and much besides, and charging him with slander 'sometimes public and sometimes surreptitious.'⁷ The letter was excerpted and translated from Latin into Dutch by one of Voetius' enemies, thus giving it wide currency in the Netherlands and adding fuel to the flames. Voetius was of course infuriated by it.

In the 'letter to Dinet' Descartes gives the text of the

University of Utrecht Senate's decree against him. It reads as follows:

> The professors reject this new philosophy [i.e. Descartes' theories] for three reasons. First, it is opposed to the traditional philosophy which universities throughout the world have hitherto taught on the best advice, and it undermines its foundations. Second, it turns away the young from the sound and traditional philosophy and prevents them reaching the heights of erudition; for once they have begun to rely on the new philosophy and its supposed solutions, they are unable to understand the technical terms which are commonly used in the books of traditional authors and in the lectures and debates of their professors. And, lastly, various false and absurd opinions either follow from the new philosophy or can be rashly deduced by the young – opinions which are in conflict with other disciplines and faculties and above all with orthodox theology.[8]

Descartes answers the charges one by one in his letter. He was of course pleased at the admission that his views upset the old Aristotelian orthodoxies, but he was especially troubled by the imputation of religious heterodoxy. He vigorously rejected this, and claimed that his views were every bit as consistent with religious orthodoxy as any other. 'Indeed, I insist that there is nothing relating to religion,' he wrote, 'which cannot be equally well or even better explained by means of my principles than can be done by means of those that are commonly accepted.'[9]

To get his own back Voetius engaged a proxy, Martin Schoock, to write an attack on Descartes. The result, entitled

The Admirable Method, appeared in 1643. It charged Descartes
with atheism on the grounds that he had set aside the traditional proofs of God's existence in order to put in their place
proofs so weak that they would encourage readers to reject the
idea of God altogether. This was a tactic that Mersenne and
others had attributed to Vanini, famously burned at the stake in
Toulouse in 1619 for his heresies. Schoock indeed likened
Descartes to Vanini several times in the course of his diatribe –
'René may rightly be compared with that cunning champion
of atheism, Cesare Vanini,' he wrote – and later confessed
that Voetius had especially encouraged this, because the other
imputation laid against Vanini, namely of homosexuality,
would suggest itself to readers too. The tactic had the desired
effect; Descartes in his turn was so enraged – and so alarmed
that the imputation of atheism would do him harm, as even the
most unfounded of accusations have a bad habit of doing – that
this time he replied directly in a *Letter to Voetius,* published by
Elzevir in May 1643 in both Latin and Dutch. And he wrote
not just to Voetius, but to the town council of Utrecht, to the
university, and to Huygens, complaining of Voetius and saying
that he sought to protect the town, citizens and students of
Utrecht against Voetius' evil ways.

His vituperation against Voetius scarcely knew bounds. He
accused him of 'atrocious insults', of being 'base and commonplace', stupid, absurd, coarse, impertinent and impudent. '[I]
declare that such criminal lies, such scurrilous insults and such
atrocious slanders are contained in your book, that they could
not be employed between enemies, or by a Christian against
an infidel, without convicting the perpetrator of wickedness
and criminality,' he stormed.[10] 'Even if the philosophy at which
you rail were unsound, which you have failed to show at any

215

point, and never will manage to show, what vice could it possibly be imagined to contain great enough to require its author to be slandered with such atrocious insults? The philosophy which I and all its other devotees are engaged in pursuing is none other than the knowledge of those truths which can be perceived by the natural light [of reason] and can provide practical benefits to mankind; so there is no study more honourable, or more worthy of mankind, or more beneficial in this life . . . I have read many of your writings, yet I have never found any reasoning in them, or any thought that is not base or commonplace – nothing which suggests a man of intelligence or education.'[11]

The imputation of atheism was, if not the most galling of Voetius' charges, certainly the most dangerous. Descartes was uncompromising in his own defence. 'You say that "René may rightly be compared with that cunning champion of atheism, Cesare Vanini, since he uses the self-same techniques to erect the throne of atheism in the minds of the inexperienced." Who will not marvel at the absurdity of your impudence? Even if it is true (and I insist it is) that I write against atheists and put forward my arguments as first rate, and even if it is true (which I strongly deny) that I reject the common traditional arguments [for God's existence], and that my own have been found to be invalid, it still would not follow that I should even be suspected – let alone guilty – of atheism. Anyone who claims to refute atheism and produces inadequate arguments should be accused of incompetence, not face a summary charge of atheism.'[12]

Voetius made the mistake of writing to Mersenne in the hope of enlisting his support against Descartes. But Mersenne was on Descartes' side, and forwarded Voetius' letters to him. This was not much of an advantage, though, for matters had already progressed too far. Voetius' response to Descartes' public letter was to sue him for libel. The authorities in Utrecht read both the 'letter to Dinet' and the *Letter to Voetius*, agreed that Descartes had libelled Voetius, and forwarded the matter to the Utrecht police court. Since Descartes lived in the province of Holland and not in the province of Utrecht, and since it was exceedingly unlikely that the authorities would be bothered to extradite him for a libel hearing, matters could have rested there. But Descartes had no intention of letting them rest. He was well connected; he knew Huygens, and the French ambassador to the Hague, one La Thuillerie; he lobbied them, and secured the desired effect – which was that the Prince of Orange himself had a quiet word with the authorities in Utrecht, and the libel action went equally quietly into abeyance.

But this was not quite enough for Descartes. As always, he wanted not just the negative, but the positive; as with his desire not just for Church tolerance, but approval, he now wanted not just to escape, but to win. He pressed for action to be taken against Schoock, and this hapless pawn was duly arrested and put into prison for two very uncomfortable days. Schoock was so traumatised by this experience that, in the jargon appropriate to the case, he sang like a canary, putting all the blame onto Voetius and showing the authorities letters from Voetius that proved it. Schoock was released, Descartes wrote a final indignant letter to the Utrecht magistrates, and at last the quarrel subsided.

The controversy had become a deeply unedifying one; from a dispute in philosophy it had degenerated into a personal squabble of a most undignified name-calling kind. During it Huygens advised Descartes to drop the matter; 'Theologians are like pigs,' he wrote, 'when you pull one by the tail, they all squeal'; but Descartes would not listen. His *amour propre* was at stake, and so were his philosophical views; which is why, when the next controversy flared over them, he was just as energetic in defending himself – though this time without quite the same degree of personal animus, because he was not so closely acquainted with the people involved.

This second major controversy took place at Leiden University. There too Descartes had a friend, Golius, and a disciple and champion, the logic professor Adriaan Heereboord. Throughout the first half of the 1640s Heereboord repeatedly proposed Cartesian theses for debate in the university, as a way of promoting and defending them. Surprisingly, perhaps, given the storm blowing in Utrecht over the same questions, the discussion of Cartesian philosophy at Leiden proceeded quietly until 1646, when a theology professor called Jacob Trigland disputed the very Cartesian assertion, put forward by one of Golius' students, that 'doubt is the beginning of indubitable philosophy' – a tenet fundamental to the *Discourse* and the *Meditations*. Trigland's argument was that premising radical doubt as the starting point of enquiry would lead students into scepticism and atheism. As a result of Trigland's intervention the Senate of Leiden University banned Cartesian philosophy, and declared that only Aristotelianism could be taught in its faculties.

This did not deter Heereboord, who continued to lecture on Cartesian themes, and in an oration argued that both Aristotle and St Thomas – that sceptical St Thomas whose empiricism required that he insert his finger into Christ's wound – used doubt as a route to certainty. What probably stung most was his remark that the Cartesian method of doubt helped to free minds from prejudices. This was too much for Jacob Revius, regent of the school of theology at Leiden University. He added his voice to Trigland's, and the latter now went further and claimed that Descartes was a blasphemer for suggesting that God might be a deceiver (in the *Meditations* Descartes strengthened the sceptical starting point by saying: in order to see whether there is anything you cannot possibly doubt, imagine that instead of being good, God is a deceiver who tries to give you false beliefs about everything. Is there anything he cannot make you falsely believe? Answer: yes – he cannot possibly make me believe the falsehood 'I do not exist'[13]). For good measure, Trigland had also accused Descartes of being a Pelagian, that is, one who does not believe in the doctrine of original sin.

Angered, Descartes wrote to the curators of Leiden University on 4 May 1647, demanding that they settle matters with Revius and Trigland, on pain of a public scandal. In his letter he defended himself earnestly against the imputation of blasphemy, but did not dilate too far on other charges; wisely so, for elsewhere in his correspondence he had committed himself to a few unorthodox positions, as for example believing in the basic goodness of human nature (which controverted the doctrine of original sin), and in the idea that everyone would eventually get to heaven (by no means a view that a self-respecting anti-Arminian orthodox Calvinist could possibly agree with, though for Descartes' fellow Catholics this thought was a commonplace).

The curators iterated their decision to forbid discussion of Cartesian views, and to require that Heereboord should confine himself to Aristotelian philosophy henceforth. When they wrote to Descartes accordingly, he replied that they had missed the point: he had demanded a retraction of the accusation of

blasphemy, and an apology. Never one to let matters drift, at
the same time he sent a complaint to his highly-placed friends,
who again spoke to the Prince of Orange. Although in combative mood, Descartes found the controversies wearing: in
May 1647 he wrote, 'As for the peace I had previously sought
here, I foresee that from now on I may not get as much of that
as I would like. For I have not yet received all the satisfaction
that is due to me for the insults I have suffered at Utrecht, and
I see that further insults are on the way. A troop of theologians,
followers of scholastic philosophy, seem to have formed a
league in an attempt to crush me with their slanders.'[14]

While quiet words were being had in government circles,
the dispute on the ground was heating up. At Christmas 1647
a tumult broke out at Leiden during a disputation between a
Cartesian who had been a student of Regius at Utrecht, and
a member of Leiden's theology faculty who had attacked the
'new philosophy'. Moreover, Revius had just published his
A Theological Consideration of Descartes' Method (in which he
makes some stinging points: '[Descartes] is convinced that he is
absolutely right about everything . . . what he means by certain
words is never what anyone else means by them'), to which
Heereboord replied by challenging Revius to a debate.

The Prince of Orange now acted. He summoned Leiden
University's rector, Frederik Spanheim, to come and see him.
The rector duly presented himself at the Stadhouder's office on
12 January 1948. The prince told him to find a way of settling
matters without further uproar, in any way that seemed best to
him. It was a delicate matter for the rector, given that he had
two schools of his university in arms against each other, in one
of which – the theology faculty – some of the professors were
distinguished and influential individuals. Spanheim took the

only course open to him, and a drastic one: he banned the discussion of any metaphysics whatever, whether Cartesian or Aristotelian. He did this despite the fact that Revius complained bitterly that he was being prevented from opposing Descartes' dangerous theories, and despite the fact that the ban on metaphysics left Descartes' physics untouched: it continued to be taught in the university as before, much to the theologians' chagrin.[15]

From this distance, both of time and mentality, it is no longer easy to appreciate the reasons why the 'new philosophy' of Descartes appeared so threatening to the theologians and traditionalists of his day. To get a sense of the acuteness with which participants in these debates felt the anxiety of the challenge they faced, it is helpful to be reminded of the world picture that Descartes' new philosophy controverted.

Religious, metaphysical and scientific orthodoxy at the opening of the seventeenth century was a synthesis of Christian theology with aspects of Aristotelian science. In the thirteenth century St Thomas Aquinas had achieved a majestic harmonisation of Aristotle's science, Ptolemy's astronomy, and Galen's medicine – which more broadly included a conception of man in his material aspects – into a single philosophy serving Christian theology. This great synthesis is known as Thomism and, even for Protestant savants after the Reformation, the framework it provided continued to shape thinking, not least about what was theologically acceptable in the way of scientific and metaphysical enquiry.

'Natural theology' concerned the existence and nature of God, and was permissible as an exercise of man's God-given reason, suitably constrained by revelation and the authority of the Church. A variety of arguments were adduced to prove God's existence and to research his nature (his omnipotence, omniscience, eternality, and so forth), and the two sets of questions were of course related – for example: if it is of the nature of God to be a necessary being, i.e. one that must exist and cannot not exist, then that fact by itself establishes that he exists. His existence can be deduced in other ways: the Cosmological Argument says that everything in the universe has a cause, so the universe must have a cause which is not itself caused by something else (at risk of infinite regress), so there must be a self-caused cause of everything; and this is God. Or, he can be proved to exist from the fact of design in all things: this is the Teleological argument. Or, he can be proved by reason alone: there is something in the universe that is the greatest or most perfect thing there is; such a thing that actually exists is greater or more perfect than such a thing that does not exist; therefore, the greatest or most perfect thing exists – and this is God.

There is not much disagreement among philosophers now that none of these arguments works, for reasons that readers might entertain themselves by investigating; and there are eloquent voices of faith which say, as for example Soren Kierkegaard does, that in any case faith is what flies in the face of argument and reason, and is not faith otherwise.[16]

But the chief source for understanding the relationship between mankind and the universe, and especially God, is the revelation of Scripture. The Reformation was precisely about the degree to which authority in this arena resided in Scripture, Protestants saying that it is the ultimate authority, Catholics saying that authority is shared between Scripture and the Church. Scripture taught that God created heaven and earth, and in them innumerable creatures, including a great angelic host – one third of which (so some authorities had it) had rebelled and followed Satan out of heaven, supporting him thereafter in his efforts to thwart God's will. After God had created Adam and Eve, Satan tempted them from their allegiance, and therefore all subsequent human beings have fallen natures. Moreover, the hosts of bad angels infect all aspects of the sublunary realm, constantly and energetically seeking to subvert finite souls from their path to God by inspiring wicked deeds, heresies, witchcraft and false knowledge, all in order to bring as many souls to damnation as possible.

To save mankind God revealed his will first, and somewhat obscurely, through the prophets, and then finally and perfectly through the sacrifice of Jesus Christ. In the light of that sacrifice all will be judged when the Last Trump sounds, an event confidently taken to be imminent by every generation of the faithful since.

These tenets, give or take a few thousand details of fine tuning (all of which, however, were individually enough to send people to the stake if they were on the losing side of a disagreement about them), had been established by theologians in the centuries after the alleged events taken as their starting point – the life and death of Jesus of Nazareth. But views of the natural world were still essentially Aristotelian. In the Aristotelian view, the material world is built out of the four elements earth, air, fire and water. The elements have four properties: hotness, coldness, wetness, and dryness, and these combine in different ways to give the chief character of the elements: thus, earth is cold and dry, water is cold and wet; fire is hot and dry, air is hot and wet. (This last speaks the Greek origin of these ideas; air might be very wet in England, but it is not often hot.) Each element has its natural place; earth, being heavy, and also morally base, tends towards the centre of the universe. Water is the same, but less so, and therefore covers earth. Air belongs between water and the lightest element, fire, whose home is a region high above the earth; it can indeed be seen twinkling in the very highest regions of space.

The elements are never encountered in their pure form, but always as admixtures, which is easily proved by chemical experiments in which they are separated or purified, e.g. by means of heat. The fact that combinations of elements can be rearranged by such means prompted alchemy, and not least its central quests of deriving precious metals from base metals, and discovering substances that would ensure longevity. An example of the reasoning employed is instructive, as offering a stark comparison to Descartes' methods. What is the most desirable and beautiful metal? Gold. As the best and nicest stuff in the world, gold must obviously be a perfect blend of the four elements, combined in perfect proportions. Obviously, therefore, baser metals needed only to have their constituent elements rearranged into perfect proportions, and they would become gold. Moreover, as a perfect compound, it is obvious that gold must be a perfect medicine too; taken in a liquid form it would surely cure all ills. Thus does greed and folly lead to bad thinking.

Apart from the 'natural motions' of the earth and water downwards, and of air and fire upwards, all motion must be the result of a mover giving things a push, just as a human being moves a ball by kicking or throwing it. If pushing stopped, things would cease to move (there was no grasp of the idea of inertia in this science). This was why there had to be a God, to get everything going, and indeed to keep it going, since obviously it is not man or any other finite being who is pushing the tides or the moon or the sun or the wind.

The stars and planets were conceived as revolving around the stationary earth, carried along in crystal spheres that had been set going by God (and were kept going, some theorists said, by 'Intelligences', superior angels charged with maintaining their correct orbits). The moon is lowest and basest of the heavenly bodies, and therefore is closest, its sphere being fastest-moving of them all. The next spheres in order of ascent are Mercury, Venus, the Sun, Mars, Jupiter and Saturn, each sphere moving more slowly than the one beneath it. These bodies are composed of a 'quintessence' – a fifth element – and they move in perfect circles around the earth, and are perfect, unchanging and incorruptible. They pour out divine music as they move, which we cannot hear while clothed in our vestments of clay, but which we will hear when we have gone to heaven.

And so the theory proceeds, through the medico-psychological theory of humours in the human body to the astrological influence of the heavenly bodies on human character and fate, and thence to the theory of the divine ordering of the world of men from anointed kingship to lowly serfdom. This last is the theory of 'degree', starting with God at the top and reaching the worm at the bottom, but with man as the connecting creature between angels and beasts, between the realms of heaven and earth. The theory was not without its subtleties; even though angels excel men in knowledge, men excel angels in the capacity to learn; even though men excel beasts in wisdom, yet beasts excel men in strength; and so on. The theory of degree admirably suited those who invented it, of course, these being the people at or near the top of the ladder.

225

Such was the world, and the beliefs, and the science, which for an accumulation of centuries had shaped the outlook even of the most educated men, until the beginning of the seventeenth century and beyond. Imagine what it must have felt like to believe all this, and then to be confronted with a novelty such as, say, the Copernican theory, which turned everything upside down. Not all the details of the traditional view furnished the minds of those such as Voetius and Revius, but most of them did; and certainly enough for them to be affronted – and more than affronted: shocked; and more than shocked: threatened – by Descartes' outlook and his way of thinking, both of which they found dramatically alien. And to see how alien the new Cartesian view must have appeared to them, one need only reflect on the startling fact that Descartes assumed very little from the traditional outlook, used hardly any of it, invoked hardly any of it, quoted none of it, and respected none of the people who relied on it, but instead actively and swingeingly rejected it as a framework for thought.[17] He adhered to just two of its principles, thinking that these were anyway so obvious that they could scarcely be regarded as distinctive components of the traditional view: one was mind-matter duality, the other was the belief that there can be no such thing as a vacuum. It was, as noted, his explicit aim to sweep traditional Aristotelian 'science' and metaphysics from the board, and to replace them with a clean, rational, jargon-free, mathematically supported, self-standing, crisply argued, fresh look at the nature of things – and he was sincere in his belief that this did not controvert basic theological commitments, but was consistent with them. Interestingly, the two main concepts he did not reject – dualism and the principle that nature abhors a vacuum – are two of the major weaknesses in his position.

9

The Princess of the Passions

No doubt the preceding chapter gives the impression that Descartes did nothing during the 1640s but engage in violent altercations over the reception of his views in the Dutch universities. True enough, these excitements absorbed a good deal of his time; but more of it was devoted to other major matters. One of them was the completion of the task of getting his principal ideas into published form; after the *Meditations* he wrote out his science and published it under the title *The Principles of Philosophy*. Another was the fostering of a valuable friendship he had formed with the highly intelligent daughter of an old enemy; the daughter was Princess Elizabeth of Bohemia, and her father (by then dead) was none other than the Winter King, Frederick, Elector Palatine, whose army Descartes had, in his small and obscure way, helped to beat at the White Mountain a quarter of a century before.

A third matter was France, and Descartes' growing sense that France was once again a safe place for him, and that he was now entitled to some reward for his eminence in the fields of science and philosophy – an official post, a title, a pension, something that would mark his place in the firmament. With this at least partly in mind he visited his native land for the first time in many years – all the old reasons for not doing so had since vanished; the war in Europe was drawing to an exhausted close, and people he might not have wished to see were no longer in the way; and moreover, something tantalising had been suggested, which he needed to pursue in person.

Descartes' friendship with Princess Elizabeth curiously brings the White Mountain back into view. The epochal event of the battle on its shallow slopes – it is a modest hill, in reality – had something mysteriously to do with Descartes' early adult life, with his military service and travels, his putative spying, his association – as spy, or would-be acolyte? – with Rosicrucian thought, his involvement in some capacity with the brutal reduction of Bohemia and Moravia, during which the Protestants of those regions were forced back into the Catholic fold at the point of a sword.

There are preciously few references in Descartes' writings, letters or recorded conversations which allude to those traumatic events, or to anything to do with his experience of war, the military, or the regions of battle he visited. It makes one wonder whether his attentive friendship towards Elizabeth of Bohemia had something more in it than is ever said: a kind of recompense or restitution, a sense of debt towards someone whose straitened circumstances, living in exile in the Hague on the generosity of the House of Orange, was the result of something that he had been party to. Certainly, his friendship with Elizabeth is not a matter of toadying or snobbery, of social climbing or a desire to cut a figure among chandeliers and silver tureens. Descartes was by no means above such things, although he professed to dislike the idea of the time-wasting aspects of court life – a profession that rings hollow in the light of his actions later – but the letters between him and Elizabeth are not about this sort of thing at all. They record a meeting of minds between a thinker and an intelligent woman, and some of the best of Descartes arises from it.

Samuel Hartlib – the Mersenne of England, in that he managed a vast correspondence among European intellectuals (and incidentally also spied for the Parliamentary cause in the English civil war) – visited the Netherlands in the winter of 1634, and recorded meeting Descartes at the house of Princess Elizabeth's mother, Princess Elizabeth Stuart.[1] Descartes' acquaintance with the Palatinate family at that point could not have been great; his presence at a levée or soirée, at which a visitor like Hartlib was also present, by itself does not imply intimacy, and there are no other references from that time to suggest that Descartes was a frequent visitor at either of the family's houses in the Hague and Arnhem. In 1634 Princess Elizabeth was only sixteen, although she was just in the process of being asked to marry King Wladislas IV of Poland – whom she refused because he was a Catholic and she was a Calvinist and, young though she was, she emphatically knew that she did not want to convert.

After his defeat at the White Mountain, Elector Frederick V of the Palatinate, the putative King of Bohemia, went into exile in the Netherlands with his wife Elizabeth Stuart. She was cousin to the Prince of Orange, who accordingly gave the exiles a home and an income. Frederick died in 1632 of the plague, caught while visiting his erstwhile lands in the Palatinate, and his widow and children were left to fend for themselves. Princess Elizabeth Stuart had four sons and four daughters by this time, and although her brother was King of England (none other than Charles I) he had troubles of his own, and anyway she felt that her eldest son's claims to the Palatinate would be best served by remaining close by in the Netherlands.

These were the family circumstances in which the gifted Princess Elizabeth grew up. She made excellent use of her time and opportunities, and even the limitations under which the family lived, by pursuing her studies. She knew six languages, including Latin, and was very good at mathematics. She read Descartes' *Discourse and Essays* and his *Meditations,* and conceived a desire to question him about the ideas they contained. She asked Alphonse de Pollot to arrange a meeting. Descartes agreed, for he had heard of her intelligence and was flattered by the interest she showed in his work. The meeting duly took place in the autumn of 1642, Descartes travelling from his home, then in Endegeest, to the Hague, along a canal which passed through 'prairies and woods' and among handsome country houses.[2] The meeting was repeated again the following spring, but it was not the meetings which mattered so much as the correspondence that sprang up between the two, and the fact that Elizabeth's questions inspired Descartes to produce a treatise he might not otherwise have considered writing, *The Passions of the Soul.*

Elizabeth's astuteness reveals itself in her question to Descartes about how, if mind and matter are so different – the first consisting essentially in thought, the second consisting essentially in spatial extension – they can interact? This was not a question that Descartes found easy to answer, and his prevarications to Elizabeth ('Well', he said, 'we experience their interaction, and God knows how it works') did not satisfy her.

A warm mutual affection arose between them. She signed her letters to him, 'Your very affectionate friend,' and he signed his to her, 'Your devoted one.' His first letter to her, though expressed in what at first looks like the conventional floweriness of courtly hyperbole, has a current of sincerity borne out by Descartes' unfailing admiration for the Princess both as mind and woman:

> The honour Your Highness does me in sending her commandments in writing is greater than I ever dared hoped for; and it is more consoling to my unworthiness than the other favour which I had hoped for passionately, which was to receive them by word of mouth, had I been permitted to pay homage to you and offer you my very humble services when I was last at the Hague. For then I would have had too many wonders to admire at the same time; and seeing superhuman sentiments flowing from a body such as painters give to angels, I would have been overwhelmed with delights like those that I think a man coming fresh from earth to heaven must feel. Thus I would hardly have been able to reply to Your Highness, as she doubtless noticed when once before I had the honour of speaking with her. In your kindness you have tried to redress this fault of mine by committing the traces of your thoughts to paper, so that I can read them many times, and grow accustomed to consider them. Thus I am less overwhelmed, but no less full of wonder, observing that it is not only at first sight that they seem perceptive, but that the more they are examined, the more judicious and solid they appear.[3]

And indeed the specific question Elizabeth had raised with Descartes was a good one: how, given his commitment to the essential difference between body and mind, can the mind make the body perform voluntary actions? How, in other words, can purely thinking stuff act upon matter, or spatial stuff, such that the latter is moved to do the mind's bidding?

The sentiment conveyed in this first letter remained in all their subsequent correspondence. At the end of 1645 he was writing in exactly similar vein, 'So seldom do good arguments come my way, not only in the conversations I have in this isolated place [he was then living at Egmond-Binnen] but also in the books that I consult, that I cannot read those which occur in Your Highness's letters without feeling an extraordinary joy.'[4]

In a book about their relationship, Leon Petit claims that Descartes and Elizabeth were in love with one another.[5] Genevieve Rodis-Lewis is inclined to agree, though in her opinion it was not a sexual passion. Sexual passions and a considerable amount of associated turmoil were no strangers to the Palatinate household in the Hague; one of Elizabeth's sisters, Louisa, had an affair with a French adventurer, to the annoyance of one of the princesses' brothers, who arranged for a set of criminals to assassinate the adventurer, whereupon the prince himself fled from the Netherlands. This is all good tabloid matter, and as Court scandals go not a bad one, though not too uncommon either. Unluckily for Princess Elizabeth, her mother thought she had been involved in inciting her brother to plot the assassination, and arranged for her to go and live with other relatives, the family of the Elector of Brandenburg in Berlin. Elizabeth left the Hague in August 1646. She and Descartes met during the course of that summer, not long before her departure, but they never saw one another again.

Nevertheless their correspondence continued. From it one sees that the affection between them was not love in Petit's sense, but something more avuncular on Descartes' side – he was the same age as her mother – and halfway between a daughter's and a friend's on Elizabeth's side. She teased him, and disagreed with him, and sought his counsel, as well as debating with him intelligently about his views; and he advised her on how to deal with her depressions, fevers, irritations, rashes, and even constipation. More to the point, he dedicated to her his scientific textbook, *The Principles of Philosophy*, when it was published in 1644:

> To her Serene Highness the Princess Elizabeth of Bohemia
> Eldest daughter of Frederick, King of Bohemia, Count
> Palatine and Elector of the Holy Roman Empire.

So Descartes begins his dedicatory epistle to Elizabeth, in it acknowledging all the claims of Frederick V and his family to the titles and territories that the Battle of the White Mountain had stripped from them. Descartes always referred to Elizabeth's mother as 'the Queen'; at the very least this demonstrates his diplomatic bent, but it is a nice curiosity in view of the history of his allegiances. Did he ever tell Princess Elizabeth where he had been on 8 November 1620, when she was two years old in Hradcany Castle on the hill above Prague's Vltava River, and the army of Duke Maximilian was just a few miles away, with him in it, bent on driving her father from his possessions?

His dedication to Elizabeth continues:

The greatest reward which I have received from the writings I have previously published is that you have deigned to read them; for as a result they have provided the occasion for my being admitted into the circle of your acquaintance. And my subsequent experience of your great talents leads me to think that it would be a service to mankind to set them down as an example to posterity . . . when I consider that such a varied and complete knowledge of all things is to be found not in some aged pedant who has spent many years in contemplation but in a young princess whose beauty and youth call to mind one of the Graces rather than gray-eyed Minerva or any of the Muses, then I cannot but be lost in admiration . . . together with your royal dignity you show an extraordinary kindness and gentleness which, though continually buffeted by the blows of fortune, has never become embittered or broken. I am so overwhelmed by this that I consider that this statement of my philosophy should be offered and dedicated to the wisdom which I so admire in you — for philosophy is nothing else but the study of wisdom. And indeed my desire to be known as a philosopher is no greater than my desire to be known as your Serene Highness's most devoted servant, Descartes.[6]

Dedications written in any century but the last tend to be high-flown and, when addressed to those in socially elevated positions, too toadying for our current taste. But there is something more than formula in this warm and personal eulogy. Over the next half dozen years he frequently praised Elizabeth to others and commented on her outstanding intellect; in a letter written in 1648 he said that he had composed his little treatise *The Passions of the Soul* 'only to be read by a princess whose mental powers are so extraordinary that she can easily understand matters which seem very difficult to our learned doctors.'[7]

The little treatise in question grew directly out of Elizabeth's dissatisfaction with Descartes' answer about the mind–body problem. Pressing him, she asked him to explain 'the manner of [the soul's] actions and passions on the body.' Her interest was not merely theoretical; she observed the effect on her health of her sensitivities and emotional states, and her interest was in part therefore practical. Her first question to Descartes about the relation of body and soul had been put in the summer of 1642, when they met; the following year she was still trying to get a straight answer out of him, and finally in September 1645 she demanded that he give 'a definition of the passions'. Descartes accordingly sat down and wrote a draft of the treatise, probably the first two thirds of the essay that was eventually revised, extended and published in 1649. It was the last of his works published in his lifetime.

The *Passions* iterates Descartes' dualism, gives a mechanistic account of the workings of muscles and nerves, and repeats his view that the pineal gland is the place in the brain where 'the soul exercises its functions more particularly than in the other parts of the body.'[8] 'Let us therefore take it,' he wrote, 'that the soul has its principal seat in the small gland located in the middle of the brain. From there it radiates through the rest of the body by means of the animal spirits, the nerves, and even the blood, which can take on the impressions of the spirits and carry them through the arteries to all the limbs.'[9] The second part of the work considers individual passions – love and hatred, desire, hope, anxiety, jealousy, confidence, despair, irresolution, courage, remorse, joy and sadness, derision, envy

235

and pity, indignation and anger, pride and shame. Given that Descartes was currently experiencing a number of these – not least the negative ones – in his battles over his theories at the universities of Utrecht and Leiden, he might well have claimed special expertise. He spoke too of laughter and tears, of blushing, of the difference between affection, friendship and devotion, and of the distinction between 'concupiscent love and benevolent love'.[10] In considering the nature of the affection that subsisted between Descartes and the Princess, Rodis-Lewis cites this very distinction, claiming that what Descartes felt for the Princess was 'benevolent love'. She is probably right.

'A distinction is commonly made between two sorts of love,' Descartes wrote, 'one called "benevolent love", which prompts us to wish for the well-being of what we love, and the other called "concupiscent love", which makes us desire the things we love. But it seems to me that this distinction concerns only the effects of love and not its essence. For as soon as we have joined ourselves willingly to some object, whatever its nature may be, we feel benevolent towards it – that is, we also join to it willingly the things we believe to be agreeable to it: this is one of the principal effects of love . . . We may, I think, more reasonably distinguish kinds of love according to the esteem which we have for the object of love, as compared with ourselves. For when we have less esteem for it than ourselves, we have only a simple affection for it; when we esteem it equally with ourselves, that is called "friendship"; and when we have more esteem for it, our passion may be called "devotion".'[11]

The most remarkable part of the transactions between Descartes and Elizabeth lies in a series of letters they exchanged from July 1645 onwards in which they discussed Seneca's

De Vita Beata, 'On the Happy Life'. Descartes proposed it to Elizabeth as a help to her in the difficult circumstances of ill-health and family pressures then besetting her, but he did so before he had read it properly himself, so when he next wrote he said that he had come to think it was not sufficiently rigorous to serve as the subject of their discussion. He therefore begins (rather characteristically) by telling her how Seneca *should* have discussed the topic. In subsequent letters he examines Seneca's arguments, iterating his complaint that the ancient author does not express himself accurately and does not properly understand what he wished to say; and after a while he abandons him altogether and sets out his own *lebensphilosophie* instead. The account he gives is as follows.

Happiness, he tells the Princess, consists in 'perfect contentment of mind and inner satisfaction.' The key question is how this contentment is to be attained. The things that promote it, Descartes says, fall into two classes: those that depend on our minds, such as wisdom and virtue, and those that depend on factors outside ourselves, such as honours, wealth and health. Echoing the acknowledgement of Aristotle that it is easier to be happy when fortunate in one's circumstances, he observes that 'a person of good birth who is healthy, and lacks nothing, can enjoy a more perfect contentment than one who is poor, ill and deformed, granting that both are equally virtuous and wise.' But even though this is so, 'a small cup can be just as full as a large one, even though it contains less liquid; likewise if we regard everyone's contentment as the full satisfaction of his desires, duly regulated by reason, I do not doubt that those who are poorest and least blessed by fortune, can be as fully contented and satisfied as anyone else, even though they do not have as many good things.'[12]

And anyone can be contented if he respects three conditions: first, if he tries to use his reason as well as he can when thinking what to do in the various circumstances he finds himself in; secondly, if he firmly adheres to what reason thus recommends, without being distracted by his passions and appetites – 'virtue, I believe, consists precisely in firmly holding to this resolution' – and lastly, if he remembers that 'all the good things he does not possess are all entirely outside his power.'[13] Descartes claims that these three principles are related to the rules of morality he had set out in his *Discourse on Method*.

In adhering to these principles, Descartes continues, there are four truths that are most useful to us. The first is that there is a God on whom all things depend, who is infinitely perfect, all-powerful, and cannot be disobeyed. This teaches us to be calm in the face of everything sent by God to test us. The second is that our souls exist independently of the body, are much nobler than body, and are capable of enjoying satisfactions not found in the physical world; which prevents us from being afraid of death, and warns us against attaching too great affection to things of this world. Thirdly, we must entertain an idea of the immensity of the universe, which is God's creation, and marvel at the fact that it exists wholly for our service. Fourthly, we must consider that although we are each individuals, yet we are all connected to one another, and our interests are so interwoven that the whole must be regarded as more important than each part. 'If someone considers himself to be part of the community, he delights in doing good to everyone,' Descartes observes, 'and does not hesitate even to risk his life in the service of others when the occasion demands. So this consideration is the source and origin of all the most heroic actions done by men.'[14]

These pious thoughts provide a Christianisation of what, until Descartes introduces them, is in substance a version of Stoic practical morality. The 'three conditions' to be observed in attaining contentment would not be out of place in the writings of the two great later Stoic teachers, Epictetus and Marcus Aurelius. But the last of the 'four truths' is not specific to any religion or ethical view, but is wholly general in the way it premises the interconnectedness of the human family. However much of a cliché this is, it has the merit of being a worthy one. Descartes was not, as the foregoing shows, always able to put it into practice in his dealings with others.

Elizabeth's witty and intelligent younger sister Sophie – who later married Ernest-August of Hanover, and gave him a son, George-Louis, who in 1714 became King George I of England – gave a pen-portrait of Elizabeth at the time of her friendship with Descartes: 'My sister, who is called Madame Elizabeth . . . loves to study, but all her philosophy cannot keep her from chagrin when the circulation of her blood causes her nose to turn red . . . She knows all the languages and all the sciences, and has a regular commerce with Monsieur Descartes, but this thinker renders her a bit distracted, which often makes us laugh.'[15]

One reason for Descartes' enjoyment of Elizabeth's intellect was that – as indeed she herself noted in her letter thanking him for the dedication of *The Principles of Philosophy* – her intellect was unspoiled by Aristotelian philosophy. Her sharp, receptive intelligence doubtless made a refreshing change from the prejudices of the traditionalists who opposed his ideas in their universities. It is an interesting consideration that, even as those battles raged, he was discussing Seneca, the happy life, and the passions of the soul with her.

The question of a happy life was not an idle matter for Elizabeth. Because of her father's famous defeat at the Battle of the White Mountain, her family was poor, and dependent on the charity of royal relatives. She had given up the idea of marriage, preferring a life of study; but even if this had not been so, the behaviour of two of her brothers, Edward and Philip, made it harder for her to contemplate a conventional marriage, whether within or outside what was in effect a widely extended single European royal family. (Another brother, Rupert, married the daughter of an English knight, and went on to become Duke of Cumberland and First Lord of the Admiralty in the British government.)

Edward converted to Roman Catholicism in order to marry Anne of Gonzaga, daughter of the Duke of Mantua. Elizabeth was deeply wounded by what she saw as his apostasy, and bewailed it in her correspondence with Descartes, seeming to ignore the fact that he was himself a Catholic. Descartes, in kindly and irenic fashion, replied that God had many ways of drawing souls to himself.

Philip's crime was of a quite different order. It was he who arranged the assassination of one Monsieur L'Espinay (some accounts say he publicly stabbed and killed L'Espinay himself), in anger at the latter's bragging that he had had an affair with his sister Princess Louisa of Bohemia. Philip was obliged to flee; he joined the army of the King of Spain.

In the resulting family tribulations, Elizabeth and her mother fell out because the Queen thought Elizabeth had encouraged Philip's misadventure. This, as noted earlier, is why Elizabeth was sent away to live with her dreary cousins at the Brandenburg court in Berlin. But the life of a boarded-out poor relation could not hold her forever. In 1667, seventeen years after Descartes' death, she entered a Protestant convent at Herford in Westphalia, eventually becoming its abbess – a position of considerable responsibility, given that in the convent's domains were 7,000 people working its farms, vineyards, mills and factories. Most notably, under Elizabeth's rule the convent became a place of refuge for people of different religions, who found shelter there from persecution.

Descartes had not been wrong to see something special in Princess Elizabeth of the Palatine, and their friendship does both of them credit. She died in 1680, aged sixty-four; she had met Descartes when she was twenty-eight. It is hard not to see something of his influence in her life, which was, at the very least, consistent with the tenets Descartes advanced in their correspondence on Seneca.

Descartes' *Principles of Philosophy* was intended to be a textbook of Cartesian science for use in schools – especially, he hoped, Jesuit schools. He started it in 1641 and it was ready for the printer in the early summer of 1644. It summarised the basics of his philosophy – the sceptical starting point, the certainty of one's own existence, the mind–body distinction, and the goodness of God which guarantees truth when we think aright – and then proceeds to set out his cosmology and mechanics. There is good reason to think that he also intended to include a section on physiology and a section on psychology. A short unfinished essay later posthumously published as *A Description of the Human Body,* written in the winter of 1647–48, and *The Passions of the Soul,* written for Princess Elizabeth, might conceivably be Descartes' late efforts to supply these respective omitted portions of the *Principles,* or at least to cover the ground there left undiscussed. But as for the main parts of the *Principles* as published, there is nothing in it which is not already in Descartes' previous works, including *Le Monde*. Gaukroger remarks that it could in fact be regarded as a rewriting of *Le Monde*, using the *Meditations* as a better metaphysical basis than was available for the original treatise.[16] The main differences between the *Principles* and Descartes' previous work lie in arrangement; he was trying to make his case as perspicuous and well ordered as he could. Another feature is that he here tries to win over those wedded to traditional Aristotelian philosophy by using some of their terminology in explaining the new conceptions of physics he was introducing, such as force, motion and rest. The manoeuvre fails; it simply made some of his opponents complain, as already noted, that he did not mean by their words what they meant – and in this they were of course right.

Central to Descartes' physics is the notion of the 'vortices'. In the second half of the seventeenth century and subsequently, when Cartesian science was being hotly debated, it was not the metaphysics of the *Meditations* and the opening section of the *Principles* which attracted attention, but his theory of vortices. And it was this theory that Newton refuted at the end of Book II of his *Principia*, preparatory to setting out his own view of how the motion of bodies occurs 'in free space without vortices.'[17]

In Descartes' view, the universe is a plenum of matter in different states – there is no vacuum, no emptiness: space and matter are the same thing. For anything to move, therefore, something else has to move, and Descartes argued that the working of this principle in the universe meant that there would be indefinitely many local swirls or vortices of matter in different degrees of coarseness or fluidity, the matter at the centre of each vortex moving more slowly than the matter on its outer margins. Because of the character of the matter that constitutes the centre of a vortex – it forms as fluid round bodies, Descartes says – the centres of vortices are suns, and their pushing action is 'what we may take as light.' The sun, stars and planets are made of coarser particles of matter, and are carried along in the vortices – the earth itself does not move, being without innate motion, but it is transported around the sun by the great fluid vortex in which it floats.

Descartes' cosmology is thus an essentially Copernican universe regarded as a plenum, in which motion occurs in the vortices according to his theory of mechanics. His mechanics, summarily put, uses only the notions of size, speed, and rest or motion. Rest and motion are states of bodies which depend upon the mechanical impulse upon them of other bodies. There are three types of matter in the vortices: firstly aether, consisting of very fine fast-moving particles that form the sun and stars; secondly, tiny, smooth spherical particles which Descartes called 'celestial matter'; and lastly, larger irregular particles that aggregate to form planets and comets.

Historians of science point out that although Descartes' theory looks like a clever way of having a Copernican cake and eating it – the earth goes round the sun, but it does not move, for it is carried sedentarily along by a vortex – its main impulse was his adherence to the principle that there is no vacuum. Descartes might be said to have done as nature did, and abhorred the vacuum. In this he was wrong, as the subsequent development of science shows; but it had two very productive consequences. The first relates to his theory of vision, which is that seeing results from pressure on the eye by the universal fluid. The sun, for example, is the centre of a vortex, and its outward pressure on the universal fluid instantaneously translates into pressure on any eye directed towards it. (John Gribbin points out that Newton exposed the fallacy in this theory by noting that if vision is caused by pressure in this fashion, then anyone could see in the dark by running fast enough. Gribbin gives Descartes his answer: no-one *can* run fast enough to see in the dark.[18]) The idea of light as waves emanating from a source, like ripples emanating from a stone thrown into a pond, was however explored later in the century by Christiaan Huygens, the brilliant son of Descartes' friend.

Secondly, the theory of vortices was the starting point for developments in physics later in the century, not least Newton's, who arrived at his own theory of gravitation by rejecting Descartes' account. Since Newton's theory involved accepting action at a distance, contrary to the apparently more sensible view held by Descartes, the contest between the Cartesians and Newtonians was for a time fierce. But Newton's rejection of Descartes' vortex theory was not just right but well-founded. He showed that it conflicts with Kepler's third law, the 'Harmonic Law', which relates the time it takes for a planet to orbit the sun to its mean distance from the sun; the law states that the closest planets move at the greatest speeds and have the shortest orbital periods, which is the reverse of what Descartes said. And Newton also showed that unless there was a constant input of energy at the centre of each vortex, vortices could not sustain themselves in being.

★   ★   ★

After many years' absence from the land of his birth, Descartes at long last found it necessary to return, at least for a visit. He had left France at the end of 1628; his father had died in 1640, and there were matters of inheritance and property to be attended to. He had written to Huygens shortly after his father's death to say that he was going to have to visit France to deal with family matters. But he did not go then, and kept putting it off, presumably until he could delay no longer.

Accordingly, with what degree of reluctance we do not know, Descartes took ship for France in May 1644 and remained there for a whole six months, mainly in Paris though with a visit to his brother and half-brother, in Rennes and Nantes respectively, to discuss the matters of family inheritances. In Paris he stayed in the rue des Ecouffes with his friend Claude Picot, a priest who managed Descartes' money affairs in France and who was – to boot – preparing to translate the *Principles of Philosophy* into French. The two of them went to Blois to visit Florimond Debeaune, who had given Descartes' mathematics such a warm reception, and to Tours to visit other friends. And he renewed personal acquaintance with a number of his oldest friends, Mydorge and Mersenne chief among them, who proved as useful as ever, this time by re-introducing him to the two men – mentioned earlier in these pages, but only now entering into deeper personal acquaintance with Descartes – who were destined to play major roles in the remainder of his life and in the future of his reputation: the brothers-in-law Pierre Chanut and Claude Clerselier.

Chanut was a career diplomat and an amateur philosopher who had helped his friend Mersenne conduct experiments on air pressure, but who – when confronted with the great Descartes – disavowed any scientific expertise, saying that it was moral philosophy rather than natural philosophy that most interested him. Nevertheless Descartes and he took to one another immediately, and Chanut sought every opportunity to advance Descartes' interests. He was almost certainly one of those who worked to get Descartes a pension from the French crown during the next few years, and when Chanut was appointed ambassador to the court of Queen Christina of Sweden in 1646 he sang the praises of Descartes to such an extent that the Queen initiated a correspondence with the philosopher, and later conceived a desire to have him at her court. That was how it came to pass that Descartes ended his life in the Queen's northern fastness, after just one dark winter in her company.

Clerselier recommended himself to Descartes instantly by the fact that, when they met, he was in the midst of translating into French the 'Objections and Replies' appended to the *Meditations*. As mentioned already, Clerselier became Descartes' indefatigable champion, protector and, after his death, executor and editor, looking after the letters and manuscripts he left behind, publishing the unpublished works and fragments, and furnishing the earliest biographers with details of Descartes' life as he saw it. Baillet claimed that Descartes regarded his friendship with Clerselier as one of the greatest pieces of good fortune he had ever had, and that he 'revealed to him the most intimate secrets of his life.'[19] Whether or not this latter is true, Descartes certainly welcomed the new friendships, and they both indeed proved of immense importance.

Paris, Blois, and friends constituted the pleasure part of Descartes' visit; but they were not enough to make him think of remaining in France permanently. In a letter to Princess

Elizabeth written from Paris in July 1644 he says, 'Although there are many people here whom I honour and esteem, I have not yet seen anything to keep me here.'[20] The business part involved visiting his brother Pierre in Rennes, and his half-brother Joachim in Nantes. He left Paris to travel in their direction just a few days after writing the above words to Elizabeth. His encounters with them cannot have been all tension and haggling, for in the baptismal register at Nantes on 9 September 1644 Descartes signed as godfather for a new nephew named René. But in a letter to Picot written some years later, in 1648, he paints what is certainly a truer picture: 'Concerning my brother's complaint, it seems to me very unjust. I said nothing in Poitou except that I have not charged him to act on my behalf in my affairs. And that if he attempts to do something in my name or as though it comes from me, I will disavow it.'

When he returned to the Netherlands in November 1644 Descartes was exhausted, and to make matters worse he found not only that his controversy with Voetius was reaching a climax, but that someone who was supposed to be a follower, none other than Henry Regius, was bringing his views into disrepute by publishing nonsensical versions of them. In a letter to Pollot he wrote, 'Since my journey to France I have aged twenty years, to the extent that it is now a greater effort for me to go to the Hague than it used to be to travel to Rome. It is not that I am sick, thank God, but I feel weak and more than ever I need comfort and rest.'[21] Nevertheless his letters to Elizabeth continued in the usual vein, intimate and cheerful; this was the period in which he was writing to her about Seneca, and sending her mathematical puzzles to solve (which she successfully did) as a way of introducing her to his *Geometry*.

Despite the debilitations induced by his 1644 visit to Paris, Descartes returned there in 1647 for another visit, not for as long as in 1644 but long enough – four months – to meet the atomist Pierre Gassendi, the *Leviathan* author Thomas Hobbes, and the young Blaise Pascal, who was not well disposed to Descartes then or later, being of the camp of Roberval and Fermat. Descartes was, however, curious to meet Pascal, about whom he had heard much.

The meeting with Gassendi and Hobbes took place at a specially arranged dinner, the intention of which was to reconcile Descartes with them, for they had been sharply critical of his *Meditations* in the 'Objections' he had, through Mersenne, invited them to write. Their objections had annoyed him – as all disagreement invariably did – and he told Mersenne that he thought Hobbes was using the opportunity of criticising the *Meditations* as a boost to his own reputation. Mersenne and Clerselier were at the dinner with Descartes and Hobbes, but Gassendi could not come because he was sick in bed at home; so when the dinner was over the whole party went to Gassendi's house to wish him well.

Pascal was a prodigy, who at the age of sixteen had written an essay on conic sections that Descartes could not but admit showed genius; so the prospect of meeting the young man was irresistible. By then Pascal was twenty-one. Descartes had two encounters with him. During the first of them Pascal was in bed with a fever and, moreover, Roberval was present, which annoyed Descartes. Pascal showed Descartes the calculating machine he had made – the first ever computer, based on the technology of knitting machines – and when Descartes rose to leave, having a lunch appointment to keep, Roberval went with him; they got into the coach Descartes had hired, and argued volubly with one another as it rumbled off down the street.

This first meeting was recorded by Pascal's sister Jacqueline, together with the way it ended: 'Monsieur Descartes took [Roberval] away with him in a grand coach, where the two of them were all alone, insulting each other, but somewhat louder than here.'[22]

At the second meeting between Descartes and Pascal, which took place the next morning, they were able to talk without interruption, and Descartes suggested to the younger man an experiment to determine the issue between his theory of the plenum and Evangelista Torricelli's vacuum-invoking theory of atmospheric pressure. Pascal carried out the experiment in the following year with his brother-in-law, Puy de Dome, famously carrying glass tubes of mercury up a mountain in Auvergne to do so.

Mydorge died while Descartes was in Paris, and he saw less of Mersenne, who was ill. But he was in the French capital for a particular reason; there were suggestions afoot among some of his friends that the Court might be prevailed upon to award him a pension in the king's name, or some other remunerative recognition for his eminence in the intellectual world. King Louis XIV was still a boy, and the government was in the hands of a regent – Louis' mother, Anne of Austria – and the chief minister Cardinal Mazarin; so it was one or both of these latter two who had been prevailed on to think of the award. The prospect of it was very attractive to Descartes. In ways that suggest that his financial circumstances were no longer what they were – perhaps his expectations from the 1644 visit to Poitou had not been fully realised – he now made a number of additional efforts to pursue either a pension or a sinecure, or at least an office.[23] As is the way with royal courts, especially those in straitened circumstances, matters moved slowly, so when Descartes saw that a pension or something similar was not going to materialise straight away, he returned to the Netherlands.

To avoid travelling back in the autumn Descartes left Paris in September. He took Picot with him for a winter's stay at Egmond-Binnen, his new place of residence, and his last in the Netherlands, for he lived there through all his few remaining years in the country. The task he was reluctantly engaged in was writing a response to the confused version of his ideas that his now former disciple, Henry Regius, was putting about. He had repudiated Regius' independent version of his ideas in the preface to the *Principles of Philosophy,* but Regius had replied with a pamphlet that Descartes could not ignore, for in it Regius persisted in giving Cartesian science the wrong kind of metaphysical grounding.[24] This made Descartes anxious because only his own metaphysics, he thought, could show that his science was consistent with religious orthodoxy.

But six months later Descartes was packing his bags for Paris again, because the pension scheme seemed to be firming up, together with unspecified but alluring hints of something more – perhaps a title or a distinguished post; and his presence was required to complete the arrangements for it. He had been told that the French Crown was minded to grant him an annual provision of 3,000 livres – six times the interest he was receiving on his property in Poitou – a handsome sum and eminently worth another journey to Paris. He was also excited by the prospect of the unspecified extras, though he said to Chanut in a letter written as he packed, 'I do not want an exacting job that would take from me the leisure to cultivate my mind, even though it would give me a great deal of honour and profit.'[25]

On his return to Paris the first thing Descartes did was to buy himself a smart green silk suit, complete with a new hat and sword, and to rent a princely apartment in the city centre, close to the Court. He was living up to his expectations, and chose not to indulge any delay in playing the part of a gentleman pensioner of the King. Alas, alas; bridges crossed before they are reached have their way of tumbling into the torrent below. Even as Descartes combed his moustaches and donned his feathered hat to visit the Court, so the Court, and indeed the whole of Paris, was thrown into a sudden dangerous turmoil by the events known as the Fronde.[26] These events were, as it happens, directly linked to the promise of his pension, and they were equally directly the reason why he never received it; although in neither case was he the personal focus of the difficulties.

As noted above, France's Louis XIV, destined for splendour, was then still a boy, and the country was being run by his redoubtable mother, Anne of Austria, and her unpopular chief minister Cardinal Mazarin. Between them they had emptied France's coffers, a large component of their extravagance consisting in the gift of pensions to many people, mainly their own families and supporters. Descartes was to have been a beneficiary of this largesse, though he might have realised that all was not well when he received not one but two handsomely embossed parchments promising the pension, but without any money to follow, for this conjunction of events quite eloquently suggested bureaucratic disorder and an empty treasury.

As a remedy for their financial difficulties Anne and Mazarin devised a beautifully simple plan, which was: to place a four-year stop on the salaries of the magistrates of the high courts, excepting those in the Parlement of Paris. The idea was, to put it mildly, not welcomed. Both the high courts and the Parlement drafted a law limiting the royal prerogative, in an attempt not only to control the Crown's powers of taxation, but to limit the centralising tendency of Mazarin's rule, in which he was extending the policy of Richelieu.

Anne and Mazarin retaliated by arresting several members of the Parlement. That was too much for the population of Paris, which immediately took to the streets, barricaded over a thousand of them – thus making the city impassable – and demanded the release of the imprisoned members of Parlement. Anne and Mazarin were forced to back down.

But only temporarily, for the Peace of Westphalia had just then been concluded, releasing the French army for service at home. Anne and Mazarin secretly left Paris and ordered the returning army to blockade the city, which it did. By this time it was clear to everyone that the Fronde was larger than a merely local conflict between Court and magistracy over money, but had turned into a major battle over the rights and powers of the monarchy. As such it shared an underlying theme with the great and much longer-lasting struggle across the Channel in England, where Charles I was about to lose his head, but the outcome was not constitutional monarchy and the growth of representative government, as in the island kingdom, but the absolute monarchy of Louis XIV, and the need for another and far bloodier revolution nearly 150 years later.

As for the immediate crisis, it was resolved at Rueil in March 1649 by a compromise between the Court and the Parlement of Paris. Anne of Austria's troubles – or rather: the troubles she caused – were not however over; there was more and worse to come, which eventually ousted her from her regency altogether. But those events lie outside the scope of the present tale.

For Descartes the Fronde was a debacle. The day that the barricades went up was 27 August 1648; there were, to be exact, 1,260 barricades, which made movement around the city not only difficult to impossible, but quite likely dangerous to a small middle-aged gentleman in a fancy green silk suit. That is why the moment he heard that the barricades were going up Descartes fled. He took immediate refuge at Picot's house, then left the country as soon as he could. The degree of his hurry can be measured by the fact that his old and trusted friend Mersenne was on his death-bed, and indeed died just a few days later on 1 September; but Descartes did not tarry to bid him farewell, or to see him to his grave.

When he had recovered his breath back in the Netherlands, which took several months, Descartes wrote an indignant letter to Chanut:

> I have thought it just as well to write nothing since my return, in order not to seem to reproach those who called me to France. But I must say that I consider them to be like friends who invited me to dinner at their home, and then when I arrived there, I found that their kitchen was in an uproar and the cooking pot was turned over, and that is why I have returned without saying a word, in order not to increase their embarrassment. But this encounter has taught

me never to undertake a voyage on promises again, even if they are written on parchment.[27]

He wrote again the next month, still smarting and annoyed:

It seems that fortune is jealous that I have never desired anything of it, and that I have tried to conduct my life so that fortune would never disoblige me if it had occasion to do so. I have proved this in the three voyages I have taken to France since I retired to this land, but particularly in the last, which was commanded on the part of the king. To convince me to do it, I was sent letters on parchment, finely sealed, that contain the most grand elegies, which I don't merit, and the gift of a handsome pension. Moreover, in the details of the letters from those who sent me the king's letter, they promise me a great deal more than that if I would come to France. Ah, but when I arrived there, the unexpected troubles made it so that instead of finding what they had promised me, I found that I had to pay one of my relatives for the postage of the letters they had sent me, and that I seemed to have gone to Paris merely to buy a parchment, the most expensive and useless thing that I have ever held in my hands.[28]

Continuing in this disingenuous vein he adds, 'This, however, bothered me little'; what bothered him more, he claims, was that those who had invited him to Paris did not want him for anything useful – the 'more' that had been hinted must have suggested to him an office, a diplomatic post, a title – for it had turned out that they merely wanted him there as a rarity, 'like an elephant or a panther'.

The letter is disingenuous because Descartes' protestations about never having desired anything from fortune, and being indifferent to its gifts and cruelties, is palpably false, and never more so than at the very time he wrote those words. If a green silk suit and the allure of finely sealed parchment do not give them the lie, then the circumstances of his writing to Chanut certainly do; for in this letter he is responding to an invitation that Chanut, by then French ambassador to Sweden, was relaying to him from the extraordinary and clever ruler of that country, Queen Christina, who wished to have Descartes come and live at her court in Stockholm. The correspondence between Descartes and Chanut on this topic, and between Descartes and the Queen herself, loudly and clearly shows Descartes' avid desire to move in elevated circles, but also his wariness about whether an invitation to do so might in reality mean that he would be a mere functionary, on the level of a tutor or governess. He wanted very much more than that. The letters he and the Queen had been exchanging since 1646 confirmed the high praises he had heard from everyone about her gifts of mind and character, and he was flattered to be her correspondent – and now, even more, to be invited to teach his philosophy to her; but he had burned his fingers by expecting too much from the great, and so he prevaricated.

Had he prevaricated longer, he would have lived longer. But the combined persuasion of the Queen, Chanut, and his own ambition, proved too much. At the beginning of September 1649 he set sail for Stockholm, sailing north away from the Netherlands, from France, and from life.

10

The Queen of Winter

Descartes had met the Winter Queen, Elizabeth Stuart of Bohemia, and played a part in her downfall; he had become a friend of her daughter, whom he loved with an at least avuncular love; and now he met the Queen of Winter in a land so cold, as he wrote to a friend, that even thought froze there.

When he arrived in Stockholm and met his employer, for that is what Queen Christina was, he was not meeting a stranger. They had been corresponding since 1646 through the good offices of Chanut, and although Descartes had written *The Passions of the Soul* for Princess Elizabeth, he had dedicated its extended and published version to Queen Christina. He did so with Elizabeth's permission; the latter, after all, had already had the more substantial *Principles of Philosophy* indited to her, and Descartes wrote to her to clear matters beforehand.

'The Queen of Winter' has a pleasing ring to it as an epithet for a female Swedish monarch, given the historical resonances; but in fact Christina was the opposite of a wintry queen. On the contrary, her northern land and its cold climate, its chilly Lutheran religion and its coolly reserved people, did not suit her. She longed for something altogether hotter: a life, a place, an experience more florid and coloured than her kingdom offered, something far warmer in sentiment and richer in texture than her life had hitherto contained. And this was not a question of Christina's wishing for passionate romance like Abelard's Heloise, or military adventures like Joan of Arc. The key lies rather in the dominating fact about Christina's story, which is that at the age of twenty-eight, in 1654, she abdicated her throne in order to become a Roman Catholic.

Two of the people who played a role in this dramatic event – a role more rather than less direct, though hidden – were Pierre Chanut and René Descartes.

Christina was born in 1626, the only child of Sweden's great (everyone agrees: greatest) king, Gustavus Adolphus, whose military reforms and innovations had made the Swedish army the most formidable in Europe, thus laying the basis for its leading role in the Thirty Years War. Gustavus had entered that war for two reasons: his sincere concern for the fate of the Protestant cause, and his desire to restore Sweden's financial fortunes by securing a Baltic empire, which meant acquiring land on the Baltic's southern shore. This aspect of his policy, however much he tried to conceal it, was transparent to the German princes who stood to lose territory in Pomerania and elsewhere to satisfy Gustavus' aims, and that proved a complicating factor in the war.

Gustavus was killed at the battle of Lutzen in 1632 when Christina was only six. Her mother, Marie-Eleanor of Branden-burg, was the sister of the ill-fated Frederick V, Elector Palatine, putative King of Bohemia, which meant that Christina was cousin to the Princess Elizabeth. Marie-Eleanor had given birth to Christina after a number of difficult pregnancies and still-births, and soon afterwards went mad. She was looked after in a place away from Court, a household that was more a private prison than an asylum; and therefore had no influence on Christina's upbringing. The man appointed as regent was Sweden's leading nobleman, Axel Oxenstierna, an exceptionally able individual who prosecuted the war with as much if not more astuteness as Gustavus would have done. So successful was he, indeed, that the Treaty of Westphalia gave Sweden much of what it wanted in the way of acquisitions: Western Pomerania including Stettin and the Oder Estuary, Wismar in Mecklenburg, and the bishoprics of Bremen and Verdun. It was a considerable coup, not least because by then Sweden desperately needed the revenues.

Christina started attending council meetings when she was fourteen. The regency council consisted of five people of whom Oxenstierna, his brother and a cousin made three, giving the regent an inbuilt majority. Christina was not always in agreement with the council. She wanted the war to end as quickly as possible, while Oxenstierna needed to secure maximum mileage for the Baltic plan. When Christina came of age in 1644 the tension between the two of them increased, made worse by Oxenstierna's swingeing reforms of the country's administration, which Christina interpreted – rightly, as it happened – as an effort by him to limit her power.

A more thorough account of Christina's reign and her conflicts with Oxenstierna would show that much of the wisdom in the case lay on his side. The truth is that she was not a good queen, and by the time she abdicated she had become deeply unpopular with her people because of the folly of some of her decisions. But the public aspect of her life was not entirely paralleled by its private side. Although she had been educated like a boy, and had a man's skills on horseback and with a gun, she was a highly intelligent woman who loved learning, and when she went on hunting trips she had the classic authors read aloud to her. In this respect she reminded observers of Federigo da Montefeltro, the hook-nosed Duke of Urbino immortalised by Piero della Francesca, who was wont to have Aristotle read to him at breakfast before taking the field at the head of his mercenary army.[1]

Christina was keen also to make her court a centre of learning and culture that would do justice to the highest Late Renaissance ideals. She invited scholars and writers, musicians and architects to Stockholm, and she had a theatre constructed to the latest technological specifications, with machinery to transform the stage from a mountain landscape to a seashore, from a forest to a ballroom.

In October 1645 Chanut visited Descartes in the Netherlands, *en route* to Stockholm to take up his appointment as ambassador there. By this time Descartes' thoughts were turning towards pensions and sinecure posts, and he lost little time in dropping a hint to Chanut that the court of the celebrated young Swedish queen might have something to offer. He immediately arranged to have a copy of the *Meditations* sent to her, and followed it with a letter to Chanut in which, in his customarily disingenuous style, he disclaimed any interest in having his name known to anyone at all, least of all the great, 'but' – Descartes was a master of these 'buts' – 'since I am already known to a multitude of Schoolmen who look at my writings the wrong way and seek ways to harm me at all costs' – he was in the midst of his great quarrels – 'I am greatly inclined to hope also to be known by people of the highest rank, whose power and virtue could protect me.'[2] He was nothing if not an accomplished writer of the insinuating letter; he continues, knowing that Christina would be sure to see these words, 'Moreover, I have heard that this Queen is held in such high esteem that, although I have often complained about those who wished to introduce me to some grand person, I cannot forbear thanking you for having spoken so kindly to her about me.'[3]

It becomes amusing after a while to observe Descartes' method of seeking social advancement, about which one could discourse at length. It can be summed up thus: 'I do not at all wish to enter Court circles, BUT should you be good enough to drop a word in Her Majesty's ear . . .' It is unlikely that Chanut was in the slightest taken in by it, but he was anyway much disposed to help, and within a short time the philosopher and the Queen were corresponding, via Chanut, on matters as abstract as the size of the universe, as intimate as the distinction between rational and sensual love, and as important as the nature of the greatest good.

In passing, it might be noted that in his letter on the nature of love, Descartes included the anecdote about how, when he was a boy, he had fallen in love with a girl who had a slight squint. 'The impression made by sight in my brain when I looked at her cross-eyes became so closely connected to the simultaneous impression which aroused in me the passion of love that for a long time afterwards when I saw persons with a squint I felt a special inclination to love them simply because they had that defect.'[4] Queen Christina, as Descartes would have known from engravings of her portraits, had a squint.

When, at length, Christina wrote directly to Descartes to tell him that she had read his *Principles*, he wrote first to Chanut – 'I received as an altogether undeserved favour the letter which that matchless Princess condescended to write to me. I am surprised that she should take the trouble to do so; but I am not surprised that she took the trouble to read my *Principles*, because I am convinced that it contains many truths which are difficult to find elsewhere.'[5] Again the words were intended as much for Christina herself as Chanut; and there was even a remonstrance in them, for it had taken Christina a long time to respond to his gift of the *Principles*. To the Queen herself he wrote, 'If a letter were sent to me from heaven and I saw it descending from the clouds, I would not be more surprised than I was to receive the letter which Your Highness so graciously wrote to me; and I could not receive a letter with more respect and veneration than I feel on receiving your letter.'[6] And then he in effect offered her his presence, should she command it – though in a suitable manner, of course: 'All who love virtue must consider themselves fortunate whenever they have an opportunity to render a service to her. Since I make a special point of being one of those persons, I venture to swear to Your Majesty that she could command nothing of me so difficult that I would not always be ready to do everything possible to accomplish it.'[7]

Christina duly invited Descartes to Stockholm, and Descartes duly prevaricated, trying to get assurances from Chanut that he would not be going with false hopes of the kind he had suffered in Paris. Other biographers and commentators read Descartes' prevaricatory letters to Chanut as evidence that he did not want to go; I read them as evidence that he did not want to go unless on genuinely good terms. And by good terms he did not mean money or position only; he wished to know whether Christina really wanted to learn his views, for he hoped that if they had official sanction from a monarch it would help them to secure more of a foothold than they had so far won – for, of course, they were still not the official doctrine of the schools, as he longed for them to be. He doubtless hoped that they might be adopted in the schools of Sweden, which would be a start.

Chanut passed Christina's invitation to him in late February 1649, and in a reply specifically intended to be read by the Queen, Descartes declared himself instantly ready to fly to her side. But to Chanut himself he privately wrote:

> I shall give you, if I may, the trouble of reading two of my letters on this occasion. For I assume that you will want to show the other to the Queen of Sweden, and I have saved something for this one which I thought she need not see – namely that I am having more difficulty deciding about this visit than I had imagined I would have. It is not that I do not have a great desire to serve this Princess. My confidence in your words, and my great admiration and esteem for the character and mind which you ascribe to her, are such that I would wish to undertake an even longer and more arduous journey than one to Sweden in order to have the honour to offer whatever I may contribute towards the satisfaction of her wishes.[8]

The reason for his 'difficulty', which Descartes then sets out in detail, is that he has learned that very few people really wished to enter into his theories, and that when they did so, although they might find them surprising at first, they soon realise how much they are simply a matter of common sense, whereupon they no longer think them important. So he has often tried to explain his views, yet met with relatively little success among the great and powerful; who in any case are much more interested in those who claim to possess secrets in astrology or alchemy, and who receive greater rewards for their impostures than serious philosophers get for their pains:

> I do not imagine that anything similar will happen in the place where you are. But my lack of success in all the visits I have made for the last twenty years makes me fear that on this one I shall simply find myself waylaid by highwaymen who will rob me, or involved in a shipwreck which will cost me my life. Nevertheless this will not deter me, if you believe that this incomparable Queen still desires to examine my views, and that she can find the time to do so. If that is so, then I shall be delighted to be so fortunate as to be able to serve her. But if it is not so, and she merely had some curiosity about my views which has now passed, then I beg and urge you to arrange it so that, without displeasing her, I may be excused from making this voyage.[9]

It has become a legend that Christina, not one to brook overmuch hesitance, stopped trying to persuade Descartes and simply sent an admiral in a ship with a force of marines to get him. It is true that an Admiral Fleming of the Swedish Navy was dispatched to the Netherlands at this time, to collect a library of 20,000 volumes that the Queen had lately bought; and the marines were there to carry them aboard ship. The idea of collecting Descartes on the way made obvious sense, and accordingly Admiral Fleming presented himself at the philosopher's home and requested his company to Stockholm. In the pace of life as then lived there was time for Descartes to write a startled letter to Chanut to ask who Fleming was and if this was all above board. In the event Descartes did not accompany the admiral and the books, but put his affairs in order in the Netherlands, and at the beginning of September began the six-week journey by land and sea to the Swedish capital.

In one respect Descartes had been wrong to think that Christina might not be eager to meet him. She was; she prepared for the meeting by reviewing what she had read of his work, and reported that she felt excitement at being in the company of so great and renowned a thinker. She requested his company the very day after his arrival, which was some time before he could compose himself and get his bearings. When he appeared – a little ageing man with a wig violently curled for the occasion – he was a visual disappointment. Her first reaction was to decide that he must be given the appearance and aura of greatness that befitted him – a title of nobility, an estate, a pension, and an entourage. It would not do for him to reside with the French ambassador indefinitely.

All this was very gratifying to Descartes, who began by thinking that he had landed on his feet after all. But two things quickly became apparent. The first was that in the enthusiasm of this first meeting with Christina he had made the deep mistake of speaking to her about her cousin Princess Elizabeth, asking Christina to help her; for Christina had a jealous temperament, and she had never liked the sound of the much more beautiful and perhaps cleverer cousin who had been the correspondent of Descartes for longer than she herself had been. And secondly – and worse, from Descartes' own point of view – while he was in the very process of making his laborious way from the Netherlands to Sweden, Christina's ardour for philosophy had cooled and been replaced by a passion for ancient Greek. Descartes had never thought the classics much use – indeed he thought they were a waste of time; their science was antiquated and false, their morals predated Christianity, and too many people quoted them in place of thinking things afresh for themselves.

But Christina waved Descartes' objections aside, and instead thought about how to occupy his time. Would he like to travel around Sweden a little, for six weeks or so, to get to know the country? she asked. He declined; he had no intention of travelling anywhere, having just made an unpleasant journey over land and sea to get there, and anyway winter was approaching and the autumn days were swiftly darkening.

Christina, to Descartes' infinite dismay, had another idea. To celebrate the peace of Westphalia a spectacular new ballet was to be performed in her brand new theatre. Would Descartes take part? Would he write the music? Would he at least write the libretto? In fact, she insisted that he write the libretto, and although he had vigorously rejected the suggestion that he perform or compose music, he had to succumb on the libretto. At least it was to a brief: the subject was the Birth of Peace – the ink was still dry on the famous (or infamous) Treaty signed at Westphalia, and the whole of Europe was in a state of exhausted rejoicing. As with all such compositions, however, the ballet had to span the range from epic to comic. Descartes, who had seen something of war, and who did not think celebrations of the ending of war were a fit subject of comedy, substituted maimed soldiers and indigent refugees for the usual band of comic wags. Conscious that the work was rubbish, he tried to destroy the manuscript; but Chanut misguidedly preserved it. Worse, the audience liked it, and demanded that Descartes write another theatrical piece, this time a straightforward play with a love interest involving a princess, a tyrant, a lover, an escape in rustic dress, and some other standard tropes.

Descartes, to whom it was clear that he had made a terrible mistake in coming to Sweden, set to work on this second commission with the profoundest reluctance, but was rescued from the task by another and more fitting scheme – to which the Queen had perhaps been persuaded by Chanut, who was privy to Descartes' groans. This was to draw up statutes for a Swedish Academy on the lines of the Academie Française founded by Cardinal Richelieu.

This was more congenial work, and Descartes – his hopes somewhat reviving – set about it with assiduity. He laid down an interesting rule in the second article of the statutes, which was that only natural-born Swedes could be members of the new Academy. Doubtless this was an insurance against his being kept by the Queen in Sweden indefinitely; he was of course already thinking of returning to the Netherlands. Predictably enough, the community of Swedish savants was jealous that the task had been put into Descartes' hands; they murmured and complained, and when they saw what he had produced they disagreed among themselves and with him about its merits. This was familiar terrain for Descartes; echoes of the controversies he had borne with in the Netherlands came loudly back to haunt him. Wearied, he told Chanut that he wanted to go home straight away. 'I am out of my element here,' he wrote to a correspondent; 'and I desire only tranquillity and repose, which are goods that the most powerful kings on earth cannot give to those who cannot obtain it for themselves.'

Doubtless Chanut once again had a quiet word with Christina, who at last told Descartes that she would begin the regular study of his philosophy with him. But she did it with a surprising twist. She had been told much about Descartes by

Chanut, and knew his habits; which meant that she knew he liked to spend his mornings in bed, reading, thinking and writing, rising only at midday. Despite this – more likely, because of this – she required that he meet her at five o'clock in the morning for her lessons. Moreover, the lessons were due to begin in January, the coldest and darkest month. What effect this intelligence had on Descartes is scarcely imaginable; nevertheless he obeyed.

Before going to Sweden Descartes had pondered on the weather there, but had taken comfort from the thought that people in very cold countries well know how to insure themselves against its worst effects. He did not like cold himself; from his earliest experience in the 'stove-heated room' where he had his first philosophical stirrings, to his habitual mornings in bed, he always carefully kept himself warm. But Christina was a hardy soul, brought up to the horse and the hunting field as well as the schoolroom, and her library at five in the morning was not heated at all. Descartes had to stand during their sessions, and he had to stand bareheaded. He was already very chilled by the time he reached the library each morning, because to get into the palace in the early hours he had to leave his coach and cross a little bridge giving access to a side entrance; and as he did so the freezing wind blew up under his cloak. 'I think,' he commented, 'that in winter here, men's thoughts freeze like the water.'

The unaccustomed hours, the bitter cold, the wretchedness of the situation, quickly took their toll. Within a couple of weeks Descartes began to feel ill. Chanut had already succumbed to fever and bronchitis, taking to his bed on 15 January. Descartes did not trust the Queen's doctors – all of them foreigners – not least because one of them, a Dutch physician called Weulles, had sided with Descartes' opponents in the Utrecht quarrels of a few years before. In any case Descartes had his own medications and nostrums to rely on. Accordingly, he nursed Chanut in the Embassy, and as his own symptoms developed he nursed himself too. Among the nostrums he used was liquid tobacco taken in warmed wine, the effect of which was supposed to be expectorant, that is, promoting the loosening and expelling of phlegm filling the lungs.

It is a sad irony that one of the last letters Descartes wrote – to a French diplomatic acquaintance then in Hamburg, who had written asking him to speak to Queen Christina about some matter – was penned on the very day, 15 January, that Chanut took to his bed with the illness that Descartes was to catch. 'Since I last had the pleasure of writing to you,' Descartes says, 'I have seen the Queen only four or five times, always in the morning in her library, in the company of Monsieur Freinshemius. So I have had no opportunity to speak about any matter that concerns you . . . I swear to you that my desire to return to my solitude grows stronger with each passing day, and indeed I do not know whether I can wait here until you return. It is not that I do not still fervently wish to serve the Queen, or that she does not show me as much goodwill as I may reasonably hope for. But I am not in my element here.'[10]

Chanut got better; at the end of January, still a little weak, he was able to leave his bed. Descartes, on the other hand, was growing worse. By the beginning of February he was definitely in trouble. On the first day of that month he personally handed a fair copy of his proposed statutes for the Swedish Academy to Christina, and later in the day went to say his confession to the chaplain of the French embassy, Father Viogue. This was in preparation for the Candlemas celebration scheduled for the next day, when the embassy staff were to hear Mass together. Although he had grown severely feverish and was having trouble breathing, Descartes attended the Mass on that day, and took Communion. His illness was noted with concern by the embassy staff, who persuaded him to go to bed. At first he refused to let them call a doctor, for the reasons already noted; but when on the next day – 3 February – he had grown so much worse that he at last allowed Weulles to visit him. It was clear to Weulles that Descartes had pneumonia, and he wanted to bleed him, which was the usual remedy for any feverish illness; but Descartes resisted, feebly crying out, 'Gentlemen! Spare this French blood!' But when he had grown too weak to resist he was bled several times, of course growing weaker as a result. He drifted in and out of febrile sleep for several days, his chest so congested with phlegm that he could scarcely breathe. His servant, Henry Schluter, kept feeding him biscuits and soup, because he knew that Descartes believed firmly in the importance of maintaining the digestive functions, and that a complete fast was to be avoided at all costs. Schluter was also able to keep the leeches away. On 8 February Descartes seemed to rally, and on the ninth was even able to have a conversation with Chanut about edifying matters of morality and providence. The next day he felt even better, so that – convinced his improvement had begun – he was confident that he would recover. He went so far as to allow himself the luxury of visitors. When they had gone he asked Schluter to help him get up so that he could sit in an armchair. In the process he collapsed in a dead faint, and when he came round whispered faintly, 'My dear Schluter, this blow means I am leaving for good!' Alarmed, Schluter called Chanut, who came hurrying in with his wife. Descartes' sister years later reported that at this juncture he dictated a short farewell letter to his brothers, asking them to maintain the annual pension he paid his old nurse. Whether or not such a letter was dictated at that moment of crisis, it is certain that by the time the priest arrived to administer the last rites Descartes was no longer able to speak. Instead he showed, by moving his eyes in response to the priest's questions, that he accepted the rites and submitted himself to the will of God.

The rites were duly administered, Chanut and his wife witnessing them at the bedside. At four o'clock the following morning, 11 February 1650, Descartes died. He was six weeks short of his fifty-fourth birthday.[11]

When his last breath left him in the small hours of that bitterly cold northern February morning, Descartes was far from the warm sunlit vineyards of Poitou where he had passed his childhood, far from the tumultuous scenes of a deeply divided Europe where he had played a mysterious part in the early years of a great war, far from the neat and comfortable Dutch life – think of the interior scenes being painted by Vermeer even as Descartes lay dying – where he had lived, under enormous skies, for two decades. His work had been finished for some time, and he had turned his attention to seeking preferment and reward, which – and this is how irony always loves to arrange things, it seems – came with fatality concealed in its cloak: for here he was, at a royal court, promised a title and a pension, a courtier to a queen who had invited him and who was capable of understanding him, yet dying far from everything that was home and friendship, in a cold strange land. It was an unhappy ending.

Scarcely anything could better summarise the bathos of Descartes' end than what then happened. Shocked by Descartes' death, and plagued with guilt, Christina decided that he must be given a state funeral, and interment in a marble tomb in the temple of Riddenholm, among Sweden's kings. His monument was to be incised with statements in praise of his thought by other great savants of the day. But all this would take time to arrange, so, as a temporary measure, on the day after his death Descartes' corpse was buried in the part of the public cemetery reserved for the 'unbaptised' – this on account of his Catholicism – and a wooden mock-up of a tombstone bearing his name and dates was erected above it. Within weeks Christina had forgotten her grand plans for a marble tomb at the side of her ancestors, and in the cold northern rain the wooden planks of the jerry-built monument began to rot quietly away.

Rumours immediately rose about the circumstances of Descartes' death. It was alleged that he had been poisoned by jealous rivals at Christina's court, or by people determined to stop him and Chanut from seducing Christina into Catholicism, as he was even then suspected of doing. Others at the Court had received death threats in connection with political intrigues or rivalries, so the idea is not wholly baseless. Still, the symptoms and circumstances of the illnesses suffered by Chanut and Descartes, and those attendant on the latter's death, do not support this hypothesis. His manservant Schluter wrote an account of his illness and death the day after he died, and what he says shows clearly that what brought about Descartes' demise was a fever with a congestion of the lungs.[12]

Even more fanciful stories were told, including one which claimed that Descartes had not died in Stockholm, but had gone to Lapland to be inducted in shamanic rites of drumbeating, and had caught pneumonia while doing so. Yet others had it that he indeed went to Lapland but did not die – not until much later, anyway, instead living in the northern wastes for years and even writing further letters to Princess Elizabeth and Queen Christina. Great men attract legend; and legends are more readily believed by the credulous than are plain facts and ordinary probabilities.

Descartes had an effect on Christina, however. He and Chanut had shown her, by their example, that Catholics were not monsters, as Lutherans were taught to believe. Buckley suggests that Descartes encouraged Christina to use the light of reason to examine the claims of religion, confident that Catholicism would recommend itself by this means.[13] In her journey to the Roman version of the faith, Christina had secretly solicited the help of the Jesuits, and in this too Descartes might have been an influence, although her first known contact with the Order did not occur until the spring of 1651.[14]

It is morally certain that Descartes had some part, even if small, in Christina's Catholic adventure. It is hard to believe that she had entertained a leading thinker who was also a Catholic in her palace for five months without once having had a conversation, or formed a thought, asked a question, or been given a hint, on a subject that was so pressing for her.

Spoken words leave a record only if there is an attentive ear to capture them and write them down: *verba volant, scripta manent*; but spoken words can also leave a legacy in action, and it just cannot be regarded as an irrelevant fact that Descartes was Christina's court philosopher for a time, even though it was a very short time, during the prelude to her abdication and conversion to Catholicism.

Descartes' small body lay in the cold Swedish ground for seventeen years. But it was not destined to remain under its rotten planks forever.[15] In 1667 it was exhumed and transported to France. The then French ambassador to the Swedish Court was allowed to amputate the forefinger of Descartes' right hand, and the rest of the body was placed in a copper coffin, made of metal from Sweden's own copper mines in the country's far north. The corpse had a number of different burial places before finally coming to rest in the church of St-Germain des Près, where it now lies – without its head, for the skull was taken from it at the original exhumation in Sweden and another put in its place. The skull was then sold and resold to various interested parties over time. The Musée de l'Homme in the Palais de Chaillot now claims to have it.[16] As if reinforcing the point about Descartes' missing head, the bust that stands above his tomb in the side chapel of Saint-Benoit in St-Germain des Près is that of Jean Mabillon, monk, historian and palaeographer who, with Bernard de Mont-fauçon, patristic scholar and also a palaeographer, lies alongside Descartes in the vault beneath the chapel.

★   ★   ★

That is the story of Descartes' life, work and death. His true monument is the modern world, of which he is one of the founders. Every philosophy student reads him, and his is a household name. That is fame. Fame is acquired in many ways, not all of them involving merit; Descartes' fame rests on great merit, and is unlikely ever to fade so long as people read history and think about philosophy, and contemplate the lifetimes of those who made a difference to both.

Appendix I

A Note on Descartes' Philosophy

Descartes is studied in universities today for his philosophical (not his scientific) views, where 'philosophy' has its present meaning as the collective label for metaphysics, epistemology (theory of knowledge), and ethics – and their various spin-offs. It is a sometimes confusing fact that in Descartes' day 'philosophy' meant what is now called natural science, and the term 'metaphysics' was used to denote what we now mean by 'philosophy'. This is why Descartes entitled his textbook of science *The Principles of Philosophy*. But here in this Appendix, as in the main body of the foregoing text, I use the word 'philosophy' in its present-day sense to mean philosophy, not science.

Descartes' philosophy focuses upon a central question in epistemology, and three related central topics in metaphysics. The epistemological question is: 'What can I know with certainty?' The related metaphysical topics are: the fundamental constitution of the universe, the relation between its basic constituents, and the question whether it includes a deity (and moreover, of a specific kind). As so often in philosophy,

Descartes' answer to the central epistemological question stands in a defining relationship to the position he takes regarding the three related metaphysical topics. The answer to the epistemological question is: I can know with certainty that I exist, 'I' being a mind or thinking thing. From there Descartes proceeds to argue, next, that it can be proved that there is a God, and moreover a good one; that error is the result of our own fallibility and pride; and that from all these considerations, responsible use of our cognitive powers will get us to truth. Along the way we are left with the difficult question of how mind and body interact but, since there is a good God, the fact that mind and body obviously do indeed interact can be left to the larger divine intellect to understand.

These central commitments of Descartes' philosophy are mentioned in due place in earlier chapters, and both they and the large debate that has come to surround them can be left to the many books and articles that the reader could consult to take matters further (see the Select Bibliography). But there are three interesting points to be made about Descartes' philosophy, one about its distinctive and famous starting point, the other two about Descartes' method of setting out his views, which might be useful to anyone proposing to embark on a more detailed study of his thought.

First, the idea behind the thesis for which Descartes is known even among those who know nothing else about him, namely, 'I think therefore I am', is not original to him. The idea, in most explicit form, is that one cannot doubt one's own existence, which provides Descartes with what he was looking for, namely, something that one knows with absolute certainty. When St Augustine wrote in the early fifth century AD that we can doubt everything except the soul's doubting ('On Free

Will' II 3:7) he was even then not inventing a new idea, and presumably Jean de Silhon, who published his *The Two Truths* in 1626 containing the remark 'it is not possible that a man who has the ability, which many share, to look within himself and judge *that he exists*, can be deceived in this judgement, and *not exist*', must have known St Augustine's remark or – independently of that – the idea itself in the philosophical tradition.

Descartes certainly knew Silhon's work, which predates his own version of the 'I cannot doubt my own existence' by between five and ten years, for he spoke approvingly of it, though he does not cite it. This is a little surprising given that Descartes owes even more than this to Silhon; for in the passage in which Silhon says that one cannot doubt one's own existence, he proceeds also to claim that God's existence can be proved from a knowledge of one's own existence – a crucial step for Descartes' thesis, given that the validation of one's responsibly acquired beliefs depends on there being not just a God but a *good* God, whose *goodness* is the guarantee that responsible use of cognitive faculties will lead to truth; a good God would not endow us with such faculties yet lead us astray – as the 'evil demon' hypothetically does in the first *Meditation* to generate the swingeing doubt Descartes needs in order to get his project going.

Secondly, it is a striking fact about Descartes' philosophical writing that it all takes a distinctively autobiographical form. One reason for this, no doubt, is that this form came naturally to him; but – more importantly – it was particularly suitable to his aims, for it is a conversational method of exposition which allowed him to explain his points by showing how he himself had arrived at them. There is a clever angle to this, of which

Descartes was of course fully aware. It is that the reader is thereby made to take the point of view of the thinker of the thoughts in question – to become the denotatum of the first person pronoun 'I' – and therefore to feel the convincing power of those ideas from the viewpoint of how they were arrived at. This was especially significant for Descartes' views because his system is such that it requires the individual consciousness to be convinced of the truth of what it thinks *from within the privacy of its own experience*, for it starts from a consideration of the contents of its private consciousness, and therefore has to find reason to trust what (appears to be) conveyed into it, by experience and reason, from an external universe.

This starting point – the Cartesian starting point of private data, from which a route to an external world has to be underpinned by a guarantee of certainty lest it be an illusion created by perceptual or ratiocinative error, or the mischief of a malign demon bent on making us believe nothing but falsehoods – was accepted by all Western philosophy until Dewey, Heidegger and Wittgenstein in the twentieth century, and was the source of endless difficulty, as was the dualistic commitment (the mind–body division) of Descartes' metaphysics. For although Descartes laboured, most notably in his *Meditations on First Philosophy*, to provide a guarantee for the route from private experience to public world, few if any of his successors could accept what he offered as guarantee, which was: the goodness of a God. (Two large assumptions have to be accepted here: first, that there is a God; and secondly, that it is good.) So Descartes had bequeathed his successors an intractable problem to which no response seemed plausible, except to the individual proposers of the various solutions that were offered in

280

epistemology: by John Locke and Bishop Berkeley, by Bertrand Russell and A. J. Ayer, and by others in between and since.

Thirdly, the reason why Descartes is such a repetitive writer – his three main works, the *Method*, the *Meditations*, and the *Principles*, all iterate the same few basic philosophical claims – is that he was especially anxious to show that his scientific views – Copernican, materialist and mechanistic as they are – do not controvert the fundamentals of the Christian faith, but are consistent with it. It happens that his endeavour was one of the helps towards freeing science from the proscribing inter-ference of religion, even though in his own day, and for a time afterwards, his desire to be believed on this score went unsatisfied by the people he most wished to convince: namely, the church authorities and the Jesuits. As he was keen to point out repeatedly, his metaphysics (his philosophy) was essential as a basis for his science – not in the sense that the latter followed from it, but because the science was licensed by the metaphysics in orthodox terms. His philosophy was thus a preface to his science; it is an irony, though only a minor one after all, that what is left of Descartes in the world of thought is that preface alone, for his science was very soon superseded by Newton and all that has followed from Newton's work.

Among the most discussed aspects of Descartes' thought are the sceptical arguments he uses in applying his method of doubt, his insistence on the essential difference between mind and matter, and his reliance on the goodness of a deity to serve as a guarantee of our enquiries. Some comments are called for on each of these, given their centrality to Descartes' philo-sophical enterprise.

Descartes' 'method of doubt' involves setting aside any belief or knowledge which admits of the least possible doubt, however improbable or absurd that doubt might be, to see what if anything is left behind. If anything is left behind, it will be so precisely because it is invulnerable to doubt: it is certain. Since Descartes' aim in the *Meditations* is to discover what can be known with certainty, the method of doubt is crucial, for it is the route to his goal. Trying to take each of our beliefs or knowledge claims and individually subjecting it to scrutiny would be an impossibly long task, so Descartes needed a completely general means of setting aside the whole corpus of dubitable beliefs, however unlikely their alleged dubitability. This he sought to achieve by employing sceptical arguments.

It is important to note that Descartes' use of sceptical arguments does not make him a sceptic. Far from it; he used them merely as an heuristic device to show that we indeed have knowledge. He is therefore a 'methodological sceptic' rather than a 'problematic sceptic', by the latter term meaning someone who thinks that sceptical problems are serious and pose a genuine threat to our ambition to acquire knowledge. It happens that many philosophers since Descartes' time have felt that he did not provide an adequate answer to the sceptical doubts he raised, and that therefore scepticism really is a problem. Descartes himself emphatically did not think so.

The sceptical considerations Descartes used are mentioned briefly in the main text, but merit iteration here. The first of them is a reminder that our senses sometimes lead us astray; perceptual misjudgements, illusions, and hallucinations can and occasionally do give us false beliefs. This might prompt us not to place reliance on what we think we know by means of sense-experience, or at the very least to be cautious in reposing confidence in it as a source of truth. But even so, says Descartes, there would be many things I believe on the basis of my current experience – such as, for example, that I have hands and that I am holding a piece of paper in them, that I am sitting in an armchair in front of a fire, and the like, to doubt which would seem to be madness, even given the senses' frequent unreliability.

Would it really be mad to doubt such things? No, says Descartes – and he here brings his second argument into play – for I sometimes dream when I sleep, and if I am now dreaming that I am sitting in front of a fire holding a piece of paper, my belief that I am so doing is false. To be able to be certain that I am sitting thus, I would have to be able to exclude the possibility that I am merely dreaming that I am sitting thus. How is that to be done? It seems very hard, if not impossible, to do it.

But even if one were asleep and dreaming, he continues, one could know that, for example, one plus one equals two. Indeed there are many such beliefs that could be known to be true even in a dream. So Descartes introduces a much more swingeing consideration: suppose that instead of there being a good God who wishes us to know the truth, there is by contrast an evil demon whose whole purpose is to deceive us in all things, even about 'one plus one equals two' and all such other apparently indubitable truths. If there were such a being, one would have a completely general reason for doubting everything that can be doubted. And now we can ask: suppose that there is such a being; is there any belief that I nevertheless cannot doubt, even if the deceiving demon makes every belief I have false, if it is possible for it to be false? And as we know, the answer is yes, there is an indubitable belief: it is that I exist.

Some critics of this procedure have argued that the sceptical arguments employed by Descartes do not work. They criticise the dreaming and evil demon argument on a variety of grounds – for respective examples, that there are indeed criteria that enable us to distinguish between dreaming and waking states; and that the evil demon hypothesis is far less plausible than most of the beliefs (such as that one plus one equals two) it is supposed to call into question. But such attempts to show that Descartes' method of doubt cannot get off the ground are misplaced. The sceptical arguments employed in the method of doubt do not themselves have to be plausible or sustainable. They may indeed be far less plausible than what they impugn; but that does not matter. They are simply a device, an heuristic, something that helps one to see how it is that when one says 'I exist' it cannot but be true. Given that in any case the aim of the *Meditations* is to demonstrate what can be known with certainty, almost any heuristic that made it possible to expose certainties would do equally as well.

Criticisms of the sceptical arguments Descartes uses are more pertinent if those arguments are employed as part of a 'problematic' sceptical attack on the possibility of knowledge or reliable belief. If a sceptical argument is less plausible than what it is used seriously to call into question, that is a *prima facie* reason for suspecting it. We can in this case legitimately ask whether sense-perception is as unreliable as the argument alleges; whether the idea of a deceiving demon is a coherent one; whether the concept of error would make sense if there were never anything to contrast it with, namely, sometimes being right or knowing the truth; whether the formulation of sceptical doubts is itself possible unless we already know something to be true, for example that responsibly employed reasoning is reliable and that we know the meaning of the words we use in framing the sceptical doubt; and so forth. But none of this applies to Descartes' argument in the *Meditations*, in which the invocation of sceptical considerations is merely a device, and does not have to survive scrutiny of this kind to do the work required of it.

The second great talking point in Descartes' philosophy, the mind–body problem, is the source of an immense debate in philosophy and more latterly also in psychology and the neurosciences. It is one of the most important questions still facing human enquiry. Put at its simplest, it asks: what is mind, and what is the relation of mind to the rest of nature? How should we best understand common-sense concepts of such mental phenomena as belief, desire, intention, emotion, reason and memory? How does the grey matter of the brain give rise to our rich and vivid experiences of colour, sound, texture, taste and smell?

Descartes gave the mind–body problem an especially sharp focus by arguing that everything that exists in the world falls under the heading either of material substance or mental substance, where 'substance' is a technical term denoting the most basic kind of existing stuff. He defined the essence of matter as *extension* (that is, occupancy of space), and the essence of mind as *thought*. Matter is thus extended stuff, mind is thinking stuff. But by making matter and mind *essentially* different in this way, he raised the seemingly insuperable problem of how they interact. How does a bodily event like pricking oneself result in the mental event of feeling pain? How does the mental event of thinking 'it's time to get up' cause the bodily event of rising from bed?

Descartes himself did not have an answer, and his successors had to resort to heroic solutions to the problem his theory had bequeathed. Their strategy was to accept dualism but to argue that mind and matter do not in fact interact, their appearance of doing so being the result of the hidden action of God; such were the views of Malebranche and Leibniz, reported in the main text above.

A much more plausible alternative, however, is monism: namely, the view that there is only one substance. Three possibilities rise to the fore. One is that there is only matter. The second is that there is only mind. The third is that there is a neutral substance which gives rise to both mind and matter. Each of the three has had proponents, but it is the first option – the reduction or annexation of all mental phenomena to matter – which has been most influential.

One materialist approach is the 'identity theory', which asserts that mental states are literally identical with states or processes in the brain. In its earliest form, it asserted that occurrences of mental phenomena are nothing other than types of brain occurrences, but this was quickly seen to be too sweeping, for a particular mental event (for example, a mental image of the Eiffel Tower) might in my brain activate one set of cells, while in yours another.

On the basis of this theory, a number of philosophers currently maintain that, as neuroscience advances, we will be able to eliminate the old-fashioned and imprecise mental vocabulary we standardly use. Research in neurology and cognitive science have built an overwhelming case for accepting a very intimate relation between mental and neurological phenomena. Neuroscientists now have highly detailed empirical knowledge of brain function and its relation to mental activity, and are able to locate the seat of many conscious processes in precisely defined brain structures.

But these advances only serve to correlate brain activity with mental occurrences; they do not explain how the former actually produces the latter. Given the persistent difficulties in identifying that relation precisely, various strategies are proposed. One is to accept that our ways of talking about mental and physical phenomena are irreducibly different, even though they are about the same thing. Imagine, for example, how sociologists and physicists would respectively describe a football match, each focusing upon features which his particular science can address to describe the same thing.

Consciousness, on the other hand, can at first appear much easier to understand than the relation between mind and body: anyone capable of thinking is after all intimately conscious of being conscious. But consciousness is by far the most perplexing mystery facing philosophy and the neurological sciences. Some philosophers, in the tradition of Descartes, think that it is too hard for human intelligence to understand. Others even claim that there is no such thing as consciousness; we are actually zombies, just very complicated ones. In defiance of these views, enquirers have profited from powerful new investigative tools, especially brain scanning devices, to watch brains at work. One result is a great increase in knowledge of brain function and a refined understanding of the correlation between specific brain areas and specific mental capacities.

The central problem remains, however, how coloured pictures, evocative smells and sounds arise in the head as if it were an inner cinema-show. One recent theory offered by neurophysiologist Antonio Damasio is that consciousness begins as self-reflexive awareness constituting a primitive level of selfhood, a powerful but vague awareness of being 'I'. Emotional relations to an evolving self and external objects then construct a model of the world, a feeling of knowing, giving each of us the sense that we are the owner and viewer of a movie-within-the-brain.

Consciousness has arisen amongst higher mammals, according to these theories, because of its survival advantage – an organism's appropriate use of energy and protection from harm are much enhanced when it is able to place itself in a map of the environment and make plans about the best courses of action in it. Creatures which are merely biological automata, even if highly sensitive to their surroundings, would not be as adaptive as creatures that are genuinely conscious.

Debate about the mind has resulted in a widespread consensus that mind is part of nature and amenable to investigation by scientific means, but there are still fundamental mysteries about what it is and how it relates to the rest of nature. The next great leap in understanding the mind will doubtless involve a conceptual and scientific revolution of such magnitude that we cannot at present envisage it.

Descartes himself never arrived at a satisfactory way of dealing with the problem whose deep intractability he had exposed. As shown in the main text, when pressed by Princess Elizabeth of Bohemia to explain how mental and physical phenomena interact, he began by offering a profoundly implausible hypothesis in which the pineal gland somehow serves as the organ constituting the required interface, but he ended by frankly acknowledging that he had no answer.

If his statement of the problem suggests anything useful, however, it might be that in talking about mental phenomena – hopes, memories, desires, intentions, feelings, and the rest – we employ a language which is wholly different from the language of physical things, and which cannot be translated into it. The example of the physicist and the sociologist describing the football match shows what this thought implies; neither has a vocabulary apt for receiving translations from the other vocabulary; the sociological concepts have no way of accommodating concepts of force, velocity, mass, radiation, and the like – nor vice versa. To try to reduce mental talk to physical talk might similarly be like mixing up the uses of very different objects – trying to fry an egg on a pencil and to draw a picture with a frying-pan, so to speak. On this view concepts of the mental and concepts of the physical are different instruments for different purposes, and trying to explain one wholly in terms of the other is therefore misguided.

Even if this answer at some level contains a measure of truth, it still does not meet the insistent thought that since brains give rise to – produce, secrete, are responsible for, cause – thoughts and feelings, there must surely be some way of explaining the latter in terms of the former's functionings, or at the very least of explaining systematically how they are related. This remains the goal of enquiry, a project that has only grown more interesting and urgent since Descartes initiated it.

The third matter inviting comment here is Descartes' claim that if we use our intellectual faculties responsibly and carefully we can reach the truth about things, because we have a guarantee available for the efficacy of such enquiry: namely, the goodness of God. In the *Meditations* Descartes offers two arguments for the existence of a God, arguments that purport to establish the existence of a God identical with the God of traditional revealed religion, namely, an all-powerful, all-knowing and entirely good God. This is convenient for Descartes' purposes because just such a God is required for the role of epistemological guarantor, especially in virtue of being good. An all-powerful, all-knowing and entirely good God is, in short, a God of all the perfections. Indeed, possession of all the perfections is essential to one of the arguments Descartes offers for his existence; this argument says that if God is a being who possesses all the perfections, then he must necessarily exist, because failure to exist would be an imperfection. Thus God's existence follows directly and necessarily from his nature. And given that some being must be the most perfect being there is, it follows by this same reasoning that this being actually exists. So, says Descartes, God exists.

Both this argument and its companion in the *Meditations* are, as are all the arguments for the existence of a deity, spurious; readers may like to examine the literature on this subject for themselves, and to reflect on the summary of the argument just given, to see why they fail. The point of interest here, though, is Descartes' reliance on such arguments. His successors in the tradition of philosophy did not find themselves able to think as he did about this matter, and he is therefore alone in saying that we can get from the contents of our minds to a world outside our heads because our inferences (if responsibly drawn; he grants that our fallen natures can lead us into error) from the former to the latter can be relied upon courtesy of the divine goodness.

Descartes' theistic commitments were almost certainly sincere, and a commitment to the existence of a suitably equipped deity would irresistibly provide solutions to such puzzles as the problem of knowledge and the mind-body problem. And Descartes happily invokes the idea of God to deal with both. But the great difficulty here is that the concept of an omniscient and omnipotent God is over-permissive. By this I mean that if there is such a being in the universe, then anything goes: anything whatever can be explained by its presence and supposed activities, from miracles (one-off reversals of the laws of nature) to all the intractable problems of science and philosophy, simply and quickly solved by saying 'God created it', 'God knows', 'God makes it happen', 'God guarantees it', and the like. And this, in effect, means that if one believes that there is an omnipotent deity, one can therefore believe absolutely anything else, for everything else is thereby made possible.

But such epistemic promiscuity is self-defeating. Karl Popper astutely pointed out that a theory that explains everything thereby explains nothing. For example: to answer the question of how the universe came into existence by saying 'God created it' is not in fact to answer the question, but to explain one mystery by appealing to an even greater mystery – exactly like saying that the universe rests on the back of a turtle, and then ignoring the question of what the turtle rests on. (Interestingly, the claims that 'God created the universe' and 'the universe rests on the back of a turtle' are in exactly the same position from the point of view of their intelligibility, testability and likelihood; there is as much – or more accurately as little – reason to believe one claim as the other. What differentiates them is merely tradition, though both have been believed in the past.) So Descartes' reliance on appeals to the existence of a deity of suitable character (where would his argument be if there were a God, but a wicked one, or even just an unpredictable one of unreliable temper, such as the deity portrayed in the Old Testament?) fails to provide the guarantee he needs, and is one main reason for the ultimate failure of his system.

One thing that cannot be denied is the pedagogical value of Descartes' philosophy. The ideas it contains are rich and full

of suggestion, but they are presented with a clarity and simplicity which, although somewhat misleading given the inner
complexity of the ideas involved, at least makes his writings
accessible. He is not alone among important philosophers in
that his works can be placed into the hands of beginners, as
they typically are; many university courses in philosophy begin
with a study of his *Meditations*, which raises a whole raft of
the most central problems in philosophy – the problem of
knowledge, fundamental metaphysical ideas of existence and
the nature of reality, the question of deity, the nature of mind
and its place in the world, and – by implication and example –
the way to conduct a philosophical enquiry into the basic
principles of things (not for nothing does the *Meditations* have
the full title, *Meditations on First Philosophy* – meaning, the
starting point of enquiry).

In the 'Letter from the Author' which begins his *Principles of
Philosophy*, Descartes advises us to read the book 'rapidly in its
entirety, like a Novel, without the reader forcing his attention
too much or stopping at the difficulties which he may
encounter in it. And after that, if the reader judges that these
matters merit examination, and is curious to know their causes,
he can read the book a second time . . .' He did not deny that
aspects of the philosophical and scientific ideas he discussed
were difficult, but he believed that they are the common
possession of all who would make the effort to enquire into
them, and he further believed that his way of discussing them –
a proceeding informed by his ideas about 'method' – would
make it possible for anyone who made that effort to grasp them
fully. In this he was perhaps too sanguine; but the advantage is
the pedagogical one mentioned.

As a result, Descartes has been read and studied very widely in schools and universities around the world, and has been the sustenance on which generations of scholars and intellectuals have been weaned. Like the thinker whose honorific suggested his own, Thales the 'Father of Philosophy' (Descartes' informal honorific, recall, is 'Father of Modern Philosophy'), Descartes' importance resides as much in the fact that he philosophised in a certain way as in the content of his thought. He did not rely on scholastic jargon and style, but philosophised from thought rather than authority. To too great an extent contemporary philosophy has slipped back into the bad old way of relying on authority, quoting and commenting on contemporary masters rather than addressing problems directly – a situation rather too like 'normal science' in Thomas Kuhn's sense, as adapted to the sphere of professional academic philosophy. So Descartes' example of someone tackling problems head on, thinking afresh, escaping the oppressive weight of tradition and thick tomes, is a good one to set before students.

Appendix II

Biographies of Philosophers and Descartes' Biography

Does a biographer ever need an excuse to write the biography of a person who made a difference to history? Surely not. Does a biographer need to explain his or her conception of what biography is, and what it is for? Surely yes: for in doing so the biographer gives readers an insight into the point of view, the methodology, and the aim of the book in their hands, given that the book – as an attempt to tell the story of a life in its times, with no act of story-telling ever being neutral – carries the impress of the teller's take on things.

When the subject of the biography is, like Descartes, a person who lived too long ago for many of the informative incidentals of life to have survived, it matters all the more to say something about these questions of approach. Here then is this author's view.

Biography is a popular genre, and for good reason. It is a form of history, illuminating the general via the particular, and making the past, even the recent past, additionally vivid by casting it in a personal light. Moreover, it satisfies a healthy form of voyeurism, in the form of curiosity about lives made notable by achievement or fate, giving us insights into how they became so and thereby providing us with direct or indirect materials for understanding our own lives – and sometimes for changing them in the light of what we learn in the process.

The popularity of biography has increased further since biographers allowed themselves frankness about their subjects' intimacies. That is a good thing: life unfolds more behind closed curtains than on public platforms, so to achieve a living sense of human history biographers have to draw those curtains aside. What they satisfy in readers by doing so is something more exigent than mere prurience or curiosity: it is the need to be more richly informed about the one thing we all have to do all the time – live from day to day with our dreams and failures, sometimes with the danger of success, but always with other people and the unforgiving passage of time.

The natural subjects of biographies are people whose lives are characterised by, for example, glamour in society, the excitement of events on battlefields or unexplored frontiers, the tenure of national or international power, or the shadows of mystery – espionage, say, or murder. It comes as a surprise therefore to find that in recent years there has been an explosion in the number of biographies of philosophers; people who, on the whole, seem to live unglamorous lives of retirement and reflection, whose victories were not won with flashing swords among enemies, or magnificent oratory on legislature floors, but in the silence of the mind. Quite a few thinkers have been hanged or burned for their views, with the added interest of a little torture thrown in beforehand, but this seems to be thin pickings as the stuff of a good read, given that what briefly involved them in such activity was nothing more than long years of study, followed by moving a scratchy pen across parchment – reading about which, one would think, is about as gripping as watching grass grow. What therefore explains the burgeoning interest in philosophical biographies?

Given that publishing houses are not charitable institutions, and that a biography of Spinoza or Wittgenstein is required to bring in its profit, it must mean that, for a large enough number of people, a story of the growth and flowering of ideas is as interesting as a cavalry charge into the cannon's mouth. And so it can prove. One main reason can be inferred from what George Bernard Shaw said of his own life: 'Now I have had no heroic adventures. Things have not happened to me; on the contrary it is I who have happened to them; and all my happenings have taken the form of books. Read them, and you have my whole story; the rest is only breakfast, lunch and dinner.'

The idea that things do not happen to philosophers as much as philosophers happen to things is captured in Isaiah Berlin's remark that the philosopher sitting in his study today can change the history of the world fifty years hence. He had in mind the likes of John Locke, whose writings were quoted verbatim and at length in the documents of the American and French revolutions, and Karl Marx, whose thought was bent to the use of revolutionaries putatively as idealistic but far less enlightened. But he could equally have cited any of the figures whose ideas altered the complexion of thought in their own time or afterwards – particularly among them Descartes – because ideas are the fuel of the machines of history, and in the form of ideologies, beliefs, sciences, political and social theories, commitments and ideals, they are the human factor (droughts and plagues have their part too) that lie behind the events that drive historical change. This remains true even when the proximate human causes of historical movement seem to be the usual pairing of cupidity and stupidity – because to be greedy for something is to believe it desirable, and to fail to understand something is in effect to be in competition with the ungrasped idea: and so the claim holds.

But this is not all that is of interest in a philosopher's life. With exceptions, most philosophers were not hermetically sealed from their times, which means that they were influenced by them, reacted to them, knew and interacted with some or all of the other best minds in them, and observed them in ways that are peculiarly interesting because of the sharpness and depth of their vision. Moreover, in many cases they were actively engaged in them. Descartes saw military service in the Wars of Religion, and was present at the Battle of the White Mountain outside Prague; and he may, as has been suggested in the body of the text here, have played even more of a part than this, as a spy or agent. Wittgenstein was also a soldier; he served on the eastern and southern fronts in the First World War, and was imprisoned in Monte Casino at its end, carrying the manuscript of his *Tractatus Logico-Philosophicus* in his knapsack. In this Descartes and Wittgenstein followed the example of Socrates, who was a hoplite – a heavily-armed infantryman – in the Athenian army at the battle of Potidiae. Spinoza's family were refugees from religious persecution, and Locke fled the England of James II to the political sanctuary of the Netherlands, where he helped bury the doctrine of the Divine Right of Kings. Bertrand Russell went to prison for his pacifist activism in the First World War, and again half a century later for his opposition to nuclear weapons. Martin Heidegger was a Nazi, and Jean-Paul Sartre a Communist; Louis Althusser went mad and strangled his wife, Friedrich Nietzsche went mad and his sister strangled his works into a shape congenial for Nazism.

Madness, the fear of madness, genius, dedication, passion (not a few great philosophers were great philanderers too), and conflict with their times, mark many philosophical lives.

Even for more peaceably circumstanced philosophers, the externals of their lives are engaging and informative. David Hume earned his sobriquet of 'le bon David' in the salons of Paris, where his wit (in both old and new senses) was greatly appreciated; and his failure to secure a Chair at the University of Edinburgh remains a reproach to that city. Immanuel Kant – the one philosopher of modern times to share the stature of Plato or Aristotle – scarcely stirred from his home city of Konigsberg in East Prussia; but given that he was an atheist in a city wracked by religious strife, in which the Pietist community from which he sprang played a leading part, there is supreme interest in the delicate and risky path he followed by remaining there. In part it explains why, in a way reminiscent of Hume whom he admired, he succeeded in getting a secure academic post only in middle age. (Kant's theological scepticism – despite his official views about the need for concepts of God, freedom of the will, and immortality of the soul, to give general point to morality – is nicely discussed in the biography by Manfred Kuehn.)

It has to be acknowledged that most philosophical biographies, with honourable exceptions to be mentioned shortly, suffer one of a pair of shortcomings. Either they are reasonably well written, because written by professional biographers, but fail to give an adequate account of their subjects' philosophical achievements; or they succeed in doing the latter because written by philosophers, but fail to be well written, because their authors' literary stock-in-trade is the academic book or paper – scarcely a thing of beauty in most hands, now that the academy has been professionalised into a slough of recondite jargons and impenetrabilities.

Examples of the former include Ernest Mossner's copious 1954 life of Hume, still the standard work, and yet unsatisfying as an account of Hume's thought, especially given that philosophical understanding of Hume was impoverished before Mossner set to work, relative to the rich resource of scholarship and debate which has flourished since. Another example is Ronald W. Clarke's 1975 biography of Russell; here the problem is that Clarke did not understand Russell's work in logic or philosophy, and had little sense of its provenance or of what it led to, and therefore of the significance of the problems Russell was addressing.

Examples now abound – it seems they multiply almost daily – of philosophers writing biographies encumbered by deficits in literary skill and the art of biography. Naming names makes invidious comparisons: but let us look at biographies nearly contemporary with the effort to which this is an appendix. One example is Terry Pinkard's life of Hegel. If one wished to get an overview of Hegel's thought – a large undertaking at best – there could be no better place to start than the helpful, accessible and well-organised account of it given by Pinkard. But the non-philosophical parts of his book do not make easy reading, and might fairly be said to do the opposite. This applies also to the otherwise excellent biography of Kant, already mentioned, by Manfred Kuehn, and although one might point a finger at restrained editing by the publishing house responsible for both, no publisher has a monopoly on philosophically sound biographies that required attention in literary respects. This matters; because no book can do its work, nor can it survive long, unless it is written well.

It is a pleasure to turn to philosophical biographies which are well written in addition to being well constructed and re-searched. By coincidence the two that spring to mind are both about Wittgenstein: Ray Monk's excellent *Ludwig Wittgenstein: The Duty of Genius* and – even more to the point – the peerless *Young Ludwig* by Brian McGuinness, the first of two projected volumes whose sequel, alas, seems destined never to appear.

Monk's biography of Wittgenstein is deservedly well known. Written with natural grace and clarity, and buoyed by Monk's admiration for his subject, it is also a useful introduction for the non-specialist to Wittgenstein's main ideas. It is better for a biography that its author feels at least a minimum of sympathy for its subject (best of all is reasonably tolerant objectivity), and Monk is an ardent Wittgenstein sympathiser. One result is that his Wittgenstein, who in reality was an egregiously unsym-pathetic character – he has variously been described as arrogant, resentful, unmannerly and pathologically egocentric, or all of these things together – comes out glossed as a tortured genius who should accordingly, in Monk's opinion, be forgiven much. Compare Monk's two-volume account of Bertrand Russell's life: Monk self-confessedly disliked Russell, and his biography of him detrimentally shows it.

By contrast, Brian McGuinness's beautifully written, deeply insightful account of the first half of Wittgenstein's life is the closest thing to a paradigm of philosophical biography in existence. It weaves life and thought seamlessly together, skilfully paints their setting and, with elegant dispassion, neither glosses nor distorts, but presents Wittgenstein as a creature of his place and time. No-one in Vienna at the beginning of the twentieth century regarded Wittgenstein as unusual or notably clever, but when he arrived in Cambridge in 1911, one of the

301

smuggest and most self-enclosed enclaves in the smuggest, most self-satisfied and complacent countries then in the world, he was a bombshell. Russell, who thought everyone he met either a fool or a genius and said so repeatedly, placed his strange-seeming little Austrian into the latter category, and Wittgenstein's reputation was made. Wittgenstein's career thereafter had much to do with resenting Russell's help – a common phenomenon. McGuinness shows where Wittgenstein's always unacknowledged ideas came from in the rich intellectual soup of German-speaking, and especially Viennese, culture of the nineteenth century – they included the repugnant Otto Weininger – and as one of the translators of the *Tractatus Logico-Philosophicus* he gives a brilliant and lucid rendition of that work's principal themes. His book is an irresistibly civilised read; the chapter on the First World War and its effects on Wittgenstein (who said of the war 'it saved my life') begins in Virgilian mode: 'Austria is now our theme, Austria and the last days of an empire and culture whose variety, whose failings, and whose charm mirrored human nature itself.'

Among the most notable contributors to the recent spate of philosophical biography is Rudiger Safranski, not an academic but a fine writer thoroughly grounded in philosophy. His intellectual biographies of Schopenhauer and Heidegger were well received, the latter not least because it gives a frank account of Heidegger's Nazism; and his more recent biography of Nietzsche followed suit. His skill lies in combining highly readable narrative with intelligent and perceptive accounts of his subject's work.

Safranski belongs to the school of thought which disdains spending too much time on a subject's sexuality, a topic hijacked by so-called 'psychobiography' which tries to analyse while describing an individual's life. In a way this is a mistake, as the case of Nietzsche shows. Joachim Kohler's *Zarathustra's Secret*, published in German a decade before it became available in English, is a study of Nietzsche's erotic life, and it proves very illuminating. Safranski ignores it – except obliquely, in a few paragraphs accepting but downplaying the significance of Kohler's thesis.

In the absence of Kohler's book this would be a fault, for as Kohler succeeds in demonstrating, it is clear that Nietzsche's masochistic homosexuality explains much that he said and suffered. Nietzsche himself pointed to sexuality as the summit of an individual's spirituality, and his concept of an ideal existence embraced Dionysian orgiastic freedom as expressed in his own day by the life of the naked, sun-kissed youths of Sicily (which Nietzsche called 'the isle of the blessed'), so lovingly photographed by Wilhelm van Gloeden. For Kohler, Nietzsche's attack on Christian morality is the product of this repressed erotic longing, and explains his ideal of the 'Superman', who overthrows life-denying inhibitions in order to live passionately and supremely.

Safranski sees the erotic in these themes too, but is more concerned with a straightforward exposition of Nietzsche's ideas. Whatever their source, these ideas are revolutionary and subversive, for they challenge the morality Nietzsche sees as based on the enslavement and weakness suffered by the Jews in exile, and which gave rise to an 'inversion' of values proclaiming that the feeble, the fearful, and those that weep and mourn, shall inherit the Kingdom. Nietzsche poured contempt on this view. Man should instead 'overcome himself', he said, by expunging the weaknesses in his nature, and aspire to live heroically and powerfully.

Nietzsche's life is a gift for the biographer, for it was undeniably an extraordinary one. A summary is instructive, as showing how little one ought to be surprised by anything in human lives that are egregious (in the non-pejorative, literal sense of this term), for it makes an instructive comparison with Descartes, who sought to remain personally orthodox even while introducing a revolution into thought. Nietzsche was a revolutionary thinker who disdained orthodoxies; and his revolution was not effected in the sphere of philosophy and science, as with Descartes, but in the psychology of an age.

Nietzsche had a start in life comparable to Descartes', in the sense at least of belonging to a class in society which ensured that he received an education commensurate with his talents. He was born in Saxony in 1844, the son of a mild-mannered pastor who died of 'softening of the brain' when Nietzsche was five years old. He was a precocious child – everyone called him 'the little pastor', an ironic label given his later views – and he easily gained entry to the distinguished Schulpforta school, and later the universities of Bonn and Leipzig. While at Leipzig he discovered Schopenhauer's thought and was for a time enthralled by it, although he later came to reject its pessimism. Even before he had completed his degree his brilliance earned him, aged just twenty-four, a professorship at the university of Basle. Soon after arriving in Basle he encountered the other great influence of his life: Wagner, first his master and ideal, and later his enemy.

Academic life did not suit Nietzsche, any more than it would have suited Descartes. His first book was regarded as so bad by the scholarly community that it was inevitable he would resign. There followed a life of solitary wandering in Switzerland and Italy, writing and thinking, publishing increasingly provocative and controversial books, until at last he produced his masterpieces, *Thus Spake Zarathustra* and *The Genealogy of Morals*. In the first, he gave a full statement of what he regarded as his greatest philosophical insight: the doctrine of 'eternal recurrence', which says that everything that happens will happen again, exactly as it happened before – and therefore one must live so that one will not mind repeating one's life endlessly.

No-one could wish to reprise Nietzsche's own life in actuality: he went irrecoverably mad ten years before his death, probably as a result of syphilis, and in the twilight of his sanity suffered as much agony as euphoria.

The lives of Wittgenstein and Nietzsche, Locke and Descartes, with their wars and wanderings, and in the first two cases their personal struggles, could not seem to be more contrasted to the externally eventless existence of the great Immanuel Kant. But Kant's biography is every bit as gripping in its own way. Moreover, the second half of Descartes' life was only marginally less removed from the centre of things than Kant's life, and it was as deliberately quiet.

It might smack of hyperbole to say that Kant is one of the greatest philosophers of all time, but it is nevertheless true. He is also, arguably, more right about many things than most philosophers succeed in being, which adds genuine importance to his greatness. He is not an easy read; his forbiddingly-entitled works – *The Critique of Pure Reason*, *The Groundwork of the Metaphysic of Morals* – some of them massive, are not the kind of thing you read in the bath or in bed. But they are extraordinary and powerful works, monuments of the mind of man, which greatly repay attentive study.

Kant did not have the advantages of a Descartes or Locke in

the matter of his birth and family circumstances. He was the
son of a harness-maker, and was brought up in poor but not
indigent circumstances. His parents were adherents of Pietism,
a form of fundamentalist Christianity which Kant himself was
too intelligent to accept. His gifts ensured that he had the best
education Konigsberg could offer, but he was not a prodigy,
and had to leave university before his Master's degree in order
to work as a tutor in various private families. After six years
he returned to Konigsberg University to satisfy the academic
requirements for becoming a 'privatdozent' or untenured
lecturer, dependent for his living on students' private fees
because only fully appointed professors received a salary. He
was thirty-one years of age when he began his academic career,
and forty-six before he finally secured a salaried position. And
it was another ten years before he produced the first of the
great works by which he is now remembered, making him
a late developer indeed – and therefore a heartening model for
all those who feel (as Saintsbury put it in speaking of Dryden)
'too gifted to find their way early in life'.

But the long years of preparation were not unproduc-
tive. Kant lectured and published much on a wide variety of
subjects, from physics to cosmology, from geography to
anthropology. In part it was a requirement of lecturers' hand-
to-mouth existence that they were jacks of all intellectual
trades in this way, but in Kant's case it was also a product of
large interests and unappeasable curiosity. This wide reading,
thinking and teaching fed into his mature work, not as its
subject-matter but as the background to the abstract reflections
they embody.

In the first of his great 'Critiques' Kant argued that the world
we experience is in part determined by our cognitive faculties,

which shape the way the world appears to us by contributing very general structural features to it – such as its spatial and temporal character, and the fact that experience is always governed by such fundamental concepts as (for example) causality. These concepts are not learned from experience, but are supplied by the mind; and they are what make experience possible.

Kant's moral philosophy builds on this basis an austere ethics of duty, in which the obligations by which we must live are identified by reason. On the great questions of metaphysics as he identified them – the existence of God, the immortality of the soul, and the freedom of the human will – Kant argued that we cannot prove any of them, but that we need to assume them to make sense of morality, so that people can be persuaded that evil-doing will be punished in a posthumous state. This view is somewhat reminiscent of Plato's contention that although religious beliefs are false they are useful as a means of controlling the unlettered.

The austerity of Kant's views and his bachelor life give a misleading impression of him. He was not a withered pedant but a sociable being who enjoyed the modest pleasures of dining out and playing billiards. Tragically, in the last years of his life Kant suffered progressive dementia, ending as a helpless child. It was almost as if the immense intellectual effort of his later years had burned away the volatile spirit of his genius; but if so, it was a wonderfully worthwhile sacrifice. By the time he died he was already famous and controversial; since then his works have become classics of philosophy along with those of Descartes, Plato and Aristotle.

The examples of Kant, Nietzsche and Althusser, with their descents into madness or dementia at the last, are untypical of the general run of philosophers, who tend to live long and enjoy an alert old age, as exemplified by Thomas Hobbes and Bertrand Russell. Hobbes sang every evening into his nineties, convinced that it cleared the lungs. Russell, by contrast, smoked a pipe into his nineties, convinced of nothing but the folly of mankind.

Descartes is among the more surprising of his kind in that, during the last years of his life, he turned his attention to seeking worldly honours, attracted by the glamour of the Court and the prospect of material advancement. In this endeavour he was cut short by the unlucky accident of pneumonia; but he might well have ended his days as a minor nobleman on a royal pension, or even on an estate – not in Sweden, given the weather problem and the fact that Queen Christina abdicated, not long after his death, to become a Catholic – but in his beloved Netherlands, or even perhaps France.

In this respect Descartes was merely human, though it has to be said that not many philosophers have much cared for what the world has been able to give. But in the essential thing – the fact that he made a major contribution to the progress of thought – Descartes' stature is unquestionable, and with it his place in history. To show that he was also a man of his time, and played a part in it, is to do no more than to complete the picture as it should be completed. That has been the intention here.

Notes

Introduction

1. *Les oeuvres de Jean-Baptiste Van Helmont*, French trans. Jean Le Conte (Lyon, 1671), Part I, ch. XVI, 'On the Necessity of Leavens in Transformations', pp. 103–109.

2. Quoted in Roger Ariew (1999), *Descartes Among the Scholastics*, pp. 13–14 and here adapted. The concepts in play are all Aristotelian. The four causes are given in Aristotle's *Physics*, Book II chs. 3–4 as material, formal, efficient, and final. For example: the material cause of a table is the wood and nails from which it is made; its formal cause is its design; its efficient cause is the labour of the carpenter; and its final cause is the aim or purpose for which it is made, e.g. to serve as a dinner table. The four elements are given by Aristotle in *De Caelo*, Books III and IV, and are earth, water, fire, and air. The first two have a natural tendency to move downward towards the centre of the earth (which is the centre of the universe), the latter two a natural upward–moving tendency, towards the periphery of the region of the universe below the sphere of the moon. Each is an appropriate mixture of the qualities hot and cold, dry and wet.

309

So, fire is hot and dry, air is hot and wet, water is cold and wet, earth is cold and dry. The 'three principles of natural things' are matter, form, and privation (Aristotle, *Physics*, Book I). Note that the full details of Borgia's memorandum by these rules outlaw the tenets of other philosophical schools, notably the Stoics and atomists, and also engage in the internecine quarrel between certain Augustinian and Franciscan doctrines, e.g. about the nature of man and the soul, thus taking sides in Scholastic disputes over 'substantial forms' and related matters.

3. As its first discoverer Willebrord Snell now has the distinction of having the law of refraction named after him (Snell's Law).

4. Hazlitt, W., 'Locke A Great Plagiarist', *Collected Works* (ed. P. P. Howe).

5. Elizabeth Haldane's 1905 biography follows Baillet uncritically, but is good on the historical context. A rash of minor French biographies came later: Samuel Silvestre de Sacy's *Descartes par lui-même* (1956) has some good illustrations; P. Frederix in *M. R. Descartes en son temps* (1959) portrays the philosopher as a bumptious and mistaken clever-clogs; while in *Descartes, c'est la France* (1987) A. Glucksman sets out to rescue the French mind from being malignly over-branded as 'Cartesian'. Even as a French cultural hero Descartes is not immune to attacks by Frenchmen. Neither Frederix nor Glucksman go the lengths of Dimitri Davidenko's *Descartes le Scandaleux* (1988), in which the philosopher is portrayed as a drunken whoring gambler ('I drink therefore I am' indeed) who infested the margins of the intellectual world of his day to (says Davidenko) little real effect.

A more balanced and relaxed survey of Descartes' life, though a speculative one, was offered by Jack R. Vrooman in 1970. It is much dependent on the earlier lives and does not seek to offer an original perspective. Genevieve Rodis-Lewis produced her *Descartes, Biographie* in 1995, translated into English as *Descartes:*

His Life and Thought in 1998. This work, whose detail, density and structural complexity make it a challenging read, not I am afraid helped by a poor English translation, makes sense only to those who already know all details of Descartes' story. In 2002 appeared the eccentric, lively, sometimes wildly wrong and sometimes pungently perceptive biography by Richard Watson, *Cogito Ergo Sum: The Life of René Descartes*. Anyone who tells you that Ovid and Seneca are Greek poets (as Watson does on his page 72) sets the alarm bells ringing permanently, and he is anyway so cavalier and opinionated that his account is best treated as a refreshing romp to be enjoyed after Gaukroger's more thorough and sober account.

Chapter 1: The Awakening

1. Alfred Barbier, quoted in Watson p. 61.
2. *See* Rodis-Lewis p. 5; and Adam and Tannery (AT) VI.46, VI.241, and III.141.
3. Descartes' snippets about his childhood are to be found in letters to Princess Elizabeth of Bohemia written in May 1645, to Hector-Pierre Chanut 6 June 1647, to Henri Brasset 23 April 1649, all *Corr.*, vol. VII, and in the *Discourse on Method*. The story of the cross-eyed girl in the letter to Chanut begins, '. . . *lorsque j'etais enfant, j'aimais une fille de mon age, qui etait un peu louche* . . .'
4. Letter to Princess Elizabeth, op. cit.
5. AT, II.378.
6. Letter of 9 February 1645.
7. AT, VI.4–5; Cottingham, Stoothoff and Murdoch (CSM) I.113.
8. AT, VI.7; CSM, I.114.
9. The letter, dated 24 June 1625, is cited by Baillet but has since been lost.
10. Gaukroger, p. 63.
11. Perhaps he hoped thereby to raise in people's minds the

suggestion that he was related (although no relationship existed) to the recently deceased (1618) and at that time famous Cardinal du Perron, royal advisor and theologian.

12. Breda did not become a formal military college until much later; evidently, when it did so it was because a de facto tradition of education in military skills already existed there.

13. See *Journal Tenu Par Isaac Beeckman de 1604–1634* (ed. Cornelius de Waard), 4 vols., (The Hague, 1939–53), I.228 and Baillet, I.43.

Chapter 2: A Night of Dreams

1. Democritus of Abdera lived approximately between 460 and 370 BC; Leucippus was an older contemporary (his dates are unknown). Between them they founded the atomic philosophy of nature, the most influential of the natural philosophies devised before Socrates (who died in 399 BC). Socrates shifted philosophical attention to ethics and politics, but with Aristotle natural philosophy again became important, and after Aristotle's death atomism was revived and revised by Epicurus. His version of it was given expression in Lucretius' famous and beautiful Latin poem *De Rerum Natura* (*On the Nature of Things*). In the seventeenth century Pierre Gassendi was instrumental in bringing atomistic ideas back into focus.

The ancient atomist argument can be simply characterised. There must be ultimate constituents of the material world (since nothing can come from nothing) which are not themselves composed of anything simpler or smaller. These are the atoms ('atom' means 'indivisible'). They exist in a void, through which they fall – with a curvilinear motion so that they can bump into each other – and constitute the larger objects we are familiar with in the world by aggregating together (having bumps and hooks, like Velcro, which allow them to stick together when they collide). Those are the basics in summary; the theory is of course richer than this sketch of it suggests, and both in its classical and Epicurean forms is interesting in light of the metaphysical problems it addressed.

2. JIB, I.244.
3. *See* Gaukroger pp. 74–89 for an account of this work.
4. Schuster, *Descartes and the Scientific Revolution* I.101.
5. Gaukroger, p. 99.
6. Baillet, p. 143.
7. AT, VI.11–13.
8. AT, VII.17.
9. AT, VI.11.
10. The notebook is the *Cogitationes Privatae*. For a discussion of the notebook, its provenance, contents and fate, *see* John R. Cole, *The Olympian Dreams and Youthful Rebellion of René Descartes* (University of Illinois Press, 1992). The psychological interpretation offered by Cole is interesting but controversial, and I shall not engage with it here, except to say that it makes far too much of too many details; and of course the theory underlying his interpretation is itself questionable.
11. The following account is taken from Baillet's report in Book II chapter 1 of his *Life*, itself based directly on the lost notebook, and therefore in all probability almost a transcription of Descartes' own words.
12. On 'exploding head syndrome' *see* the article by Dr Joel Saper (Director of the Michigan Head Pain & Neurological Institute in Ann Arbor) in the *Detroit Free Press*, 24 October 2000. I (ACG) also experience this syndrome, but only when excessively tired.
13. This diplomatic rider might have been aimed at the lawyers in his family, but it was certainly intended for the priests and prelates of his Church.
14. AT, VI.27.
15. Letter of 9 October 1649, AT, V.430.

16. AT, X.212–15.
17. AT, VI.18–19.
18. Ibid., p. 20.
19. G. Rodis-Lewis, p. 44.
20. Quoted ibid., p. 45.
21. The whole of chapter 8 of Book 2 of the *Traité* is devoted to this theme; *see* Rodis-Lewis p. 46.
22. AT, VI.22–23.

Chapter 3: The Mystery of the Rosy Cross

1. Frances Yates' *The Rosicrucian Enlightenment* (1972). This invaluable study is my guide in what follows.
2. Elizabeth I called Duke Frederick 'cousin Mumpellgart', this being his family name, and he presumably provides the original for 'cosen garmombles' in Shakespeare's *Merry Wives of Windsor*; 'Garmombles' being the German duke who hires horses at the Garter Inn – an allusion to the duke's visit to Elizabeth in the 1590s. *See* Yates, p. 44.
3. Ibid., p. 49.
4. Ibid., p. 51.
5. Ibid., p. 56.
6. Both the *Fama* and the *Confessio* are translated in the appendices to Yates op. cit. For this passage *see* pp. 297–8.
7. Yates, pp. 73–81.
8. Ibid., p. 132.
9. *See* Berkeley's *Notebooks*; he deleted the phrase from his manuscript of *The Principles of Human Knowledge*. *See* relevant discussion in A. C. Grayling, *Berkeley: The Central Arguments* (1986).
10. Yates, p. 137.
11. Bacon's *Novum Organon* had appeared in 1620, promoting the use of inductive inference in empirical science, and his *Advancement of Learning* had just appeared in 1623. In the latter

he set out to show 'the excellency of Learning and Knowledge', and to 'deliver it from the discredits and disgraces which it hath received; all from ignorance; but ignorance severally disguised, appearing sometimes in the zeal and jealousy of Divines; sometimes in the severity and arrogancy of Politiques; and sometimes in the errors and imperfections of learned men themselves.' And then he explains these obstacles to knowledge (here quoting his observations only of the first kind): 'I hear the former sort say, that Knowledge is of those things which are to be accepted of with great limitation and caution, that the aspiring to overmuch knowledge was the original temptation and sin whereupon ensued the fall of man, that Knowledge hath in it somewhat of the serpent, and therefore where it entereth into a man it makes him swell; SCIENTIA INFLAT: that Solomon gives a censure, that there is no end of making books, and that much reading is weariness of the flesh, and again in another place, that in specious knowledge there is much consternation, and that he that increaseth knowledge increaseth anxiety, that St. Paul gives a caveat, that we be not spoiled through vain philosophy, that experience demonstrates how learned men have been archheretics, how learned times have been inclined to atheism, and how the contemplation of second causes derogate from our dependence upon God, who is the first cause.'

12. The Treaty of Ratisbon was a major affair, and one of the chief players in it was Pope Gregory XV. He helped Ferdinand II with money and diplomatic aid in the conquest of Bohemia and Moravia, and supported the savage repression of Protestantism there, sending Carlos Caraffa as nuncio to Vienna to advise on the best means to be used. Gregory was largely responsible for ensuring that Ferdinand's promise to Maximilian of Bavaria was kept in the matter of transferring the Electorship of the Palatinate to him – both the electoral right and the territories – thereby securing a Catholic majority for elections to the Imperial

throne. As a reward for Gregory's help, Maximilian gave him the Palatinate library of Heidelberg, 3500 items strong, containing much occult literature. Pope Gregory immediately sent a deputation to transport the library back to Rome, where it was housed in the Vatican library as the 'Gregoriana'. About a thousand of these books and manuscripts found their way back to Heidelberg in 1815 and 1816 as gifts from Pope Pius VII to mark the end of the Napoleonic Wars.

13. Baillet, pp. 51–3.
14. Ibid.
15. Quoted in Cole, pp. 25–6.
16. Gaukroger, p. 108.
17. Yates, op. cit., p. 150.
18. Despite the immense care Descartes took always to soothe and placate Catholic, and especially Jesuit, opinion – or at least to try to – knowing that his views could so easily be branded as dangerous along with the rest, he was ultimately unsuccessful. For all his assiduity in orthopraxy and avowed orthodoxy, and for all his wooing of Jesuit opinion, his works ended on the Index of Forbidden Books – in company, it has to be said, with almost every other book of any interest ever written – and the universities were forbidden to teach his doctrines. But that lay in the future.

Chapter 4: Nine Years of Travel

1. Would a study of these Huguenot troubles reveal that they were provoked by those who wished to weaken France's endeavours in the Grison lands?
2. We learn this from a letter written in 1638; AT, II.388.
3. Descartes discussed in two letters the pluses and minuses of living in Italy, his views obviously formed during this long visit. AT, II.623.
4. *See* his account of avalanches in his *Meteors*, and the references to

Mount Cenis, AT, II.636. He reported seeing the avalanches in May, hence the dating of his return journey.

5. B. de Grammont, *Historiarum Galliae*, Bk XVIII (Toulouse, 1643) iii, pp. 208–9. *See also* J. S. Spink, *French Free Thought from Gassendi to Voltaire* (New York, 1960), Ch. 1 *passim* and pp. 28–33.

6. Grammont, ibid.

7. Moreover, they in part anticipate the philosophical views of Hegel and F. H. Bradley, particularly in respect of the conceptual need for an Absolute as reconciler of contingent contradictions.

8. William L. Hine, 'Mersenne: naturalism and magic', in *Occult and Scientific Mentalities in the Renaissance* (1984), edited by Brian Vickers, pp. 165–176.

9. Didier Kahn, *Entre atomisme, alchimie et theologie: la reception des theses d'Antoine de Villon et Etienne de Clave contre Aristote, Paracelse et les 'cabalistes' (24–25 aout 1624)* (London, 2001), and *see also* Gaukroger, p. 136.

10. William H. Huffman, *Robert Fludd and the End of the Renaissance* (London: Routledge, 1988) and Allen G. Debus, 'The chemical debates of the 17th century: The reaction to Robert Fludd and Jean Baptiste van Helmont', in M. L. Righini Bonelli and W. R. Shea (eds.), *Reason, Experiment, and Mysticism in the Scientific Revolution* (New York, 1975), pp. 19–47.

11. Gaukroger, pp. 140–41.

12. The *Rules* are to be found at AT, X.359 et seq.; the best English version is Cottingham et al., vol I, pp. 9 et seq.

13. AT, X.350–412; Cottingham, pp. 9–39.

14. Baillet, I, pp. 162–3.

15. Ibid., p. 165.

16. Ibid., p. 166.

17. Watson, p. 147.

18. Ibid., p. 149.

Chapter 5: Animals on the Moon

1. 'He played no further part in the war in the way hypothesised here' – that is, as an intelligence operative; I make this claim because, continuing with reliance on circumstantial evidence as before, I see neither cause nor opportunity for him to do so, but on the contrary so much concentration on his scientific and philosophical work, and so deep an immersion in affairs as different as family life and bitter personal controversy, that it becomes quite implausible to think that he was continuing intelligence work, for the Jesuits or anyone else, in his new circumstances. His friendship with Constantijn Huygens and the protection he later received from the highest authorities in the Netherlands suggest reasons for their regard additional to his reputation as a savant; in fact, Huygens – adviser to the Stadhouder, and therefore in a sense something close to being the Prime Minister of the United Provinces – very early gave Descartes his protection and interest. But this creates a puzzle: if Descartes had been active in the pro-Habsburg Jesuit interest even in a relatively minor capacity, why would the authorities in the United Provinces, allied to France and hostile to the Habsburgs, give Descartes welcome and protection? A possibility – and this has to be the merest conjecture, based on trying to keep the story consistent – would be that Descartes turned State evidence, as the modern jargon has it; that is, in return for being allowed to leave France for liberal exile in a friendly state, he abjured any activities inconsistent with French interests, and perhaps told Cardinal Berulle, in that famous and puzzling interview, what he knew. The secrecy of his movements and addresses for his first years in the Netherlands would then need to be explained not as anxiety to avoid French government hostility or surveillance, but the attentions of individuals who might have come to bear grudges as a result of his activities in the hypothesised role. In the

absence of hard evidence all this is, of course and to repeat, mere conjecture – but it is hard to resist making it, given the sheer number of circumstantial hints in favour of there being more to Descartes' story than the overt facts say. Still: from this point on in his story the hypothesis plays no further role.

2. Descartes lived at twenty-four different addresses (at least twenty-four, one should say; and quite a few more, if one takes short stays into account) in the Netherlands during his twenty years there – and, in the early years of his sojourn at least, he kept them secret.

3. *See* Universiteit te Franeker 1585–1811: bijdragen tot de geschiedenis van de Friese Hogeschool onder red. van G. Th. Jensma, F. R., H. Smit, F. Westra; redactieraad: M. H. H. Engels . . . [et al.].

4. He was right. *See* 'Vector analysis of fast focusing by hyperbolic and spherical lenses' Albert Y. Shih, Shunting Shih *Proc. SPIE* vol. 3889, pp. 842–8, *Advanced High-Power Lasers*; Marek Osinski, Howard T. Powell, Koichi Toyoda (eds) (2000). Their abstract reads: 'The delivery of a high-power laser beam to the target area, either via fibre systems or free-space optical trains, requires an effective focusing optical element at the end of the delivering system. It can be derived that a hyperbolic lens has the optimal surface to achieve the best focusing effect. Using this type of lens, the rays representing the beam can make a large angle with respect to the axis and the incidence angle on the lens surface is far from normal. As a result, the ordinary scalar field theory with paraxial approximation is not valid in this case. In order to understand the performance of a hyperbolic lens, it is necessary to use the vector field theory and apply the Huygens principle directly in the model. Using this method, we were able to show the performance of a hyperbolic lens is much better than that of a spherical lens.'

5. AT, I.13–16.

6. AT, I.24.
7. AT, I.154–5.
8. Ibid.
9. And *see* the other warm expressions of affection and indebtedness in Descartes' letters to Beeckman quoted earlier, during and shortly after the Breda period. 'Love me and rest assured that I would forget the Muses before I forgot you, for they unite me to you in a bond of eternal affection' he wrote to Beeckman on 24 January 1619. Eternity did not last longer than the growth of his ambitions.
10. Beeckman died 20 May 1637. A Protestant minister called Andreas Colvius wrote to tell Descartes of Beeckman's demise, and Descartes replied saying that he was sorry to hear it; he 'had been' one of Beeckman's best friends, he rather pointedly added, but since life is very short in comparison to eternity it scarcely matters whether it lasts a few years more or less.
11. *See* Simon Schama, *An Embarrassment of Riches passim* for an account of Amsterdam and the Netherlands in the seventeenth century; it furnishes a striking background to Descartes' 'exile' there.
12. *See* the booklet published for a 2003 exhibition of the university library of Leiden called 'Descartes and Leiden: friends and foes, admirers and adversaries'.
13. Written on 5 May 1631, this letter shows Descartes attempting to emulate the high literary style of de Balzac's own celebrated manner; the work on which de Balzac's fame rests is his *Letters*, published in 1624, a number of them written from the Netherlands where he had travelled extensively. Descartes' imitation of the manner and content is conscious.
14. AT, VI.41–2.
15. AT, I.254–5.
16. AT, I.140–41.
17. AT, I.236–7.

18. Note that Newton had an even more literal version of such a view; he thought that since his principles would result in the universe going out of kilter after a time, a God was needed to put it back on course again – to keep the laws steady, so to speak.
19. AT, XI.34–5.
20. Ibid., pp. 31, 33, 34.
21. Ibid., p. 36.
22. Ibid., p. 37.
23. Ibid., pp. 120–21.
24. Ibid., p. 130.
25. Ibid., p. 132.
26. Ibid., pp. 241–2.
27. AT, I.176–7.
28. Actually, the idea that there could be insensate creatures which nevertheless appear 'outwardly normal' is very dubious; a comparatively short stretch of observation would serve to show that they do not appear outwardly normal at all, and so the sceptical argument relying on this consideration weakens further. The best response to the other-minds sceptic is to be found in P. F. Strawson's *Individuals* (London, 1959).
29. AT, I.250.
30. Ibid., pp. 270–71.
31. Ibid., p. 271.
32. Ibid., p. 272.
33. Galileo Galilei, 'Letter to the Grand Duchess Christina of Lorraine', 1615.
34. AT, I.281–2.
35. Ibid., p. 282.
36. Ibid., p. 282–3.
37. Ibid., pp. 287–8. The allusion to the Antipodes concerns the Church's effort to deny their existence and proscribe belief in them – until of course the intrepid explorers who sailed around

the world settled the matter out of hand. The Liege text cited by Descartes was communicated by him to Mersenne in full in August 1634 (*see* AT I.306), and it reads: 'The said Galileo, therefore, who had confessed at an earlier interrogation, was summoned to the Sacred Tribunal of the Inquisition, interrogated and detained in custody. He clearly showed himself once again to be still of the same opinion, though he pretended that he put forward his view only hypothetically. The outcome is that after discussing the matter thoroughly, the Most Eminent Cardinals of the Commissionary General of the Inquisition have pronounced and declared that the said Galileo is under strong suspicion of heresy, in so far as he seems to have followed a doctrine which is false and contrary to Holy and Divine Scripture, namely that the sun is the centre of the universe and does not rise from sunrise to sunset, whereas the earth does move and is not the centre of the universe. Or he has been of the opinion that this doctrine could be defended as a probability, even though it has been declared to be contrary to Holy Scripture.'

38. AT, I.258.
39. Ibid.

Chapter 6: Francine

1. Baillet, II.91.
2. Watson, p. 182.
3. AT, I.510.
4. Ibid.
5. AT, II.340; Watson, p. 189.
6. Baillet, II. 90; his account makes scarlet fever (also called scarlatina) most probable, though there are other febrile diseases that it could have been, with closely similar symptoms. Baillet says that Francine's body was 'covered in purple'; ibid.

7. AT, III.279.

8. Baillet, ibid. In a collection called *Illustres Francaises* published in 1876 Descartes is depicted holding out his arms to Francine at her bedside, the legend reading, 'His daughter aged five years, died in his arms. He was inconsolable.' *See* Rodis-Lewis, p. 141.

9. Gaukroger takes the view that the relationship between Descartes and Helena Jans was never close, and he cites the Clerselier report to show that Descartes regretted the liaison. Although the evidence is scanty this does not seem to me persuasive, and that, quite the contrary, Descartes kept up relations with her at least during the span of Francine's life. *See* Gaukroger, pp. 294–5.

10. AT, III.278–9.

11. Ibid., p. 280.

Chapter 7: *The Shape of Snow*

1. AT, I.338.

2. Ibid., p. 339.

3. Ibid., pp. 339–40.

4. Gaukroger, p. 299.

5. AT, VI.2–3.

6. Ibid., p. 20.

7. Ibid., pp. 31–2.

8. If the major premise were available, Descartes' argument would be a simple syllogism: 'Everything that thinks, exists. I think. Therefore I exist.' Arguments with suppressed or hidden premises are known as 'enthymemes', and the vague supposition that many of one's inferences are enthymematic – supported by hidden premises of a kind anyone would accept – is often correct, but also a common source of fallacy in informal reasoning. Possibly Descartes relied on hidden assumptions about

the necessary conditions for anything to think – among them, obviously, that it must first exist – to establish his point. But if so he is in breach of the terms he had set for an enquiry into an indubitable first truth. That might seem a pettifogging point, for of course the assumption in question is inescapable; but if it is absolutely secure foundations you require – and that is what Descartes was after – just such quibbles have to be taken very seriously.

As it happens, Descartes himself acknowledged – in response to contemporary criticism – that his 'I think therefore I am' was not an enthymematic syllogism, and subsequent philosophers have attempted to understand it in different ways: as a direct intuition, as a 'performative utterance' (the mere assertion of it being proof of its truth), as a 'presuppositional implication' showing that, since it is a presupposition that one exists if one thinks, then the fact that one is thinking is sufficient for the truth of 'I exist'. And so on. *See* e.g. Marjorie Greene, *Descartes* (University of Minnesota Press, 1985) and Roger Scruton's essay on Descartes in A. C. Grayling (ed.) *Philosophy: A Guide Through the Subject* (Oxford University Press, 1995).

9. On this score, Descartes is in the right. His doubt is after all only 'methodological' – that is, it does not have to be plausible in itself; it is only a device to get us to see a certain point – namely, what cannot be doubted even if you use the most absurd and swingeing sceptical challenge to try to infect your beliefs with uncertainty. But there is a separate and important point at stake: whether such a degree of scepticism is intelligible quite apart from the methodological use that Descartes puts it to. And the answer seems to be 'no'. How – for one example of how an argument to this effect might begin – could one even possess the language in which to frame the doubt, if what such scepticism suggests were true?

10. Op. cit., pp. 32–3.

11. He explains this view in a letter to Lazare Meyssonnier of 29 January 1640 thus: 'I will answer the question you asked me about the function of the little gland called *conarion* [pineal gland]. My view is that this gland is the principal seat of the soul, and the place in which all our thoughts are formed. The reason I believe this is that I cannot find any part of the brain, except this, which is not double. Since we see only one thing with two eyes, and hear only one voice with two ears . . . it must necessarily be the case that the impressions which enter by two eyes and two ears, and so on, unite with each other in some part of the body before being considered by the soul. Now it is impossible to find any such place in the whole head but this gland . . .' Descartes is wrong to think that the pineal gland is the only single structure in the brain. AT, II.19.

12. Consciousness seems, in one way, the easiest thing in the world to understand, for anyone capable of thinking about it is intimately conscious of being conscious – we are immediately acquainted with our own consciousness, which attends every moment of our aware experience and thought. Similarly, the consciousness of others is obvious in their faces and behaviour, and most people well know how to read and respond to them as conscious beings – this indeed is the ordinary experience of everyday social interaction.

   At the same time, consciousness is the most perplexing mystery facing science and philosophy. It is such a difficult problem that for a long time philosophers put off thinking about it, and scientists ignored it entirely. Some, as noted, follow Descartes in thinking that it is too hard for human intelligence to understand. Others even claim that there is no such thing as consciousness; we are actually zombies, just very complicated ones. In defiance of these variously pessimistic and implausible views most students of the problem – philosophers, neuro-scientists and psychologists, working together – have profited from the availability of powerful new investigative tools, especially brain scanning devices, to watch both healthy and damaged brains at work in the processes of learning, sensing, remembering, reasoning, and feeling. One result is a great increase in knowledge of brain function, in the sense of a refined understanding of the correlation between specific brain areas and specific mental capacities. Aristotle thought that the brain is a device for cooling the blood (after all, one wears a hat to keep warm in winter), and that the seat of the mind is the heart (where, when one sees the beloved, tumult occurs); if nothing else, recent science has settled conclusively what everyone since Aristotle has believed to the contrary.

But all this knowledge does not amount to an understanding of consciousness, which is far too protean and varied a phenomenon for simple matchings between conscious states and activity in this or that brain structure. Above all, no degree of accuracy in tracing a given mental event to a given brain event can by itself explain how coloured pictures and evocative smells and harmonious or discordant sounds arise like a (scented) cinema-show in the head. This problem – the problem of qualia – is the hardest and most central problem of consciousness, and it still waits solution.

13. Some of these innovations, including the use of superscripts to represent squares, cubes and the rest, were anticipated by François Viete at the end of the previous century. Descartes claimed not to know the work of the earlier mathematician, and this became a point of contention; *see* below.

14. AT, X.359, et seq.

15. AT, VI.77.

16. AT, I.560.

17. AT, I.455.

18. Gaukroger, p. 323.

19. Ibid., p. 331.

20. AT, II.24–5.
21. AT, III.437.
22. AT, II.188–9.
23. Rodis-Lewis, p. 120.
24. AT, VII.9; *see* Gaukroger, p. 323.
25. AT, IV.540.
26. AT, VII.7.
27. AT, II.288.
28. AT, II.437.
29. AT, I.362, 367.
30. Rodis-Lewis, p. 124.
31. Carl Boyer, *A History of Mathematics* 2nd edn revised by Uta Merzbach (John Wiley, 1991), p. 346.
32. E. T. Bell, *Men of Mathematics* (1937) ch. 3 *passim*, 'Descartes: Gentleman, Soldier, and Mathematician'; *see also* the discussion in Bell's *The Development of Mathematics* (McGraw-Hill, 1945).
33. Boyer, op. cit.

Chapter 8: Descartes Contra Voetius

1. AT, I.649. *See* Vrooman, p. 141, Gaukroger, p. 333.
2. AT, I.435, 437.
3. AT, VI.62–3.
4. AT, II.480.
5. AT, III.528.
6. Ibid., p. 529.
7. AT, VII.563–603 *passim*; this quotation 576. Descartes' account of the details of the affair is at 582–595.
8. Ibid., pp. 592–4.
9. Ibid., p. 581.
10. AT VIII.8 *Letter to Voetius passim*.
11. Ibid., pp. 25–36, 42.
12. Ibid., p. 175.

13. The sceptical starting point is set out with clarity and brilliance in the first *Meditation*. *See* AT, VII.17–23.
14. AT, V.15–16.
15. Much of the circumstantial detail of these various disputes is taken from the *Conversations with Burman*. Frans Burman was a young theology student who visited Descartes in the spring of 1648, trading on the fact that Descartes and Burman's father were old friends. Burman made a careful record of his conversations with the philosopher, in which they discussed the disputes in detail – Burman had been a student at Leiden all during the previous five years of trouble there. This record was written down in Latin by Johannes Clauberg, and text of the *Conversations with Burman* we now have is a transcription of this lost Latin original. Because the copy was rediscovered only in 1895 some question arises about its authenticity, though the internal and external evidence would appear to support it well enough. One thing that critics mention is that the Descartes who appears in Burman's record is a frank, reasonable and very pleasant individual, obviously much maligned by his foes yet perfectly Christian in his attitude to them. The faint aroma of whitewash accordingly clings to this picture, which might of course be explained by the fact that Burman was on Descartes' side – and that the family friendship must have counted on Descartes' part too.
16. I refer readers to the discussion in A. C. Grayling, *What is Good?* (Weidenfeld and Nicolson, 2003), ch. 4 *passim*.
17. Or almost all: when it came to proving the existence of God – a necessary plank in his argument because, without the guarantee of a good God to ensure that the responsible use of our faculties will lead us to truth, it is not enough merely to be certain that one exists – he makes use of some pretty dusty old arguments; *see* the third and fifth of the *Meditations* which votaries of the old tradition would have recognised instantly.

Chapter 9: The Princess of the Passions

1. *See* G. Turnbull, *Hartlib, Dury and Comenius* (London, 1947) p. 167.
2. Rodis-Lewis, quoting Sorbiere, p. 151.
3. AT, II.662–4.
4. AT, IV.330.
5. Leon Petit, *Descartes et la Princesse Elizabeth: roman d'amour vecu* (Paris, 1969).
6. AT, VIIIA.1–2, 4.
7. AT, XI.323–4.
8. AT, XI.351–3.
9. Ibid., p. 354.
10. Ibid., p. 373 to the end.
11. Ibid., pp. 388, 390.
12. AT, IV.264–5.
13. Ibid., pp. 265–6.
14. AT, IV.290–94.
15. Quoted by Watson, p. 206. Watson's idiosyncrasies make his account of the Descartes–Elizabeth story one of the best things in his book.
16. Gaukroger, p. 364.
17. Isaac Newton, *Principia*, Book II, section IX.
18. John Gribbin, *Science: A History* (London, 2002), p. 118 note.
19. Baillet, II, p. 242. Since it is from Clerselier that the story comes about Descartes' regret at having had anything to do with Helena Jans, a question mark must be raised at this claim. Clerselier did a great deal to massage Descartes' posthumous reputation in the right direction, going so far as to insert pious qualifications to some of his writings, and no doubt working to give the impression that, but for the repented lapse with Helena, Descartes was a man of exactly the required impeccable virtue that a great genius should be.

20. AT, V.66.
21. AT, IV.204–5.
22. AT, V.72.
23. Watson has interesting details of the Descartes family finances in the 1640s; *see* pp. 244–8 of his book. It is part of Watson's case that though Descartes was comfortably placed because of his inheritances, enough to rent the chateau of Endegeest in the early 1640s, his brother and half-brother – trained lawyers in senior positions in their local Parlement – made sure that he did not get a sous more than they were obliged to give him under the terms of wills and other legal agreements. This is almost certainly true – there was little love lost between the brothers. It is likely that whatever Descartes got from the family resources was enough to sustain him during the 1630s and 1640s. But either the amount was getting to be insufficient by the late 1640s, or Descartes' sights were by then set higher; he had after all begun to move in courtly circles, visiting a princess regularly, and the expense of clean linen and smart clothes, a horse or even a carriage (an exceedingly expensive item, even to rent), and constant travel between the major cities of the United Provinces, what with servants coming too – all this might have made the idea of more money a considerable point. Whatever the circumstances, it is clear that he sought more money at this time, and was prepared to undergo great inconvenience – travelling all the way to Paris – to get it.
24. Gaukroger, p. 408.
25. In translating this passage Watson has 'a great deal of money and profit' where Descartes writes 'a great deal of honour and profit'. Apart from changing the character of Descartes' ambitions to something less praiseworthy, it unsettles the reader wishing to trust Watson's information. The passage in the letter to Chanut of 21 February 1648 reads: '*Et j'avoue que je ne souhaiterais pas un emploi penible, qui m'otat le loisir de cultiver mon*

esprit, encore que cela fut recompense par beaucoup d'honneur et de profit.'

26. In fact there were two sets of events known by this name, distinguished as the Fronde of the Parlement and the Fronde of the Princes, this latter taking place after Descartes' death.
27. AT, V.288–9.
28. Ibid., pp. 328–9.

Chapter 10: The Queen of Winter

1. The mannishness of Christina has been a focus for debate among scholars, who note that when she was born she was first announced to be a boy, and it was only later on the night of her birth that the midwives concluded that she was in fact a girl. This suggests either hermaphroditism, or a genital malformation. Ambiguous sex and sexuality have consistently been attributed to Christina, and observers noted that apart from her mannish air and masculine proclivities, she had a curious voice, which sometimes dropped very low and at other times sounded like a woman's. Whatever the truth, since intelligence is not a gendered commodity, the signal fact of her high intellectual gifts is independent of these curiosities.

    An excellent account of Christina and her life appeared as this book was about to go to press: Veronica Buckley, *Christina Queen of Sweden* (London: Fourth Estate, 2004). I was fortunate to secure a proof copy and to be able to make some use of it.
2. AT, IV.535.
3. Ibid.
4. AT, V.57.
5. Ibid., p. 290.
6. Ibid., p. 294.
7. Ibid.
8. AT, V.326–7.

9. Ibid., p. 329.

10. AT, V.460–7.

11. The accounts of Descartes' death given by Baillet and later biographers vary widely, and the earlier they are the more dramatic embellishments they seem to have. The most reliable account seems to be that of Henry Schluter, Descartes' man-servant, who wrote a letter to friends in the Netherlands saying, 'Yesterday [his letter was dated 12 February 1650] between three and four in the morning Monsieur Descartes died. On February 3rd at four o'clock in the morning, on the way to meet the Queen in her library, which he did even when it was extremely cold – the Swedes say it has not been so cold in many years, which is possibly what caused his death – he was stricken by a bad fever. He said it came from the phlegm which was so heavy on his stomach that he believed it was extinguishing his natural fires. He was terribly cold, had a bad headache, and could eat nothing but a few spoonfuls of brandy. Then he slept for two days. On Friday he had wine sop. He complained of burning heat and pain in his side that got worse every day, and could hardly breathe. He refused to believe that it was pneumonia. On Monday the Queen sent her physician who prescribed bleeding among other remedies, but Monsieur Descartes said he had too little blood left, and that he wanted his medicines only from the kitchen. He refused to let the physician come again. But on Tuesday he let himself be bled three times, but it did no good because his blood was corrupted and yellow. He will be buried at four o'clock this after-noon.' AT, V.576–7. *See also* Baillet, II, p. 423, Rodis-Lewis, pp. 201–3, Watson, pp. 307–10.

12. AT, V.576–7.

13. Buckley, p. 201.

14. Ibid., p. 189.

15. Almost all the following account is taken from Gaukroger, who

acknowledges G. A Lindeboom, *Descartes and Medicine*, for the details. *See* Gaukroger, p. 417.

16. Ibid., quoting E. Weil, 'The skull of Descartes' in the *Journal of the History of Medicine* II (1956) pp. 220–21.

Select Bibliography

Descartes' Works

Adam, Charles and Tannery, Paul (eds), *Oeuvres de Descartes*, 2nd edn (Paris: Vrin, 1974–86). (This is abbreviated AT in the endnotes.)

Adam, Charles and Milhaud, Gerard (eds), *Correspondance*, 8 vols (Paris, 1963)

Aliquie, F. (ed.), *Oeuvres philosophiques de Descartes*, 3 vols (Paris: *Classiques Garnier*, 1963–73)

Cottingham, John, Stoothoff, Robert and Murdoch, Dugald, *The Philosophical Writings of Descartes*, 3 vols (Cambridge: Cambridge University Press, 1984–91). (This is abbreviated CSM in the endnotes and most of the quotations from Descartes' writings are taken from the excellent translations in these volumes.)

Biographies and General Works

Adam, Charles, *Vie et Oeuvres de Descartes* (Paris, 1910)

Akerman, Susanna, *Queen Christina of Sweden and her Circle* (Leiden: Brill, 1991)

Ariew, R., *Descartes and the Last Scholastics* (New York: Cornell University Press, 1999)

Ariew, R. and Grene, M., *Descartes and his Contemporaries: Meditations, Objections and Replies* (Chicago: University of Chicago Press, 1995)

Artigas, M. and Shea, W. R., *Galileo in Rome* (Oxford: Oxford University Press, 2003)

Ayers, Michael and Garber, Daniel, *The Cambridge History of Seventeenth-Century Philosophy*, 2 vols (Cambridge: Cambridge University Press, 1997)

Baillet, Adrien, *La Vie de Monsieur Descartes*, 2 vols (Paris: Daniel Horthemels, 1691) (facsimile reprint, Geneva: 1970; New York: Garner, 1987)

Beeckman, Isaac, *Journal*, ed. Cornelis de Waard, 4 vols (La Haye, 1953)

Baker, Gordon and Morris, Katherine J., *Descartes' Dualism* (London: Routledge, 1996)

Betts, C. J., *Early Deism in France* (The Hague: Nijhoff, 1984)

Bouwsma, William J., *The Waning of the Renaissance* (Yale: Yale University Press, 2002)

Boyer, Carl B., revised by Merzbach, Uta C., *A History of Mathematics*, 2nd edn (New York: John Wiley and Sons, 1991)

Brockliss, L., *French Higher Education in the Seventeenth and Eighteenth Centuries: A Cultural History* (Oxford: Oxford University Press, 1987)

Buckley, Veronica, *Christina Queen of Sweden* (London: Harper-Collins, 2004)

Chappell, Vere and Doney, Willis, *Twenty Five Years of Descartes Scholarship* (New York: Garland, 1987)

Clark, G. N., *The Seventeenth Century* (Oxford: Oxford University Press, 1947)

Clark. G. N., *War and Society in the Seventeenth Century* (Cambridge: Cambridge University Press, 1957)

Select Bibliography

Cole, John R., *The Olympian Dreams and Youthful Rebellion in René Descartes* (Illinios: University of Illinois Press, 1992)

Cottingham, John, *Descartes* (Oxford: Blackwell, 1986)

Cottingham, John, *The Cambridge Companion to Descartes* (Cambridge: Cambridge University Press, 1991)

Cottingham, John, *A Descartes Dictionary* (Oxford: Oxford University Press, 1993)

Dainevillle, F. de, *Les Jesuites et l'education de la societe Francaise, la naissance de l'humanisme moderne* (Paris: Beauchesne, 1940)

Dear, Peter, *Mersenne and the Learning of the Schools* (New York: Cornell University Press, 1988)

Dicker, Georges, *Descartes: An Analytical and Historical Introduction* (Oxford: Oxford University Press, 1993)

Garber, Daniel, *Descartes' Metaphysical Physics* (Chicago: University of Chicago Press, 1992)

Gaukroger, Stephen, *Descartes: An Intellectual Biography* (Oxford: Oxford University Press, 1995)

Geyl, Pieter, *History of the Dutch-Speaking Peoples 1555–1648* (London: Phoenix Press, 1961)

Gilson, Etienne, *La Liberte chez Descartes et al theologie* (Paris: Libraire Felix Alcan, 1913)

Greengrass, M., *France in the Age of Henri IV* (London: Longman, 1984)

Grene, M., *Descartes Among the Scholastics* (Wisconsin: Marquette University Press, 1991)

Haldane, Elizabeth, *Descartes: His Life and Times* (London: John Murray, 1905)

Hausman, David and Alan, *Descartes' Legacy: Minds and Meaning in Early Modern Philosophy* (Toronto: University of Toronto Press, 1997)

Huppert, G., *Public Schools in Renaissance France* (Illinois: University of Illinois Press, 1984)

Koyré, A., *From the Closed World to the Infinite Universe* (Baltimore: Johns Hopkins Press, 1957)

Langford, J. J., *Galileo, Science and the Church* (Indianapolis: St Augustine's Press, 1998)

Lenoble, Robert, *Mersenne et la nassance du mecanisme* (Paris: Vrin, 1943)

Lindeboom. G., *Descartes and Medicine* (Amsterdam: Rodopi, 1978)

Machamer, P., *The Cambridge Companion to Galileo* (Cambridge: Cambridge University Press, 1998)

Maland, David, *Europe at War 1600–1650* (London: Macmillan, 1980)

Mancosu, Paolo, *Philosophy of Mathematics and Mathematical Practice in the Seventeenth Century* (Oxford: Oxford University Press, 1996)

Mersenne, Marin, *Correspondance* (eds) Cornelis de Waard, Pintard, R., Rochot, B., and Baeliue, A., 17 vols (Paris: Presses Universitaires de France, 1932–88)

Neel, Marguerite, *Descartes et la Princesse Elisabeth* (Paris: Elzevir, 1946)

Nye, Andrea, *The Princess and the Philosopher: Letters of Elisabeth of the Palatine to René Descartes* (Oxford: Rowman and Littlefield, 1999)

Orcibal, Jean, *Le Cardinal and de Berulle* (Paris: Cerf, 1965)

Parker, G., and Smith, L. M. (eds), *The General Crisis of the Seventeenth Century* (London: Routledge, 1978)

Pennington, D. H., *Europe in the Seventeenth Century*, 2nd edn (London: Longman, 1989)

Pintard, René, *Le Libertinage erudit dans le premiere moitie du XVIIe siecle* (Paris: Boiven et cie, 1943)

Popkin, R. H., *The History of Scepticism from Erasmus to Descartes* (Assen: 1960)

Reinhard, Marcel, *Henri IV ou la France sauvee* (Paris: Hachette, 1943)

Reith, Herman R., *René Descartes, The Story of a Soul* (Lanham: University Press of America, 1986)

Renn, J. (ed.), *Galileo in Context* (Cambridge: Cambridge University Press, 2002)

Select Bibliography

Ridley, F. A., *The Jesuits: A Study in Counter-Reformation* (London: Secker & Warburg, 1938)

Riggs, David, *The World of Christopher Marlowe* (London: Faber and Faber, 2004)

Rodis-Lewis, Genevieve, *Descartes: His Life and Thought*, trans. Jane Marie Todd (New York: Cornell University Press, 1995)

Schama, Simon, *An Embarrassment of Riches: An Interpretation of Dutch Culture in the Golden Age* (London: Vintage, 1997)

Sebba, Gregor, *The Dream of Descartes* (Illinois: Southern Illinois University Press, 1987)

Shapin, Steven, *The Scientific Revolution* (Chicago: University of Chicago Press, 1996)

Sirvin, J., *Les Annees d'apprentissage de Descartes* (New York: Garland, 1987)

Smith, Pamela H., *The Business of Alchemy: Science and Culture in the Holy Roman Empire* (Princeton: Princeton University Press, 1994)

Varaut, Jean-Marc, *Descartes: Un Cavalier Francais* (Paris: Plon, 2002)

Verbeek, T., *Descartes and the Dutch: Early Reactions to Cartesian Philosophy 1637–1650* (Illinois: University of Illinois Press, 1992)

Vrooman, J. R., *René Descartes: A Biography* (New York: 1970)

Watson, Richard, *Cogito, Ergo Sum: The Life of René Descartes* (Boston: Godine, 2002)

Webster, C. (ed.), *The Intellectual Revolution in the Seventeenth Century* (London: Routledge, 1974)

Wedgwood, C. V., *The Thirty Years War* (London: Jonathan Cape, 1938)

Westfall, R. S., *The Construction of Modern Science: Mechanisms and Mechanics* (New York: John Wiley, 1971)

Westfall, R. S., *Essays on the Trial of Galileo* (Rome: Vatican Observatory Publications, 1989)

Williams, Bernard, *Descartes: the Project of Pure Enquiry* (London: Penguin, 1978)

Wilson, M. D., *Descartes* (London: Routledge, 1974)

Yates, Frances, *The Rosicrucian Enlightenment* (London: Routledge, 1972)

Index

Page numbers in *italics* denote note

Adam, Charles, 7, 99, 107
Admirable Method, The, 215
Aemelius, Anton, 210
Albert of Austria, Archduke, 39
alchemy, 224
algebra, 200
Althusser, Louis, 298
Amsterdam, 151
Andreae, Johan Valentin, 85; *The Chemical Wedding of Christian Rosencreutz*, 83–4, 85, 87, 97–8
animals: Descartes' view as soulless automata, 35, 159–60
Anne of Austria, 249, 251, 252, 253
Antipodes, 172, *321–2n*
Aquinas, St Thomas, 221
Aristotelianism, 90, 122, 131, 132, 150, 218, 223–6
Aristotle, 2, 221, 237, *312n, 362n*; *De Caelo, 309n*; *Physics, 309n*
Arminian controversy, 41–4, 211–12

Arminius, Jacobus (Jakob Hermanzoon), 41–2, 212
atheism, 121–2
atomism, 49, *312–13n*
Augustine, St, 278–9
Aurelius, Marcus, 239
Ayer, A. J., 281

Bacon, Francis, 5, 6, 14, 67, 90, 92, 128; *Advancement of Learning, 314–15n*; *Novum Organon, 314n*
Baillet, Adrien, 6–7, 27, 28, 34, 65, 66, 68, 93, 94–5, 108, 131, 132, 133, 175, 177, 246
Barberini, Cardinal, 199
Barbier, Alfred, 19
Bayle, Pierre, 118, 119
Beaugrand, Jean, 106, 200, 201–2
Beeckman, Isaac, 49–54, 130, 144; background and scientific insights, 49–51; death, 150, *320n*; falling out with Descartes, 53,

341

Beeckman, Isaac – *cont.*
148–50; friendship and influence
on Descartes, 37, 47, 50, 52–3,
144, 149–50, *320n*; topics
collaborated on with Descartes,
50–2
Belgium, 39
Bell, E. T., 206
Bellarmine, Cardinal, 114, 165,
167–8
Benedictines, 29
Berkeley, Bishop George, 90, 281
Berlin, Isaiah, 297
Berulle, Cardinal, 9, 130–1, 131–2,
132–4, 135–8, *318n*
Béthune, Maximilien de (duc de
Sully), 19
biographies of philosophers,
296–308
Bitauld, Jean, 122
Bohemia, 60, 61–3; challenges
Ferdinand's authority with
selection of Frederick as king
of Bohemia, 55, 63; defeat of
Frederick V and persecution
of Protestants, 64–5; and
'Defenestration of Prague', 46,
61–2
Boltzmann, Ludwig, 75
Borel, Pierre, 7, 131
Borgia, Francisco, 2
Boyer, Carl, 205–6
brain, 191–2, 286–7, 289, *326n*
Breda, 36, 37
Brotherhood of the Rosy Cross *see*
Rosicrucianism
Bruno, Giordano, 103, 113
Buckley, Veronica, 273

Bucquoy, comte du, 65, 94
Burman, Frans, *328n*

Cabala, 82, 83, 87, 90, 92, 102
Calvinists, 45, 212
Cardano, Geronimo, 195
Cartesian philosophy, 218–19,
277–294 passim, *see also*
Descartes, Philosophical and
Scientific Theories
Casale, 134, 135
Castelli, 167
Catholic League, 58, 59
Cats, Jacob, 145
causes, 2, *309n*
Chandoux (chemist), 131, 132
Chanut, Pierre, 176, 245–6, 255,
260, 262, 263, 268, 269, 271, 272
Charles I, King, 138, 252
Charles IX, King, 23, 24–5
Charlet, Père Etienne, 26
Charron, Pierre, 77–9
Chastellier, Père, 26
Chastillon, Gaspard de, 46
Chatellerault, 17, 20, 115
*Chemical Wedding of Christian
Rosencreutz, The* (Andraea), 83–4,
85, 87, 97–8
Cherasco, Treaty of (1631), 135
Christian of Anhalt, 57–8, 60, 61,
63, 64, 86, 87, 89
Christina, Queen of Sweden, 144,
257–69; background, 258–9; and
Catholicism, 258, 273–4, 308;
correspondence with Descartes,
99, 246, 255, 257, 261–2; and
Descartes' death, 272; invitation
to Descartes to come to

Stockholm, 176, 246, 255, 262–5; mannishness of, *331n*; reign, 259–60

Cicero, 30

Clarke, Ronald W., 300

Claves, Etienne de, 122

Clerselier, Claude, 131, 176–7, 245, 246, *329n*

Cogitationes Privatae (notebook), 69, *313n*

Coligny, Admiral, 24

comets, 161

compass, 53–4

Compendium Musicae (Descartes), 51

Confessio Fraternitatis, 83, 85, 87–9

Confession of Faith, 41–2

consciousness, 194, 287–8, *325–6n*

Copernican model, 113, 114, 164, 165, 166, 167, 168, 169, 226

corpuscularianism, 49

Cosimo II (Grand Duke of Tuscany), 167

cosmology, 242–3, 225

Counter-Reformation, 5, 13

Courtmour, Baron de, 46

Crollius, Oswald, 86

Cumberland, Duke of, 240

Damasio, Antonio, 287

De Bagni, Cardinal, 199

de Balzac, Jean-Louis, 153, *320n*

de Viau, Théophile, 121

Debeaune, Florimond, 204–5, 245

Dee, Dr John, 84, 86, 87

'Defenestration of Prague', 46, 61–2

degree, theory of, 225

Democritus of Abdera, 49, *312n*

Desargue, Girard, 204

Descartes, Jeanne (sister), 17, 19

Descartes, Joachim (father), 17, 19, 180

Descartes, Pierre (brother), 17, 19, 26, 247

Descartes, René

Personal Life: attends coronation of Ferdinand II, 55, 61; baptism, 18; biographies of, 6–8, *310–11n*; birth, 5, 18; and Cardinal Berulle, 9, 131–4, *318n*; and Catholicism, 3–4, 11, 29, 73; childhood and upbringing, 16–22; composes libretto for Queen Christina's ballet, 266; correspondence with Queen Christina, 99, 246, 255, 257, 261–2; death, 5, 99, 271, 272–3, *332n*; and death of daughter, 180–2; and death of mother, 22; decision to abandon study of letters and go travelling, 32–3; decision to leave France for Netherlands and reasons, 102, 130–9, 143; draws up statutes for a Swedish Academy, 267, 269; education at La Flèche, 13–14, 22–3, 26–8, 31–2; enlists in Prince of Orange's army in United Provinces, 9, 36–8, 45–6; exhumation of body and transportation to France for burial, 274; falling out with Beeckman, 53, 148–50; falls ill in Sweden and nurses own symptoms, 268–70; family background, 16–17; fathers illegitimate child (Francine) and relationship with, 175, 177–8,

Descartes, René, Personal Life – *cont.*
179; finances, 250, *330n*;
friendship and correspondence
with Princess Elizabeth, 22, 144,
227, 228–9, 230–4, 236–7, 241,
247–8; friendship with Beeckman
and influence of, 37, 47, 50,
52–3, 144, 149–50, *320n*; and
Fronde, 253–4; graduates from
Poitiers with canon and civil law
degree, 33, 34, 35; health, 21–2,
207–8; intelligence agent
hypothesis, 9–11, 46, 54–5, 96,
100–1, 115, 298, *318n*; invited
by Queen Christina to
Stockholm, 176, 246, 255,
262–5; Italian journey, 107–8,
111–14; Jesuit loyalty, 28, 99,
100; joins army of Duke
Maximilian in Bohemia and
involvement with Battle of White
Mountain, 9, 46–7, 53, 54, 63–4,
93, 228, 298; likening to Vanini,
119, 215, 216; living in the
Netherlands, 9, 56, 141, 142–3,
147, 150–4, 155, 207–8, 250;
living in Paris, 116; living in
Sweden, 265–8; moral code and
principles, 77–8, 79, 188; motto,
11; nervous breakdown in youth
hypothesis, 33–4; pension from
French crown debacle, 246,
249–52, 254; relationship with
Helena Jans, 178–9, 180, *323n*;
return visits to France, 245–7,
248–50, 251; and Rosi-
crucianism, 81, 82–3, 93–102;
stays at Saint-Germain-en-Lay

between school and university,
33, 34–5; and Thirty Years
War, 56
**Philosophical and Scientific
Theories**: achievements and
contributions, 3–4; and anatomy,
155, 159; animals as soulless
automata, 35, 159–61; battles
over theories at Utrecht and
Leiden universities, 213–14,
219–20, 236; and comets, 161;
compass experiments, 53–4;
cosmology, 242–3; described as
'Father of Modern Philosophy',
3; dispute with Voetius, 11, 146,
210–11, 213–18, 247; existence
and goodness of God, 197–8,
238, 278, 280, 289–91, *328n*;
'four truths', 138–9; freeing of
science from theological
interference, 123; and Galileo
affair, 162–3, 170–3, 183, 187; on
happiness and love, 236, 237–8;
and hydrostatics, 51–2; 'I think
therefore I am' dictum, 188–90,
197, 278–9, *323–4n, see also* God;
importance of, 293; increase in
reputation due to Mersenne,
105–6, 125; interest in medicine
and prolonging of life, 208;
mathematics and geometry, 4, 32,
47, 50–1, 53–4, 105, 125,
186–7,195–6, 197, 205–6;
mechanistic view of nature, 130,
156–8; method of doubt and
sceptical arguments employed,
78–9, 190, 195, 281–5, *342n*;
method and rules for conducting

effective enquiry, 14, 67, 69, 77, 112, 126–8, 132, 195, 196–7; and mind-body interaction (dualism), 190–2, 194, 197, 226, 232, 235, 238, 278, 285–9; night of dreams, 69–74, 75, 76, 96, 97, 98, 126; notational innovations, 195–6; optics and discovery of law of refraction, 4, 107, 125–6, 147–8, 186; pedagogical value of philosophy, 291–2; philosophy, 4, 277–93; principles observed in studies, 77; reasons for being a threat to traditionalists, 221, 226; regarded as outmoded by some *philosophes*, 5; on vision, 243–4; vision in 'stove-heated room', 66–9, 74–7; vivisection and ill-treatment of animals, 159–61; and vortices, 242–4; wanting to avoid theological offence, 163, 169, 171, 172, 173, 210, 214, 226, 281

Writings: autobiographical form of, 279–80; *Compendium Musicae*, 51; *A Description of the Human Body*, 241–2; *Discourse on Method* see *Discourse on Method*; *Exercises in Good Sense*, 105; on Index of Forbidden Books, *316n*; *Meditations on First Philosophy* see *Meditations on First Philosophy*; *Le Monde* 154–61, 162, 169, 173, 183, 186, 242; *The Passions of the Soul*, 230, 234–6, 241, 257; *Principles of Philosophy*, 194, 227, 233–4, 241–2, 245, 292 ; *Rules for the Direction of the Mind*, 74, 105, 112, 126–8, 196; use of

pseudonyms, 97, 101; *The World*, 130

Description of the Human Body, The (Descartes), 241–2

d'Etoiles, Vasseur, 116

Dialogue Concerning the Two Chief World Systems (Galileo), 161–2, 168–9

Dinet, Jacques, 213

Discourse on the Method and Essays (Descartes), 15, 67–8, 75, 125, 173, 184–94, 218, 238; allegations of plagiarism over *Geometry* section, 200–1; autobiographical details, 13–14, 15, 21, 22, 31, 105, 187–8; contents and theories in, 4, 185–94, 197–8; contribution made by, 3; criticism of *Geometry* and *Optics* sections by Paris mathematicians and Descartes' response, 199–204; Descartes' reaction to favourable responses to, 204–5; distribution of copies, 198–9; process of publication, 184–5; written in French instead of Latin, 198

Dome, Puy de, 249

Donauworth, 56–7, 61

doubt: Cartesian method of, 218–19; Descartes' method of, 78–9, 190, 195, 281–5, *342n*

dualism (mind-body correlation), 190–2, 194, 197, 226, 232, 235, 238, 278, 280, 285–9

Edward (brother of Princess Elizabeth), 240

Eleanor, Queen, 16
elements, 2, 223–4, *309–10n*
Elizabeth I, Queen, 85, 86
Elizabeth, Princess (of Bohemia), 146, 230–5, 239–41, 257, 265, 288; becomes abbess of Herford convent, 241; correspondence and friendship with Descartes, 22, 144, 227, 228–9, 230–4, 236–7, 241, 247–8; death, 241; dedication to in *The Principles of Philosophy*, 233–4, 257; family tribulations, 240; intellect, 239; interest in mind-body problem, 230–1, 235
Elizabeth Stuart of Bohemia, 16, 229–30, 240, 257
Elzevir, 184–5, 209
Epictetus, 239
Epicurus, *312n*
Espinay, Monsieur L', 240
Evangelical Union, 57, 58, 59, 63
Exercises in Good Sense (Descartes), 105
'exploding head syndrome', 73

Fama Fraternitatis, 83, 85, 87–9
Faulhaber, Johann, 93, 97, 101
Ferdinand II, Emperor, 10–11, 55, 61, 62, 63, 65, 68, 135
Fermat, Pierre de, 5, 106, 187, 200, 201, 202
Ferrand, Michel (great-uncle), 19–20, 115
Ferrier, Guillaume, 126
Ferrier, Jean, 147, 148
Fleming, Admiral, 264
Fletcher, John, 45

Florence, 113
'Florentinus de Valentia', 90
Fludd, Robert, 82, 95, 123–4
Fontanier, Jean, 121
Foscarini, Paolo Antonio, 114
France, 10–11; conflict with Habsburgs, 108–11, 134–5, 136–7, 138; Huguenot rebellion, 110–11, 138
Francine (Descartes' daughter), 175–6, 179–80, 207, 211
Francini brothers, 35
Franeker, 144–5, 146, 150
Frederick I, Duke, 85
Frederick IV, Elector Palatine, 57
Frederick V, Elector Palatine, 16, 55, 57–8, 63, 64–5, 82, 85–6, 87, 89, 227, 229
Freemasonry, 98
Fromondus, Libertus, 199
Fronde, 251–3

Galileo, 5, 113, 161–9, 170, 171, 183; arrested and prosecuted by the Inquisition, 103, 114, 162, 164, 165, 169, 171, *322n*; and compass, 53; defence of Copernican model, 166, 167, 168; *Dialogue Concerning the Two Chief World Systems*, 161–2, 168–9; discoveries as thorn in doctrinal flesh, 165–6; and Mersenne, 106, 173; *Il Saggiaore* (*The Assayer*), 168; and telescope, 165–6; telescopic discoveries, 166
Garasse, Francois, 119, 121
Gassendi, Pierre, 106, 173, 248, *312n*

Gaukroger, Stephen, 7–8, 97, 186, 207, 242
Gillot, Jean, 176
God, 221–3, 224–5; Descartes and existence and goodness of, 197–8, 238, 278, 280, 289–91, *328n*; Kant and existence of, 307; and Scripture, 222–3
gold, 224
Golius, Jacob, 151, 152, 155–6, 218
Gomarists, 42, 43, 44
Gomarus, Francis, 41
gravitation theory, 244
Gregory XV, Pope, *315–16n*
Gribbin, John, 244
Grisons, 109, 110, see also Val Telline
Grotius, Hugo, 42, 43, 44
Gustavus Adolphus II, King of Sweden, 135, 142, 258

Haak, Theodore, 98–9
Habsburgs, 10, 142; conflict with France, 108–11, 134–5, 136–7, 138
happiness, 237
Harmonic Law, 244
harmonics, 51
Harriot, Thomas, 125, 200
Hartlib, Samuel, 98, 99, 229
Harvey, William, 5
Heereboord, Adriaan, 218–19, 220
Hegel, George Wilhelm Friedrich, 300
Heidegger, Martin, 298, 302
Henri III, King of France, 25
Henri IV, King of France, 23–5, 58; assassination, 27, 28, 59; and

Evangelical Union, 58, 59; founding of La Flèche, 25–6; internment of heart at La Flèche, 27–8
Hermeticism, 82, 83, 90, 92, 128
Hobbes, Thomas, 5–6, 203, 248, 308
Holland 41, 42, 43 see also Netherlands
homosexuality, 121–2
Hooke, Robert, 147–8
Hortensius, Martin, 152
Huet, Daniel, 99
Huguenots, 137–8; and Edit of Nantes, 19, 25; rebellion of in France (1627), 110–11, 138; and St Bartholomew massacre, 24
Hume, David, 33, 299, 300
Huygens, Christiaan, 152, 244
Huygens, Constantijn, 16, 125, 152–3, 208, 217–18, *318n*
hydrostatics, 51–2

'I think therefore I am' dictum, 188–90, 197, 278–9, *323–4n*, see also God
identity theory, 286
inertia, 49
Inquisition, 165, 168; attitude to science in Italy, 113–14; prosecution of Galileo see Galileo
'Irenaeus Agnostus', 89
Italy: attitude of Inquisition to science, 113–14; Descartes travels in, 107–8, 111–14

James I (VI of Scotland), 63, 64, 85
Jans, Helena, 175, 176, 178–9, 180, 207, *329n*

Jesuits: as advisors to Habsburgs, 10, 28; championing of Catholic faith, 28, 29; conception of education, 26; demonising of Rosicrucianism, 82; Descartes' loyalty to, 23, 28, 99, 100; education methods, 29–31; employment of Descartes as intelligence agent hypothesis, 10, 54–5, 96, 100–1; and Henri IV, 25; and La Flèche, 26; *Ratio Studiorum*, 2
Jesus Christ, 223
John George of Saxony, Elector, 58, 63, 64
John Paul II, Pope, 112
Julich and Cleves, duchy of, 59

Kant, Immanuel, 299, 300, 305–7
Kelley, Edward, 86
Khunrath, Henricus: *Amphitheatre of Eternal Wisdom*, 86, 87
Kierkegaard, Soren, 222
Kohler, Joachim, 303
Kuehn, Manfred, 300
Kuhn, Thomas, 293

La Flèche, 14, 22–3, 30–1, 198; Descartes at, 13–14, 22–3, 26–8, 31–2; founding of by Henri IV, 25–6; internment of Henri IV's heart at, 27–8; topics studied, 30
La Haye, 17–18, 20
La Rochelle, 138; and Treaty of, 138
Lamormaini, Wilhelm, 10
Latin, 30, 198
Le Vayer, Le Mothe, 124

League of Lyons, 110, 111
Leibniz, Gottfried Wilhelm, 69, 96, 192, 193–4, 286
Leiden University, 151–2; accuses Descartes of being a blasphemer, 219–20; banning of Cartesian philosophy, 218, 219; banning of discussion on any metaphysics, 221
lenses, 127, 142, 147, 159, 175, *319n*
Letter to Voetius, 215, 217
Leucippus, 49, *312n*
Libavius, Andreas, 89
'libertine', term of, 116–18
'libertine crisis' (1620s), 118–19
Lipstorp, Daniel: *Specimina*, 7
Locke, John, 6, 281, 297, 298
Loretto, 112–13
Louis XIII, King, 108–9, 110, 138, 198
Louis XIV, King, 118, 249, 251, 252
Louisa of Bohemia, Princess 232, 240
Luynes, duc de, 209
Lyons League, 110

Mabillon, Jean, 274
McGuinness, Brian, 301–2
Malebranche, Nicolas, 192–3, 194, 286
Mantua, 134–5
Marie-Eleanor of Brandenburg, 258–9
Marlowe, Christopher, 10
Marx, Karl, 297
Massinger, Philip, 45

mathematics: Descartes' interests and theories in, 4, 32, 47, 50–1, 53–4, 105, 125, 186–7, 195–6, 197, 205–6, *see also* Mersenne, Fermat and Pascal

Matthias, Emperor, 59, 60, 61, 62

Maurice of Nassau *see* Orange, Prince of

Maximilian of Bavaria, Duke, 9, 46, 53, 54, 57, 58, 63, 64, *315–16n*

Mazarin, Cardinal, 249, 251, 252

Medici, Catherine de, 16, 24

Medici, Marie de, 59, 108, 136

Meditations on First Philosophy, 67, 79, 188, 194, 208–10, 218, 284, 292; as a classic text, 6; criticism of, 248; decision to circulate before publication, 205; dedication, 209–10; on God's existence, 198, 219, 280, 289–90; 'letter to Dinet', 213–14; Preface, 203–4; publication of, 209; use of first person singular, 14–15

Meier, Michael, 123

'Menapius', 89, 90

Mersenne, Marin, 245; admiration of Descartes, 139; advertises Descartes intellectual virtues, 105–6, 124–5; as conduit of philosophical and scientific exchanges, 129; correspondence with Descartes, 148, 155, 156, 161, 162–3, 163–4, 169, 170–2, 181–2, 209; death, 253; dispute with Fludd, 82, 123–4; and Galileo, 106, 173; influence on Descartes, 130; *L'Impiété des Déistes*, 121; mechanistic conception of nature, 129; offers to publish *Discourse*, 185; opposition to Rosicrucianism, 82, 92–3, 95, 100, 106; philosophical and scientific views, 128–9; 173; *Synopsis Mathematica*, 106; and Voetius, 216

'Mersenne prime', 106

meteorology: in *Discourse*, 186

Metius, Adrien, 145

Metius, Jacques, 145

mind/matter correlation *see* dualism

Monas Hieroglyphica (Dee), 86

Monde, Le, 154–61, 162, 169, 173, 183, 186, 242

monism, 286

Monk, Ray, 301

Montaigne, Michel Eyquem de, 78, 107–8, 112

Montfauçon, Bernard de, 274

Morin, Jean-Baptiste, 204

Mossner, Ernest, 300

Mydorge, Claude, 106–7, 124, 125, 126, 245, 249

Nantes, Edict of (1598), 19, 25

'natural theology', 221–2

nature: mechanistic conception of, 128–9, 130, 156–8

Naudé, Gabriel, 91–2, 124

Netherlands, 37–8, 143; Arminian controversy, 41–4, 211–12; Descartes in, 9, 56, 141, 142–3, 147, 150–4, 155, 207–8, 250; as Europe's leading country for arts and sciences, 146

Nevers, duc de, 134

Newton, Isaac 3, 84, 242, 244, *321n*

Nietzche, Friedrich, 298, 302, 303–5
Noel, Etienne, 198–9

Oath of Abjuration (1581), 38
Occasionalism, 194
occultism, Renaissance, 129
Oldenbarnevelt, Johan van, 41–3,
    44, 45
Olympica, 96–7
optics: Descartes' work on
    hyperbolic lenses, 147–8, *319n*;
    and *Discourse*, 186; and discovery
    of law of refraction by Descartes,
    4, 125–6
Orange, Prince of, 36, 40, 42–3,
    44–5, 217, 220, 229
Oratory, 135–6
Oxenstierna, Axel, 259

Pacioli, Luca, 195
Palma Triumphalis, 91
Parallelism, 194
parhelia, 161
Paris, 130; banning of debate on
    Aristotelianism, 122; decree
    passed outlawing views contrary
    to ancient approved authors, 122;
    and the Fronde, 251–3; 'libertine
    era', 116–17
Pascal, Blaise, 5, 106, 248–9
Passions of the Soul, The (Descartes),
    230, 234–6, 241, 257
Paul V, Pope, 167
Peace of Augsburg (1555), 56–7
Pell, John, 98
Perron, Cardinal du, *312n*
Petit, Leon, 232
Petit, Pierre, 203

Philip (brother of Princess
    Elizabeth), 240
Philip II, King of Spain, 39
Philip III, King of Spain, 40, 41, 58,
    59
Philip Ludwig of Neuberg, 59–60
philosophers: biographies of,
    296–308
Picot, Claude, 245
pineal gland, 192, 235, 288, *325n*
Pinerlo, 135
Pinkard, Terry, 300
Plato, 117
Pollot, Alphonse, 180–1, 230, 247
Popper, Karl, 291
predestination dispute, 41–4, 211–12
Principles of Philosophy, The, 194, 227,
    233–4, 241–4, 245, 292
Protestant Union, 85

qualia 191–2, *326n*

rainbows, 4
Ratisbon, Treaty of (1623) 94,
    315–16n
Ravillac, 28
Reformation, 13, 222
refraction, 205; discovery of law of
    by Descartes, 4, 125–6
Regius, Henry, 210–11, 212–13,
    247, 250
Reneri, Henry, 144, 145–6, 151–2,
    182, 183, 184, 210
Revius, Jacob, 219, 220, 221
Richelieu, Cardinal, 111, 134, 135,
    137–8, 198
Roberval, Gilles, 106, 203, 248,
    249

Index

Rodis-Lewis, Genevieve, 20, 21, 77, 232, 236

Rosencreutz, Brother, 88–9

Rosicrucianism, 14, 74, 81–103, 128; and attacks on and demonising of by Church, 82, 84, 89, 91; and *The Chemical Wedding of Christian Rosencreutz*, 83–4, 85, 87, 97–8; and *Confessio Fraternitatis*, 83, 85, 87, 89; and Descartes, 81, 82–3, 93–102; and *Fama Fraternitatis*, 83, 85, 87–9; features of, 88, 90–1; following, 89–90; opposition to by Mersenne, 82, 92–3, 95, 100, 106; panic over in France (1623), 82, 91–2, 94–5; roots back into Renaissance, 84; vanishing of after defeat of Frederick, 82, 91; 'A Warning Against the Rosicrucianism Vermin', 91

Royal Society, 98

Rubens, Peter Paul, 10

Rudolf II, Emperor, 55, 56–7, 58–9, 60, 61

Rules for the Direction of the Mind (Descartes), 74, 105, 112, 126–8, 196

Russell, Bertrand, 281, 298, 300, 301, 302, 308

Safranski, Rudiger, 302–3

St Bartholomew massacre (1572), 24

Saint-Germain, Peace of, 23

Saint-Germain-en-Lay, 33, 34

Sargent, Thomas, 175

Sartre, Jean-Paul, 298

Savoy, Duke of (Charles Emmanuel), 109

scarlet fever, 179

sceptical arguments: employment of in Descartes' method of doubt, 78–9, 190, 282–5, *342n*

Scheiner, Christopher, 161, 169–70

Schluter, Henry, 270, 272–3, *332n*

Scholasticism, 2

Schoock, Martin, 214–15, 217

Schopenhauer, Arthur, 302, 304

Schurman, Anna Maria van, 145–6

Scripture, 222–3

Seneca, 241, 247; *De Vita Beata*, 236–7

Shaw, George Bernard, 297

Silhon, Jean de, 279

Snell, Willibrord 4, 125

Snell's Law, 125

Socrates 298, *312n*

Soly, Michel, 209

Sophie of Bohemia, Princess, 239

Spain, 38, 39–40, 45, 108–10, 142

Spanheim, Frederik, 220–1

Spinola, Ambrogio, 36, 39

Spinoza, Benedict de, 298

Staurophorus, Rudophilus: *Raptus Philosophicus*, 97

Stoic ethics, 79

Studion, Simon: *Naometrica*, 86–7

Sweden, 65, 142; Descartes in, 265–8; *see also* Christina, Queen of Sweden

Swedish Academy, 267, 269

Synod of Dort (1619), 44, 46, 212

Tartaglia, Niccola, 195

telescope, 165–6

Thales, 3
Thesarus Mathematicus, 96, 97
Thirty Years War (1618–48), 5, 9,
    10, 46, 56, 141, 142, 258; roots
    of and causes 56–65
Thomas, St, 218
Thomism, 221
Tilly, Count, 64
Torricelli, Evangelista, 249
Toulouse, 119, 120
Traité de la Lumière, 155
Traité de l'homme, 155
Trigland, Jacob, 218, 219
Tronchet, Madame du, 179

Ulm, 93
Union of Arras, 38
Union of Utrecht, 38
United Provinces, 38–41, 109, 141;
    see also Netherlands
Urban VII, Pope, 168
Utrecht University, 145, 146, 152,
    183–4; rejection and banning of
    teaching of Cartesian philosophy,
    213, 214; rejection of Descartes'
    philosophy, 213–14

vacuum, 226, 243
Val Telline, 108, 109–11, 134, *see
    also* Grisons
van Dam, Cornelis Heymeszoon,
    151
Van Helmont, Jean-Baptiste, 1, 2
van Hooghelande, Cornelius, 98
Vanini, Giulio Cesare, 119–21, 215,
    216

Venice, 112
Viete, Francois, 195, 200, *326n*
Villebressieu, Etienne de, 7, 126
Villon, Antoine, 122
vision: Descartes' theory of, 243–4
Visscher, Anna Roemers, 145
Voetius, Gisbert, 210; battle with
    Regius, 211, 212–13; dispute
    with Descartes, 11, 146, 210–11,
    213–18, 247
Voltaire, 5
vortices, 242, 242–3
Vrooman, J. R., 207

waardgelders, 43, 45
Wassenar, Jacob, 98
Wassenar, Nicolaes: *Historich Verhal*,
    98
Watson, Richard, 99, 133, 178,
    179
Wedgwood, C. V., 8
Weininger, Otto, 302
Westphalia, Treaty of, 252, 259, 266
White Mountain, Battle of, 64–5,
    68, 82, 83, 89, 91, 93, 227, 228,
    240, 298
Wittgenstein, Ludwig, 75, 298,
    301–2
Wok, Peter, 86
World, The (Descartes), 130
world-view, 1–2, 221–6
Wotton, Sir Henry, 110

Xanten, Treaty of (1614), 60

Yates, Frances, 84, 87, 90, 91